# The New Breed
## Irish Rugby's Professional Era

# PATRICK McCARRY

# MERCIER PRESS
IRISH PUBLISHER – IRISH STORY

MERCIER PRESS

Cork

www.mercierpress.ie

© Patrick McCarry, 2015

ISBN: 978 1 78117 331 2

10 9 8 7 6 5 4 3 2 1

A CIP record for this title is available from the British Library

Printed and bound in the EU.

# CONTENTS

INTRODUCTION     5

1.   DESTINY UNCLAIMED: THE 2011 WORLD CUP     7

2.   A WHOLE NEW WORLD: RUGBY GOES PRO     18

3.   THREE LONELY AMIGOS: HICKIE, ELWOOD AND CLOHESSY     28

4.   BLACK AND BLUE: NEW ZEALAND TEACH IRELAND A
BRUTAL LESSON     36

5.   MUNSTER PLANT A FLAG     47

6.   ULSTER'S SHORT-LIVED DYNASTY     66

7.   EXILES: PASTA, PARTIES AND GREEN ROVERS     71

8.   LEINSTER STRUGGLE TO KEEP UP     80

9.   GATLAND GIVES IRELAND A FIGHTING CHANCE     92

10.   MIXING IT WITH THE BEST: IRELAND 2002–2009     101

11.   TREE-HUGGERS: IRISH CLUB RUGBY ON ITS KNEES     111

12.   'PURE JOY': ROB KEARNEY     118

13.   LEINSTER COME OF AGE     128

14.   'EVERYONE THAT COULD JUMP SHIP, DID': CONNACHT'S
REFUSAL TO LIE DOWN     138

15.   DOUBT: O'GARA, HART AND SEXTON     149

16.   'COMPLETELY ALIEN': THE NEXT GENERATION OF IRISH
RUGBY STARS     162

17. ROAD TO RECOVERY: INJURIES AND THE SPECTRE
    OF RETIREMENT                                                173

18. FRENCH FLIRTATIONS AND THE RISE OF RUGBY WAGES              186

19. A TRIP TO FRANCE: GRENOBLE VERSUS RACING                    193

20. THE SPECIALISTS: IRELAND'S FOREIGN LEGION                   217

21. DIVERGING PATHS: JAMIE, LUKE AND FEZ                        229

22. FINDING THAT ONE PER CENT: STRENGTH AND
    CONDITIONING, ANALYSIS, AND SHEER MOTIVATION                237

23. 'ELBOW, APPLE, CARPET, SADDLE, BUBBLE': CONCUSSION
    TAKES CENTRE STAGE                                          255

24. THE ABERRATIONS                                             272

25. 'IT'S TIME LADS GREW UP': HEARTBREAK AGAINST
    NEW ZEALAND                                                 282

26. ANDREW TRIMBLE: OVERNIGHT SUCCESS, NINE YEARS ON            288

27. FAIRYTALES AND 'KILLER DRILLS': SIX NATIONS 2014            293

28. ANIMAL INSTINCT: INTERPROVINCIAL BATTLE RAGES ON            301

CONCLUSION                                                      313

ACKNOWLEDGEMENTS                                                317

INDEX OF KEY PLAYERS AND PERSONNEL                              318

# INTRODUCTION

Ireland went along to the 1995 World Cup for the ride. Coached by Gerry Murphy and captained by Terry Kingston, they were a team that lost more often than not. They were a sixty-minute team in an eighty-minute world. The 1990s had been, thus far, bleak – six wins, a draw and twenty-two defeats, including failures against Italy and Namibia, and hidings at the hands of New Zealand, France and Australia.

Arriving in South Africa for the tournament, they were grouped with Wales, Japan and New Zealand. Before a ball was kicked, it was readily accepted that the final match in this grouping, against the Welsh, would determine whether they stayed on for another week or headed home to their day jobs. And so it proved, as they huffed against the All Blacks, only to be blown away, and won ugly against Japan. The 24–23 win over Wales was hard viewing, but Ireland made it into their third consecutive World Cup quarter-final. France thrashed them six days later. Nobody would miss them. Elsewhere in the tournament, players such as Jonah Lomu, Matt Burke and Joost van der Westhuizen offered a dynamic glimpse of the direction in which southern hemisphere rugby was going. The game was, in effect, amateur, but South Africa, Australia and New Zealand had worked out sponsorship, advertising and corporate employment that allowed their leading lights to train professionally. Their star men played the same game as Ireland, but – when it came to pace, power, fitness and skill levels – they were on a higher plane. South Africa beat New Zealand 15–12 in a tense, draining final. To this day, the Kiwis complain about a phantom waitress called 'Suzie', who served up tainted meals that prompted half their squad to suffer food poisoning. The Springboks, welcomed back into world rugby in 1992 following the end of apartheid, were world champions.

Within two months of that World Cup final, rugby had turned professional. The Irish Rugby Football Union (IRFU) initially opposed professionalism, voting against the International Rugby Football Board (IRFB) motion declaring the game 'open'. At the forefront of the IRFU's logic was the desire to maintain the status quo of noble amateurism, and the fear that a professional game would bankrupt them. The club scene, played out in the All-Ireland League (AIL), dominated the rugby landscape, but the IRFU was certain it could not bankroll ten or twelve professional clubs.

The provinces – Munster, Ulster, Connacht and Leinster – took part in an annual competition, the Irish Interprovincial Championship, but matches rarely attracted crowds of over 1,000. Even if the four provinces became professional – the lesser of the two evils in the union's eyes – it would mean at least a hundred full-time pros. As was reported at the time, the English Rugby Football Union (RFU) would agree to pay its top players £60,000 a year if the game turned professional. The IRFU did their maths. Irish players could not demand similar wages, and those at Test-match level totalled thirty at most. Agreeing to professionalise the provinces – where gate receipts barely reached £800 per match – would potentially cost £3 million a year.

The IRFU's objections, like its national team, were passionate, boisterous and filled with curse words, before running out of steam. The IRFB motion passed on 26 August 1995. Within a month, Ireland had a professional rugby team.

# I

## DESTINY UNCLAIMED: THE 2011 WORLD CUP

To a degree, I suppose we have failed to do ourselves justice but you're not promised anything. Just because in the four games we have played, we've produced two decent performances and two okay performances, you're not owed anything. You have to go and earn everything you get in Test rugby.

Today we were off the pace and we go home as a result of that. That's the bitter disappointment of it but you have to suck it up. We haven't performed on the big stage and it's very, very disappointing. Collectively [with Ireland] and personally, I won't get the opportunity again and that really sucks but, you know, life goes on.

*Brian O'Driscoll, 8 October 2011 (following Ireland's World Cup exit)*

Beating Australia at Eden Park during the 2011 World Cup had changed everything for the Irish team. Their troubles – underwhelming Six Nations, devastating injuries to David Wallace and Felix Jones, four warm-up losses on the bounce – were washed clear with a 15–6 victory over a talented Wallabies team in Auckland, New Zealand.

The Irish back row of Stephen Ferris, Sean O'Brien and Jamie Heaslip were embraced in turn by Paul O'Connell – a gumshield grin from a man who had inspired their rugby journeys and was now their teammate on a momentous night. Veteran out-half Ronan O'Gara, and Johnny Sexton, his rival for the No. 10 jersey, had finished the game side by side, in the 10–12 axis. The exhausted, beaming face of Cian Healy was broadcast on giant screens as he accepted the man-of-the-match award. Brian O'Driscoll,

Ireland's captain and backline talisman, sought out midfield partner Gordon D'Arcy for a hug.

It was the fourth World Cup of the professional era (the seventh since 1987's inaugural World Cup tournament), yet the win over Australia had been Ireland's first against a southern-hemisphere powerhouse. For all the advances the country had made since its reluctant entry into the world of professional rugby in 1995, Ireland had failed to fire at the highest level. There had been humiliating exits in the pool stages in the 1999 and 2007 World Cups, and meek surrenders in 2003's last eight encounter with France.

Declan Kidney, Ireland's coach at the World Cup, was in the process of transforming the team from one-off heroes to consistent challengers and champions. Three players epitomised the team's winning mentality and growing sense of justified entitlement – O'Connell, O'Driscoll and O'Gara. Each man had played a key role in slaying the Aussies. That night, in an Eden Park bedecked in green, each man took the acclaim.

Up in the stands, at the media tribune, an Irish supporter stood on a vacated table for a better view and clearer photos. Clambering down a minute later, he muttered 'Fucking hell. Fucking hell' to no one in particular. His team were on the brink of something special.

***

My journey with the team had begun eight days earlier, on 9 September 2011, at New Plymouth Boys High School. I was living in Vancouver, Canada, when *Inside Rugby* magazine editor Mark Cashman offered me work on the tournament's official match programmes. Upon learning the *Irish Mirror* needed a World Cup correspondent, I arranged a freelancing fee and booked my ticket for the host country.

Arriving into New Plymouth via Los Angeles, Auckland and Highways 1 and 3, I had already missed the week of team bonding and white-water rapids in the South Island's adventure capital, Queenstown. The squad had decamped to the North Island for their World Cup opener against the United States Eagles, team of former Ireland coach Eddie O'Sullivan. I had chugged up and parked, two streets away, in a borrowed Nissan hatchback that had had a former life as a New Zealand Postal Service rural delivery vehicle. The car comfortably took a single mattress, yet had a nasty habit of picking up zero radio signals for large stretches on the road.

Declan Kidney was three years into his tenure as Ireland's head coach and would be facing off against his former superior in the national set-up. Both men said all the right words and delivered the appropriate platitudes, but O'Sullivan had a score to settle. He would have his team wound up to spring at the Irish from the start. Battle commenced at 6 p.m. at Stadium Taranaki, with the US team determined to do their country proud on the tenth anniversary of the 11 September terrorist attacks in New York.

Kidney had made the decision to go with Sexton and twenty-two-year-old Munster scrum half Conor Murray as his halfback pairing. Ireland's World Cup opener would be Murray's third cap, but his first start. It was the sort of selection gamble that defined Kidney's latter years as Ireland coach, but an aspect of his management for which he was rarely credited. On that wretched, rainy evening in New Plymouth, Ireland laboured for fifty-five minutes before a two-try burst – from Rory Best and Tommy Bowe – made the game safe. They pressed for a bonus-point score in the closing stages, but Paul Emerick picked up an intercept try in the final minutes before saluting the rain-sodden US fans in the south terrace. That score, a demented 'Captain America' display from Todd Clever, and a banner that told Russian rugby fans just who won the space race would be the United States' tournament highlights as they packed for home. I arrived at my car shortly before midnight and found both wing mirrors had been kicked off. They would not be travelling back to Auckland. A shaky start all round.

With this win, Ireland had ended a four-game losing run that had started at Murrayfield on 6 August. But as much as the Irish players sought to accentuate the positives in the post-match mixed (interview) zone, fears of a 2007 World Cup repeat (bad to worse) were hard to shake. 'Given the day that was in it,' Geordan Murphy mused, 'we knew they were going to hit us all day long. And they did. Smash us and smash us.' The fullback insisted Ireland could step up a level to beat Australia, but added it would do the squad 'the world of good' if people begged to differ.

The Australian media were in no doubt that Ireland possessed another level but felt the Wallabies were penthouse dwellers. The consensus was for a tight first half before Quade Cooper, Will Genia and their like would run roughshod over a tiring Irish team. *The Sydney Morning Herald* declared Kidney's charges were looking forward to the game as much as an irregular brusher would a trip to the dentist's chair.

There was a snap to the Irish press briefings in the lead-up to the Wallabies match. Gordon D'Arcy shut down questions with brio and one-word answers, while Sean O'Brien bristled at suggestions that Rocky Elsom had greatly influenced his career during the Australian's stint at Leinster. Team captain Brian O'Driscoll held his tongue when asked by an American rugby journalist where he kept each of his 120 Test caps. The centre explained that his cap collection was much, much smaller than the journalist might think, and consoled the apologetic writer afterwards: 'No, no. You'd be surprised how often I'm asked that question.'

Kidney brought in Healy, O'Brien, Rob Kearney and Eoin Reddan for the Saturday-evening clash with Australia. Robbie Deans' men had beaten Italy 32–6 in their tournament opener, and had scrubbed New Zealand 25–20 in Brisbane in their final match before the tournament. Nine of the match-day twenty-two had featured in the Queensland Reds' Super Rugby victory over Canterbury Crusaders, including captain James Horwill and laid-back No. 8 Radike Samo. Samo had made an amiable interviewee in the lead-up to the game, but provided a newspaper cutting for the Irish dressing room by admitting he had never heard of O'Brien, who at the time was the European player of the year.

Kidney had a much greater motivational stroke, and it was very much a case of making the best out of a bad situation. The World Cup had been the carrot for hooker Jerry Flannery to chase as he strove to regain fitness following ongoing issues with his calf muscles. A hugely popular character within the squad, Flannery had been out of Test rugby for eighteen months before returning in time for Ireland's warm-ups. He made three appearances off the bench and started in the home defeat to England to prove his fitness ahead of the final squad selection. He was a second-half replacement in the US game, but he broke down in the team's Tuesday training session before the Australia match. His World Cup was over; he would be flying home after the Eden Park game. The coach had one final task for Flannery and it would prove to be emotional. 'I didn't say, "I think I should present the jerseys with a bit of a waterfall going on,"' Flannery recalls. 'Deccie just said it to me – that he'd like for me to give out the jerseys. There was no planning put into it, I didn't give it a second thought at all. I had just thought it was a pretty cool thing to have been asked. Deccie had tried to make clear how important and how special it was to play for Ireland in a World Cup and for me to give those jerseys out the day before the game.

'I was injured at the time, when he asked, and said, "Yeah, yeah, of course." I didn't think too much about it at the time and didn't realise the magnitude. When I got injured, we were playing Australia that weekend so you don't want to be that mopey bastard walking around and feeling sorry for yourself. You know that everyone has spent so long training for this thing, this one game. You try to put a brave face on it. I remember the lads that weren't involved in the Australia game said, "We're going to the gym. Do you want to come down?" Listen, I went down and trained with them. I was on crutches. I came back and literally got back in time for the meeting. I came in to the meeting and as I was handing out the jerseys I said, "I'll probably never ever be in this room again." It just started striking my head – this was it for me; it was over – as I was shaking hands with the lads and wishing them all the best. I suppose I probably got a bit emotional.'

Stephen Ferris later recounted how he struggled to hold back tears as he took his No. 6 jersey from Flannery – a friend, teammate, warrior, and a damn fine player. Ireland would be going into battle without him.

'I was almost watching them during pre-season as I was injured all the fucking time and I'd seen how hard they grafted and how hard they worked for each other,' Flannery continues. 'When I did manage to get fit ... I thought I'd have to retire, I didn't think I'd get to the World Cup. When I went out to play the first warm-up, I know we lost our four games of the build-up, but every game I went out I thought, "This is probably my last ever game of rugby." I really didn't think I was going to get through it. So by the time we had gotten through those four games I thought, "Jesus, I'm back. This is amazing." For me, the World Cup experience was incredible. I couldn't get enough of it.

'When I retired, I could have been very bitter and felt like I had worked my bollocks off and gotten nowhere but, in the end, I had a really good experience to finish on and to see the lads get that result was great.'

Sexton and O'Gara shared the scoring burden against the Wallabies. Healy, in front-row partnership with Best and Mike Ross, was immense, and Kearney won his aerial duel with Kurtley Beale after a tailspin start. The Irish back row gave a glimpse of a brutish, ball-carrying future, and Ferris left an indelible mark on the match by picking Genia up like a rag-doll and marching him back towards the Wallabies' try line.

Ferris says, 'At the time, I never realised I had lifted him up and back ten yards. It was only when I saw the replays, and clips on YouTube, that I knew what I had done. Another ref might have called it for being offside, from the Wallabies scrum put-in, but it was worth the risk. Eoin Reddan had snipped at Genia already so that was the red flag for me to get on him. I snapped in and drove him back and the boys came piling in behind me. I can just remember Donncha O'Callaghan shouting, "Give it to him Fez, give it to him." Seconds after that, I was lying on his back and giving him banter.

'It was right on half-time and was a definite statement of intent. We went in level at the break but knew we had them rattled. Johnny Sexton kicked us ahead on fifty minutes and we never looked back.'

At the time, the Irish economy had been three years into a recession that had seen unemployment soar and led to mass emigration of more than 87,000 people a year. It felt as if half that number were in Eden Park that night and all of them hoarse from the contest. There were so many moments in that game – from tackles to breaks, men picking themselves up from one hit and seeking the next – and so many reasons to be proud. They were showing the world that Ireland was a force – they were there to win, not just to take part.

The post-match briefing was a giddy affair for the Irish press corps. We threw the daintiest veil over our delight as the Aussies asked their captain and coach, 'What went wrong?' Suggestions by an Australian journalist that Ireland's play around the breakdown had bordered on illegal all night were met with an incredulous 'Fuck off' by an Irish voice. Kidney and O'Driscoll showed greater decorum. The captain, in particular, refused to acknowledge that the victory was his greatest in a green jersey, saying, 'We were mentally in a place where we felt we owed ourselves a big performance and we owed the Irish public one. There has never been a shortage of drive with the guys. It doesn't come and go. It's either in you or it's not. You look at the individuals, and I'm not going to question the drive or desire of people like Paul O'Connell or Ronan O'Gara; I've seen it for the past ten years. And with the younger guys you can see it with your Sean O'Briens, Cian Healys and Stephen Ferrises. I know I'm naming guys but I think it's throughout.'

Speaking in a buoyant mixed zone, after the vanquished Australians had trudged off, O'Brien declared, 'The first scrum of the game was solid and strong and we were going forward a bit. It gets into your head. We knew it was going well and we had these [where we wanted them].' He added, 'We can play better rugby than we did tonight. There's a lot of talent and belief in this squad. Top of the pool is the target, there's no point saying anything else.'

Sexton dedicated the victory to the thousands of Irish supporters that were present at Eden Park to witness their triumph. 'We thought that there might be a few more Australians out there,' he said, 'especially when you consider that they're just across the road whereas we have to travel halfway across the world just to get here. The way the economy is going at the moment, travelling here is not the easiest thing to do, so we wanted to go out there and put in a performance for them.'

The final word at Eden Park went to O'Driscoll, as he remarked, 'It's a good win but I'm not sitting here with the Webb Ellis [Cup] beside me. We're in a pool stage and we need four wins. We'll enjoy the moment but not get lost in it.'

Ireland decamped to Rotorua, duly dispatching Russia 62–12 and wrapping up the bonus point after thirty-eight minutes, before travelling on to Dunedin to take on Italy. Encased in Dunedin's 31,000-seater stadium – 'The Glasshouse' – Irish fans made it a home away from home. Many had filled the town's bars from midday and were making their own fun in the stadium's stands, regardless of the on-field action. Italian coach Nick Mallett later remarked, 'There had to be a lot of New Zealanders with green jerseys on, because I don't believe that there are that many Irish people that have enough bloody euros left to come out here.' Ireland were only 9–6 up at the break, but had attacked the Italians to a pulp. Gaps appeared after the break and the Irish players profited.

The 36–6 triumph was Ireland's most fluent to date, and added to a growing sense of belief in the country's chances of finally progressing beyond a World Cup quarter-final for the first time. Mallett challenged journalists to pick a weakness in the Irish side, as Ferris proclaimed that his teammates should be ambitious. He added, 'We talked a couple of months ago about how England, four years ago, didn't have the best of form coming into the competition but ended up getting into the final. Hopefully we can go one step further.'

Wales, with former Ireland coach Warren Gatland at the helm, were up next. Respective drop-goal and penalty misses from Rhys Priestland and James Hook had cost them against South Africa, as they lost their opening pool game 17–16. Away from the big cities for their remaining matches, the Welsh ground out a win over Samoa and beat Namibia and Fiji with panache. Gatland had stoked the fires before Ireland's Grand Slam win over Wales in 2009 by suggesting that both sets of players had a healthy dislike for each other. The Welsh, however, were almost reverential in their comments about the Irish players and were offering up no easy ammunition in the build-up to the quarter-final clash in Wellington. The furthest any player went was when the languid Alun Wyn Jones labelled the relationship between the camps as one of 'frenemies'.

Kidney selected the same starting fifteen for the match at 'The Cake Tin', Wellington's stadium. Australia's defeat by Ireland had opened up the top half of the World Cup draw for the northern hemisphere contenders. The winners in Wellington would meet either England or France, who would face off in Auckland later that evening. Once again, the Irish fans swarmed the host city on match day, and there was a rousing reception at the Intercontinental Hotel as Ireland made their way onto the team bus. A crowd of some 2,000 Irish fans crowded the reception area and car park from 11 a.m. until the squad took the short bus journey to the stadium shortly after 3 p.m.

Welsh centre Jamie Roberts had broken into Cardiff Blues two months shy of his twenty-first birthday. In 2007, in a bar with two of his closest friends, he had watched his country get eliminated from that year's World Cup. Four years on, Roberts was the destructive star of the Welsh midfield. He had teamed up brilliantly with O'Driscoll during the 2009 Lions tour to South Africa, and was part of a youthful Welsh backline that had scored seventeen tries in four pool matches. Kearney acknowledged Roberts' threat but offered a simple plan to counter his brute force: 'The key to his game is he just runs hard and direct, and you just have to hit him hard and direct and stop him. There's no huge science to stopping a direct runner; you just need to hit him.'

Donncha O'Callaghan stepped up to confront Roberts less than ninety seconds after the quarter-final kicked off. The Irish lock was steam-rollered and Mike Phillips kept his team ticking over until winger Shane Williams dived over in the corner. Priestland converted and the tone was set. Ireland camped inside the Welsh twenty-two for the remainder of the half, and three times punted for attacking five-metre line-outs rather than kick the penalties on offer. Each time they came up short as the Welsh defence held firm. O'Gara was given all the time he wanted, but Wales were confident he could do them no harm if they dropped back covering defenders. The ball-carrying threat of O'Brien, Healy and Ferris was negated as Wales tackled in pairs – one went high while the other attacked the ankles. The Irish trio made forty-four carries between them for a total of forty metres gained.

Keith Earls got Ireland back in the game after the break, but Phillips restored the Welsh lead six minutes later as D'Arcy switched off and the scrum half sniped over in the corner. Kidney threw on Sexton and Reddan, but Ireland looked spent after knocking on the door for so long with scant reward. When Jonathan Davies raced clear to score for Wales with seventeen minutes remaining, making it 22–10, the game ended as a contest. Tom Jones' 'Delilah' rang out around The Cake Tin. Ireland had fallen short at the quarter-finals again.

'Everyone is gutted in the dressing room,' said Murray post match. 'We are very disappointed with our performance and the way we approached the game. I think we got beaten up by Wales in certain aspects of the game.' Best, who had featured in the unmitigated disaster that was the 2007 World Cup, reflected on a massive opportunity that had slipped by in

Wellington: 'Overall the World Cup will be a bit of a failure for us because we wanted to win this. We didn't crow about it like we did four years ago, but we felt that, deep down, we had the firepower in our squad to do it.'

Kidney looked upon his team's 2011 World Cup quest as a beacon of hope for a country brought to its knees by recession. He took the defeat extremely personally: 'You get a sense of how much people are feeding off it and you really want to go well for everybody – not just ourselves but everybody at home and all the support out here. That just makes the hurt all the greater.'

Kidney considered what was likely to be the end of an era for Ireland's golden generation and its star players – O'Driscoll, O'Connell and O'Gara. 'I'm especially disappointed for them,' he said, 'because they will see it as their last chance. A lot of them will wear the green again, but in terms of World Cups, many of them were looking to finish up this World Cup on a high.'

A year on, reflecting on Ireland's exit, O'Driscoll mused, 'We had a great opportunity to do something special, and we didn't achieve it.' O'Driscoll, O'Connell and O'Gara – the iconic trio of Ireland's first generation of professionals – would not play together for Ireland again. They would endure career-threatening injuries, concussion worries, controversial axing and on-field heartbreak over the next three years. It would get better, but for what seemed like the longest time it would get worse. Much worse.

# 2

# A WHOLE NEW WORLD:
# RUGBY GOES PRO

The genie was out of the bottle, and we couldn't do anything about it.

*Syd Millar (former IRFU chairman) on rugby's transition to professionalism*

'A lot of modern people think the game was invented in 1995,' remarks former Ireland captain and manager Donal Lenihan. 'It's a much better game now, but you can't forget history.'

The Cork native made his Test debut in 1981 and was a virtual ever-present in the second row, right up to his final appearance in 1992. In between, he played for an Irish team that won two Triple Crowns and three Five Nations championships. He also represented Cork Constitution and the British & Irish Lions, and went on to manage Ireland during the coaching reign of Warren Gatland (1998–2001).

'I was pretty lucky with injuries over my career,' says Lenihan. '[In 1990] I had a disc out of my neck and lost a lot of power down my left-hand side as a result. I've had stitches, bumps and breaks, and have two new hips at this stage, with a new knee on the way. I played forty-six consecutive internationals before I got injured. Fifty caps, back then, was an unbelievable milestone. Players seem to get there in three weeks now. Ireland would have four games in the Five Nations and one autumn international.

'The World Cup changed all that. It was the catalyst behind the big changes that were coming. It was well known that the European unions did not want the World Cup. The southern hemisphere countries were the driving force behind it. The IRFU were not behind the concept of the tournament in 1987. Once the decision was made, they had to participate. However, that did not mean that you had to put all of your resources behind it. Ireland were in good shape at the time.

'By late 1986 I had taken over the captaincy from Ciaran Fitzgerald. We had beaten Romania 60–0 that November, before beating England 17–0 in the Five Nations the following February. We lost narrowly away to Scotland and beat Wales so, really, had left a Triple Crown behind us.

'Our preparation for the World Cup was shite. The IRFU wanted us to play no matches in the six weeks leading up to the tournament. A lot of the forwards were based in Dublin, so they took it upon themselves to sort out sessions. One of them was scrummaging against Lansdowne out at their grounds one night. All organised by the players. We had beaten Wales earlier in the year but lost to them in New Zealand. They ended up third, having lost to the hosts, but knocked over Australia in the play-off. That could have been us.'

Ireland were steadily on the wane as the decade progressed. The Triple Crown win of 1985 was, for almost two decades, the last blinking beacon of Irish success. When the squad for the 1989 British & Irish Lions tour to Australia was announced, Ireland had just four representatives out of thirty – Lenihan, Brendan Mullin, Paul Dean and Steve Smith.

Two years on, with the next World Cup nearing, there were contract issues, with the player-participation agreement a sticking point. Lenihan says, 'We could see in New Zealand, in 1987, that their players were all in adverts for tractors and televisions. We were still on the equivalent of two-and-sixpence as our daily allowance. The Australian players were all with Italian clubs in their off season, and they weren't doing it for their health. We had no professional sport in Ireland ... Australia already had a pro ethos. They had rugby league, Aussie Rules, cricketers, swimmers and basketball players that were all pros. It was inevitable, for them, that things would change.

'I was working as a bank manager in 1991, and there were initial squabbles about players getting compensated for time off work. The big issue was image rights. Basically, you were being asked to sign away your life. We refused to sign right up until the last minute. You have to look after the players, and the World Cup took the game to a new level. That World Cup brought home the possibilities of where the game could go. We should have been in the semi-final that year, but [Australian out-half] Michael Lynagh thought otherwise.'

On 23 June 1995, a day before the World Cup final between hosts South Africa and New Zealand, the rumbling debate on professionalism in rugby roared into the open. Rupert Murdoch's News Corporation announced the £360 million SANZAR (South Africa, New Zealand and Australia Rugby) deal to broadcast provincial and national rugby in South Africa, New Zealand and Australia all the way up to 2005. As the *Independent* reported, media mogul Kerry Packer and former Wallaby prop Ross Turnbull were fronting a breakaway 'rugby circus' that would be known as the World Rugby Championship (WRC) and would feature 900 of the game's best players. The cream of that bountiful crop were in line to receive £100,000 a year. The English RFU met with four leading Test players and thrashed out an alternative proposal of £60,000 a year. The IRFU tentatively crunched numbers and believed they could offer £30,000 (punts) and a company car, if amateur push gave way to professional shove. In a bout of uppercuts, combinations and low blows, Ireland padded out a gentle jab.

The first major victory for the unions came in South Africa, three weeks after the Springboks' World Cup triumph. A meeting with player representatives was hastily arranged when reports emerged of the entire Springbok squad agreeing a deal in principle to play WRC. 'We are in a Wild West situation, with a lot of cowboys in town,' declared Edward Griffiths, chief executive of South Africa's rugby union. The union convinced twenty-five of South Africa's twenty-eight elite players to sign on. In New Zealand, young stars such as Jeff Wilson and Josh Kronfeld rowed in behind the New Zealand Rugby Union (NZRU). When the Australian players opted out of any deals with the WRC threat, the roof fell in and the circus left town.

The IRFB (rebranded World Rugby in 2014) called a meeting at the Ambassador Hotel in Paris, on 26 August 1995, and invited all its member unions to attend. After years of lobbying on both sides of the aisle, the issue would come to a head. Ireland were represented by Syd Millar and Tom Kiernan, two men who had served their country with distinction on the field and were the IRFU's power brokers. Griffiths and Louis Luyt flew the professionalism flag for the South Africa delegation.

'We were well aware that something like this would come up,' Millar recalls, 'but we did not expect that Scotland, England and Wales would join the southern hemisphere nations. The southern hemisphere were concerned about Packer and Murdoch, who had the broadcasting rights to rugby league. Both the Australians and New Zealanders reckoned their players would soon be gone to league. That was their reasoning.'

The Irish delegation anticipated a brusque debate about professionalism, and were determined to fight their corner. Payments could be arranged for the national team, they argued amid line-drawing and harrumphing. Payments for club and provincial players should be revisited, and even regulated, at a later date. There were accusations from Australian delegates, Millar says, that Five Nations unions had been clandestine in player payments. 'Certainly in Ireland,' he adds, 'we were not paying players. Whether the English clubs were, I don't know, but there were claims of this, that and the other. If players were getting paid, it wasn't an extraordinary amount. The Welsh clubs always provided beer money, if you'd like to put it that way.'

Calls to make all forms, and levels, of rugby open for payments blindsided Millar, Kiernan and several other union heads. 'I was recorded saying at the time that I wouldn't change my business so radically without certain safeguards or structure,' says Millar. 'The change was that no one gets paid to everybody gets paid … We knew – we were not daft – that professionalism had to happen, but it was a matter of doing it in a controlled way and doing it properly.'

After hours of heated debate, the IRFB amateur committee chairman Vernon Pugh called for a vote on 'open' rugby. Four unions – Ireland, France, Argentina and Japan – were not in favour, but the plates were shifting. With England, Scotland and Wales on board, the three southern-hemisphere heavyweights were tugging the war in their favour. Pugh, according to Millar, suggested a second vote should be taken, stressing that a unanimous result was in the best interests of the game. The IRFB got the unanimous vote they wanted. It was time for unions and clubs to get the wallets out.

The council agreed to repeal the bye-laws and regulations relating to amateurism, and replace them with new bye-laws and regulations. The key aspects of the new regulations included contracts, limitations on sponsorship and advertising, eligibility of players for international teams, player availability, movement of players, age, reinstatement of rugby league players, testimonials, broadcasting rights, anti-doping, and procedures/sanctions.

The vote in Paris meant that the following was agreed:

1. New bye-laws and regulations (recognising agreed principles of an 'open' game) be submitted for consideration and approval at a special meeting of the council in Tokyo, Japan, on 28 September 1995.

2. Following approval of such new bye-laws and regulations, the existing bye-laws and regulations relating to amateurism then be repealed.

\*\*\*

The year 1995 marked the 150th anniversary of rugby union's rules first being committed to print. At a show of hands and the stroke of a pen, a proud tradition of amateurism was extinguished. In the book *From There to Here*, author Brendan Fanning recounts a conversation with a colleague about the reaction of an English delegate outside the Ambassador. 'He had his hands resting on the wall, and was rocking back and forth – not exactly nutting the wall but making contact with it just the same. He was absolutely devastated.'

The South African delegation returned home with all the rubber stamps they needed. 'The fact that rugby was becoming professional wasn't perhaps as earth-shattering as it was around other areas of the world,' says former Springbok media manager Alex Broun. 'These guys were the top sportsmen in the country. They were bigger than any cricketers, bigger than any soccer players. They were the top guys in the country, and the basic understanding was that these guys should be paid and paid very well for what they're doing.

'Francois Pienaar, Joost van der Westhuizen, Chester Williams, Joel Stransky, these guys – especially after they won the World Cup – were gods in South Africa. [About] the fact that they were being paid officially now, everyone went, "Well absolutely. They should be." The switch to professionalism happened very, very easily. It was almost like, "Okay, now we can declare this openly." But they were already pretty open, to tell you the truth. The payments were called gratuities or expenses, but they were now called wages. I think South Africa hit the ground running, quicker than New Zealand, Australia or anywhere else in the world. The only country that was similar was France, because people were being paid so much there.'

Ireland hit the ground with a bloodied nose and dusty cuffs. Their next Test was in three months' time – Fiji were coming to Dublin – and they needed to sign national-team players to contracts as soon as possible. The IRFU set up a contracts committee, led by Bill Lavery, and negotiated with a players' representative group of Mullin, Philip Danaher and Denis McBride. 'The first union contracts were modelled on professional cricket contracts,' Lenihan reveals. 'There was no real starting point, so they just switched rugby for cricket, made some minor changes and there you have it.'

There were four basic contracts. The first two dealt with Irish players who were playing with AIL clubs and the interprovincial series with Leinster, Munster, Ulster and Connacht. Category A was full time (approximately £25,000 a year), Category B was part time (£7,500 climbing to £10,000, dependent on appearances and bonuses) and Category C was a £5,000 developmental deal. The fourth contract was for Ireland internationals playing club rugby abroad. The union's photocopier would be kept humming with that last one over the next three years.

Kiernan, meanwhile, threw himself into the establishment of a new club competition. 'We needed something to compete with the English and French clubs at a higher level of competition,' says Millar. 'Hence the European Cup, to give our provinces a chance.' Heineken – drinks brand and leading global brewery – attached its name to the competition. The AIL was at the peak of its powers, and many clubs believed they should be allowed to compete alongside the likes of Bath, Toulouse and Leicester. Garryowen were vocal supporters of the super club concept – two sides in Limerick, two in Cork, three in Dublin and one apiece from Connacht and Ulster. Cognisant of spreading their paid professionals thinly, the union held firm to the notion of a new Holy Trinity – clubs feeding provinces, which, in turn, supply the national team with able, capable bodies.

Lenihan continues, 'Simple decisions ended up having massive consequences. The Scottish Rugby Union had a massive debt to service with Murrayfield. The IRFU let Lansdowne Road fall down and invested in the national team. Saying that, we were extremely lucky. We had a history of four provincial sides, and it was easier for fans to get on board.'

On 16 December 1995, four months after rugby's switch to professionalism, Leinster defeated Munster 19–15 at Thomond Park in front of a sparse crowd. Varying reports from the match give the attendance at anything between 700 and 1,300. One thing is for sure, not many Irish rugby fans were on board. Progress was slow.

\*\*\*

Leinster's first professional match was at Milan's Stadio Comunale Giuriati on 1 November 1995. Official figures record 1,200 in attendance, but Leinster manager Jim Glennon gauges the crowd at half that. Niall Woods had returned from a club-rugby stint in Australia, having missed out on World Cup selection earlier that year. 'It was an experience,' he remarks. 'Atrocious refereeing, atrocious pitch, no one there. Wednesday afternoon. I remember thinking they can't be that good, as there was not a huge amount of rugby in Italy. Saying that, Italy had beaten Ireland before the World Cup in a friendly. In the end we won by three points and Diego Dominguez missed seven of ten kicks, so they could have easily beaten us.' Woods blazed in a second-half try from fifty metres out. Alan McGowan converted, and added a penalty that proved crucial in a 24–21 win.

Munster's introduction to the new era was a 17–13 Heineken Cup win over Swansea at Thomond Park later that afternoon. Anthony Foley, who featured against Swansea, does not remember anything too professional about the travel arrangements. 'We trained on Tuesday and Thursday nights and cadged lifts or piled into a minibus to go to and from Cork.' Foley had just turned twenty-two, and was part of a Munster pack built around elder statesmen such as Peter Clohessy ('Claw') and Mick Galwey ('Gaillimh'). Lenihan says, 'Claw and Gaillimh went to bed one Saturday night as amateurs and woke up pros on a Sunday. Some fellas couldn't believe their luck. They were playing a game they loved, as a hobby, and now they were getting paid for it. Some knuckled down and tried to make the most of it, while others were near the end of their playing days and enjoyed the ride for a couple of years. There was an amateur ethos very much in place. Many were not going to change their social activities because you paid them a few bob at the same time. It took a long time for the clubs, players and unions to understand what professionalism was.'

Defeat away to Castres in their second, and final, pool match meant Munster missed out on the semi-finals. With Ulster not receiving a competitive invite until 1996/97, Leinster were Ireland's sole representative in the knockout stages. Tries from Conor O'Shea and McGowan, who also kicked thirteen points, were enough to squeeze past Pontypridd. The semi was against Cardiff at Lansdowne Road on 30 December. Woods comments, 'We got a cheque after that Pontypridd game for £180 (punts), which we were technically not supposed to get.' Members of the Leinster branch were summarily scolded for jumping the gun (by three months) with player payments.

Leinster arranged an extra training run despite grumbles from some players about a disrupted Christmas. Woods was struggling with a hamstring issue in the week leading up to the semi-final and was ruled out on the morning of the game. O'Shea, on loan from London Irish for the competition, took his place on the left wing. A crowd of more than 7,300 filed into the crumbling confines of Lansdowne Road. Seeking the heat of company on a horrendous, biting day, most converged in the East Terrace. Both packs heaved and mauled to a standstill, but Cardiff's forwards were canny at working the ball into scoring positions. Halfbacks Adrian Davies and Andrew Moore slotted drop goals, and Hemi Taylor and Mike Hall added tries to make a lead the hosts could not surpass.

The Welsh side soaked up the acclaim from a small band of travelling supporters – about 200 – but lost 21–18 to Toulouse after extra time in the final on 7 January 1996.

\*\*\*

Irish rugby followers seeking solace in the international team were usually drip-fed two wins per calendar year. Ireland's first game in the professional era had been a 44–8 victory over Fiji at Lansdowne Road on 18 November 1995. The following month, with the interprovincial championship and Heineken Cup out of the way, Ireland travelled to the United States to prepare for the 1996 Six Nations. The tourists, coached by New Zealander Murray Kidd, played their only Test at Life University in Marietta, Georgia, and were grateful to Paul Burke for his penalty-scoring contributions off the bench, as they won 25–16. Upon arriving home, they had their first rugby contracts to sign.

The IRFU offered contracts to twenty-nine of the thirty players who had travelled to America. Eddie Halvey was, briefly, off to Saracens, so he was not considered for the deal. English-born players such as Jim Staples, Simon Geoghegan and Chris Saverimutto were based in the Allied Dunbar Premiership, so were offered lesser packages for the sole duty of representing their country. Geoghegan secured an additional stipend for turning out with Connacht in Europe. The union was offering six full-time contracts of £25,000 per province, with twenty-two more part-time contracts of £7,500. Players such as Nick Popplewell, Paul Wallace and Paddy Johns signed, but representatives acting on their behalf, including hooker Terry Kingston, were already pressing for pay increases and further meetings with the union.

A four-try performance against Wales, at Lansdowne Road, brought Ireland its sole Six Nations triumph. They fell at home to Scotland, while there were away losses to France and England. The autumn internationals brought a heavy defeat by Samoa – 40–25 and five tries to one – and a close call against Australia, eleven days later. Ireland led 9–6 at the break, but a try from out-half David Knox and steady kicking from Matt Burke saw the Wallabies home with 10 points to spare.

Breaking point arrived on 4 January 1997, at a half-empty Lansdowne Road, as Italy rallied for a 37–29 win. Kidd was sacked three days later.

# 3

## THREE LONELY AMIGOS: HICKIE, ELWOOD AND CLOHESSY

After a pleasant fifty-five-minute chat, Denis Hickie tries to derail this book. 'The first full-time professionals in Ireland', he says, 'were myself, Eric Elwood and Peter Clohessy.' To a large, correct-answer-in-a-table-quiz extent, he is right.

I meet the former Leinster and Ireland winger at a coffee shop in Sandyford Industrial Estate, where he now works for a renewable-energy company. Our only previous interview had been in the same estate, but in the lead-up to the 2013 British & Irish Lions tour to Australia. Hickie had been in contention for the 2001 Australian tour, only for a foot-and-mouth outbreak – which led to the postponement of Six Nations matches – to smear his shop window. He was selected in 2005 for the doomed tour of New Zealand, but had the cold comfort of being part of an unbeaten midweek team. As an interviewee, Hickie has a gift for detail and recollection in all areas but two – dates and final scorelines.

The stealthy St Mary's winger was only twenty years old when he became one of only three Irishmen to earn national contracts in the first round of offers in 1996. Connacht out-half Elwood and Munster prop Clohessy were the others.

'Ronan O'Gara was given a contract a year after,' recalls Hickie. 'Paul O'Connell was a good few years after, and Brian O'Driscoll was only offered a deal in 1999. Gordon D'Arcy got a semi-pro deal around the same time. So they're not the first set of full-time professionals; they're the second. People just assume they are because they have been around a long, long time. They're not really the end of the first era, I'm afraid.'

Nice one, Denis.

The IRFU had only so many Ford Mondeos and full-time contracts to hand out in its first two years dealing with a game turned professional. Hickie had helped St Mary's College to a Leinster Senior Schools Cup in 1994, and played with University College Dublin (UCD) the following year. He was drafted into St Mary's AIL side in 1996, and, at the same time, was secured by the union as a long-term prospect for wing. He joined Elwood (then aged twenty-seven) and Clohessy (thirty) in the top tier with a Category A contract. There had been offers from the Courage League (now the English Premiership), but Hickie was focused on making the breakthrough into Brian Ashton's Ireland.

He says, 'The AIL games were the big ones back then – so you had the situation where you had smatterings of professional players at the different clubs. All the Leinster players, then, would train together, but there were so few national and provincial contracts that you might only have six or seven guys at a training session. There were only about thirty players contracted over the whole of Ireland. Most of the lads were in England. The amount of professionals left in Ireland, per team, was quite small. Sessions were mainly built around the area of strength and conditioning, which was a relatively new concept.

'We had blocks of time with Leinster, then blocks of time back with our club, then back again. You would train with Leinster in the day and often with your club in the evening. There would be a block with Leinster for the Heineken Cup, then another international block. The AIL was still the big competition, all the way up until 2000, when the players, really, stopped becoming available. I won the league with St Mary's in 1999/2000, but that was the last real year Leinster players were really allowed to play for their club. Players are always allowed to play for their club if they're not required by Leinster, but that was the last season where you would split your priorities. Your province would not let you [play] anyway, unless they wanted you to play games to get match fit.'

The Dubliner remembers 1996 until early 2000 as a period of disorganisation, frustration and shifting plates on the Irish rugby landscape. 'Everybody was finding their feet at a professional level, and there was an element of luck that the provincial system was already in place; you weren't setting up new franchises. The prioritisation of the games was an interesting element. Club games were getting 10,000 people to them. Clubs like Garryowen and Frank Hogan were interested in the Heineken Cup, and they organised fixtures against teams like Bath to raise their credentials. That idea – Irish clubs playing in Europe – was more of a Munster idea. They had so much dominance around then. Shannon, Garryowen and, to a lesser extent, Cork Constitution. They were loath to hand that over to a provincial set-up.

'Munster, at the start, spent a lot of time trying to nail down a coach. They had the split, too, with the Limerick and Cork bases, which was hard for the coaches to get their head around. That was why there was more opposition. With Leinster it was more a case of a fait accompli. Same with Connacht and Ulster.' Leinster manager Jim Glennon and branch chief executive Eddie Wigglesworth brought in Mike Ruddock as head coach. 'Mike really started us off and put all the structures in place,' says Hickie, 'and it was difficult for him as he would often have seven, eight guys for a training session during the day. He came in not really knowing the club system, and was trying to organise players to come in for sessions, trying to be professional. In those first Leinster teams he took charge of, he would have had a nationally contracted player, myself, and provincially contracted players that were full-time, part-time, guys with no contracts at all, and other guys with no intention of getting professional contracts, coming to the end of their career and with jobs and families. Mike had to juggle all that.'

He adds, 'When Leinster played Leicester Tigers [at Lansdowne Road in 1996], you had this mishmash of guys who were working through the day, professionals and guys wanting to be professional. We had David

O'Sullivan, who played open-side for Skerries. He was a carpenter, but had a part-time deal with Leinster. He was going directly up against England's Neil Back.

'It was no wonder Irish provinces struggled in Europe. You would go to play teams in France like Toulouse, who were professional for years before the game turned professional. Great club sides with great heritage. Ditto for clubs like Leicester and Bath in England. We were a team thrown together and evolving, so it took a while to catch up.'

The backline associated with Leinster in the 2000s, halfbacks aside, is often Hickie, D'Arcy, O'Driscoll, Shane Horgan and Girvan Dempsey, but it took the arrival of Matt Williams and fellow Australian – and backs coach – Alan Gaffney for the quintet to be formed. Hickie recalls, 'Shane Horgan came in through the youths set-up, whereas myself and Girvan Dempsey arrived through the schools path. Brian came in on the back of the Under-19 World Championship [in 1998]. He was in the schools set-up but played really well over there [in France], and they won that so he came straight in. We also had Kevin Nowlan, who rose from the St Mary's J6s [sixth team] to the Ireland team in a short time.

'Gordon D'Arcy was identified as a talent as far back as 1998 when Warren Gatland wanted him to tour South Africa. He couldn't go as he was doing his Leaving Cert. D'Arcy became a crucial part of that Leinster backline for years. Things solidified under Matt, and that was the season [2001/02] we won the Celtic League. That was the first year things really became organised.'

Journey's end for Leinster arrived at Murrayfield in 2009 with the Heineken Cup final win over old rivals Leicester. Hickie was two years retired by that stage – a semi-final defeat by Munster in 2006 was the closest he came to European glory. 'This was a goal at the start of my career, and I couldn't have done it with a better bunch of guys,' O'Driscoll told Sky Sports after the 19–16 win, before he name-checked Hickie as an integral part in the province's rise. 'That cup was for guys like Denis, who had put in so much and had been such an integral part of the fabric and growth of Leinster over the years,' chimed in Dempsey.

Hickie continues, 'Leinster becoming a winning team was a combination of a lot of factors. In 1997 to 1999, we did as well as we could have done. You were basically talking about a semi-professional outfit for at least two of those years. Winning home matches was probably the limit of what we could have hoped to achieve, especially if you consider how hard it still is to win away matches now. We were going to Toulouse and playing in front of 20,000 people, where Leinster at that time were playing in front of 1,000 people. It was a full club set-up; like going to Toulouse now, only we were not like Leinster are now. There was a lot of talk like "Irish teams can compete in Europe", but we were so far behind in terms of structure. I don't think it was a case of the [Leinster] players all getting together to change something. There was a lot involved – personnel, professionalism, fitness, conditioning, resources.'

Hickie made a try-scoring Ireland debut in a 1997 Five Nations win over Wales in Cardiff. He had already been training with the national team for over a year at that stage. 'Something that encapsulates that era for me was the early days of training, where you would go off and do military camps and fitness sessions,' he says. 'Murray Kidd was the Ireland coach, before Ashton came in, and I was called in for training as a nineteen-year-old. The game had just turned professional, so they had us down in the Curragh army camp.

'One day you are an amateur and the next you're professional. There was no understanding of … yesterday I was a guy who trained twice a week, now that I'm a professional I have to be training twice a day. I had to go to the gym. I had never done that before. You had to go flog yourself there and be on the pitch twice a day for really long training sessions – two-and-a-half-hour sessions, twice a day. You went from two or three rugby units a week to ten or eleven, and yet your body hasn't changed. They equated paying you with you being out training forty hours a week.

"Here's your cheque, now get out there and train from 9 a.m. to 5 p.m." It was ridiculous. Physically, guys were breaking down.'

Hickie's first seven caps arrived under Ashton, the former Bath coach. He was fortunate, in many ways, to miss the developmental tour to New Zealand and Samoa in the summer of 1997. While David Wallace, Malcolm O'Kelly and Rob Henderson emerged with credit from a tour with a solitary win and eight chastening defeats, many who made the trip fell by the wayside. 'To be perfectly honest with you,' says Hickie, 'Brian was appalled by how far back we were skills-wise. He was appalled at how bad our skills were, and he was right. Zero skill level. There was no skills training.'

Hickie got 'banged up and didn't play particularly well' on a losing tour to South Africa in 1998, and was dropped by Gatland. He missed the World Cup – and exit at the hands of Argentina – the following year, and returned to the squad in February 2000, two weeks after Ireland were caned 50–18 by England at Twickenham.

Capped sixty-three times by his country, Hickie admits he has all of his games on video, and his father is in the process of transferring them to DVD. 'It would be hilarious,' he remarks, 'to look back at the pace of the game when I started. It was a different world.' Eddie O'Sullivan arrived with Gatland in 1998, and replaced the New Zealander in 2001. The 2003 World Cup, and another quarter-final, showed Ireland had progressed somewhat, but trophies began to fill the IRFU's Lansdowne Road cabinet as Triple Crowns were claimed in 2004, 2005 and 2007. Hickie remarks, however, that celebrating 'Triple Crowns meant we weren't winning championships'. He feels the real sign of Ireland's international advance arrived in the autumn internationals during the final five years of his career.

'The first thing was that our competitiveness against France improved. We couldn't dream of beating France in the 1980s and 1990s. We nearly beat them in Paris in 1998, did the job in 2000 and beat them in Lansdowne

Road the following year. That was one indication that we were going in the right direction.

'The real milestone was being able to compete in the November games. We beat Australia on a heavy day in 2002. That was the first time Ireland had beaten Australia in over twenty years. We then beat South Africa in 2004 and beat them well in 2006. They really started realising that you were getting places. Growing up, there was never a hope of beating South Africa and Australia. We didn't win them all, but we were competitive. We ran the All Blacks close a couple of times. Look at it now when Australia and South Africa come to play us. We're the favourites; if we don't beat them, it hasn't been a great year. Charting those games is charting our progress.'

Hickie recalls – before glancing at his watch and realising he has been chatting with me for almost an hour – going to watch Ireland as a supporter in 1996 as they were beaten 22–12 by the Wallabies. Ireland led 9–0 at the break but fell away at the end. 'No surprise really,' says Hickie. Has he kept his winners' medals and commemorative caps? Yes. Does he possess any framed pictures of his time as a rugby player? No, but he might chase up Inpho Photography's Billy Stickland for one. Has the game provided any lasting friendships? Yes, with former Leinster, Ireland and St Mary's teammates.

Asked if he misses the post-match dressing room as much as his friend Brian O'Driscoll does, Hickie explains that the need fades with each passing year. 'When you finish, immediately you miss the lads. You miss the big days. But, as time goes on, you have the recognition that it was a special time in your life. You had the opportunity to do a lot of great stuff with really amazing people. Having played professionally, I'm able to look back on that period of my life with a great deal of fondness. And, because of the era I played in, I got to experience some great years in the club game – three or four years when the clubs were at their highest level and the atmospheres at games were so memorable. All volunteers, the coaches, all amateur players and a great sense of club community. Going down on the train for All-Ireland League games in Cork and Limerick, and even more fun on the train back. Now I can look back on both periods of time. I feel really lucky that I was able to play both, because I got the best of both.'

Before I allow Hickie to head back to his new life, I fight my corner that O'Driscoll, D'Arcy and O'Gara were the first full full-time players. 'They're guys who first started when the game was fully professional, rather than in that transition period. They were in full-time squads with a fully professional tournament [Celtic League] on the horizon.' Satisfied, I offer to pick up the tab, before realising I never even ordered the coffees.

# 4

## BLACK AND BLUE: NEW ZEALAND TEACH IRELAND A BRUTAL LESSON

Justin Marshall had been working in an abattoir when the game went professional in New Zealand. The scrum half began his playing career at Southland before moving on to Canterbury. 'When I started in 1992 we were paid petrol money and a bit for a few drinks after the match,' he explains. 'There was always food laid on. I was working in what you'd call a slaughterhouse in deep Southland. It's all about sheep in New Zealand. I started off as a labourer and ended up as a link in the slaughter-board chain. Southland were in the second division back then. They got promoted, but within a year I went from playing in front of a few hundred to 30,000 in Super Rugby. Those days gave me a grounding, an appreciation of where I had come from.'

Ian Jones had been juggling a career as an electrician in 1992, when Ireland arrived in New Zealand to play his All Blacks in an end-of-season tour. 'We would have got together a week before a Saturday game and trained pretty hard on the Wednesday and Thursday,' he says. 'Another run-out on Friday. Professionalism, I suppose, is a state of mind. A lot of us would have been training hard with our clubs and on our own.

'The game in Dunedin was far closer than we would have wanted. We changed a few things for Wellington, raised our game and won with some points to spare.' New Zealand had fifty-three points to spare, as they cantered in eleven tries to a solitary, converted response by Neville Furlong.

At around the same time, All Blacks winger Jeff Wilson had put a semi-professional career in cricket on hold in 1992 to play rugby for his country. 'Goldie' had played Ireland at the World Cup, but failed to see out the game after getting poleaxed in the first ten minutes. 'There was an up-and-under ten metres from our line,' he says. 'I claimed the ball, landed and the whole Irish pack went ploughing into me. I was trampled on and took a couple of shots to the head. It was the old days, so anything stood. I was done by half-time. There was still that passion about playing the All Blacks. For countries, we knew, it was always their biggest game. You could see their focus during the Haka. They threw everything at us from the start. It took us a while to settle and get things done.'

He adds, 'The 1996 and 1997 group had a lot of experience and guys at the peak of their powers. You had Sean Fitzpatrick, Michael and Ian Jones, Zinzan and Robin Brooke. We went over to South Africa and won there, twice. Everyone was starting to embrace professionalism, and it suited us that John Hart came on as our coach. He was ideally suited for that changing landscape.'

In November 1997 Justin Marshall was all set for his twentieth international cap when the All Blacks embarked on a northern hemisphere tour. He had come into the team following the 1995 World Cup and had only experienced one defeat – by South Africa in Johannesburg – as an All Black. Before starting the tour, New Zealand wrapped up the Tri Nations and claimed the Bledisloe Cup. Fitzpatrick was tour captain, but the wily hooker was battling with a slew of injuries and niggles. He rarely trained during the month-long trip, and faced fitness tests each Friday. He failed each one, but made his ninety-second and final appearance, off the bench, against Wales on 29 November. It was his first outing as sub in a black jersey. Despite the presence of world-class veterans Jones and the Brookes (Robin and Zinzan), and Frank Bunce in the squad, Hart opted for Marshall as his captain. The retired scrum half, now a commentator with Sky Sport NZ, recalls, 'It was an easy introduction for me. Each week they expected Fitzy to play, and he took the press conferences. He would get the bad news the day before, or [on the] morning, and all I had to do was lead the teams out. There were leaders across the field too, so it was never a case of me having to call all the shots.'

At its conclusion, the tour would see the All Blacks' top talents complete an eleven-month season. Stradey Park in Llanelli, against the local Scarlets team, had been their first stop on the tour. Hart had fielded a strong team, and the All Blacks ran out 81–3 victors. Moving on to the next weekend in Dublin, the players were relatively fresh. Ian Jones, for one, was looking forward to running out at Lansdowne Road again. 'I had played for the All Blacks there before, against Leinster in 1989, and had the chance to run out there again for the Baa Baas [Barbarians]. I was there for that wonderful Test match in 1989 when Willie Anderson approached Buck [Shelford] in the Haka,' he declares.

Ireland had yet to beat the All Blacks in thirteen attempts, stretching back to a 15–0 reverse at the same Dublin venue in 1905. 'There is a lot more pressure captaining your country against a team that has never beaten you,' Marshall maintains. 'You always want to be on the right side of the fence when the game is done. The other side has a chance, each time, to create history.'

Jones takes the reasoning further. 'Most All Blacks have a keen sense of history. "Not on my watch" was a phrase we had as players, and I'm sure that extends to the current crop.'

As game day approached, New Zealand upped their training-ground intensity. To them, Ireland were the first of four stepping stones towards a year of utter dominance. Wilson says, 'We were on a roll coming into that game. I can honestly say, we knew there was a challenge in front of us, but there was never a point where we considered the fact we might lose. That meant, as a group, we got to enjoy playing Ireland in that great stadium. I'm grateful to have played at a time when those old stadiums, with their great history, were still in one piece.'

Hart opted to omit Jonah Lomu, scorer of two tries against Ireland at the World Cup, from the match-day squad in anticipation of bruising encounters with England. Glen Osborne took his place on the left wing. Fitzpatrick was ruled out on the Friday morning before the match but the team had trained with Norm Hewitt as hooker for most of the week. He was set for a long-awaited Test debut.

Brian Ashton, in contrast, was scattering out Test caps like confetti. Ten months into a six-year contract, the Irish coach was keen to shake up a struggling team. He rewarded some of the players who had shone during a hellacious developmental tour to New Zealand and Samoa (played seven, lost six) that summer. Kieron Dawson, David Erskine, Conor McGuinness, John McWeeney, Kevin Maggs, Kevin Nowlan and Malcolm O'Kelly were all slated for Ireland debuts. The pack had four British & Irish Lions – captain Keith Wood, Nick Popplewell, Paul Wallace and Eric Miller – and the experienced Eric Elwood was at out-half.

Leinster winger Denis Hickie had missed the summer tour through injury. He had scored two tries in his first three Test matches, and had experienced his first run-in with the IRFU blazers hours before his debut against Wales. He recalls, 'The night before your first game you can't sleep anyway, but I had just gotten to sleep when the alarm went off. I went down the street in my pyjamas. We were all out, standing there, because the alickadoos [non-playing members of a union or club – also known as 'committee men' or 'blazers'] had had late drinks in one of the bedrooms and were smoking cigars that set off the alarms. You couldn't make it up … It's just the way the game was run. It was an amateur game that, overnight, became professional.'

A win over Wales in Cardiff had been Ashton's sole success during the Five Nations. A swathe of senior players had withdrawn from the New Zealand and Samoa tour, downgrading its importance, but increasing the Englishman's frustration. One particular bugbear, apart from his chagrin at the players' lack of basic skills, was the union's failure to ensure he returned to Ireland with four provincial head coaches in place. Mike Ruddock and Warren Gatland had been installed at Leinster and Connacht, respectively; Clive Griffiths had looked set for Ulster, before walking away. Griffiths' fellow Welshman, John Bevan, had gone a step further – he had a meeting with the senior Munster players at Thomond Park – but changed his mind. 'I was bloody furious,' Ashton told Fanning, in *From There to Here*. 'We were getting thrashed left, right and centre on the other side of the world, with two provinces without full-time coaches.'

The tour convinced Ashton that Ireland's future lay in blooding young talents and sourcing foreign players with Irish ties, while retaining a core of experienced, proven heads. Based in England, he was an infrequent spectator at AIL games (two over two seasons), but watched Heineken Cup footage of the provinces and noted the stand-out talents. Form rather than reputation would be the central tenet on his team. Having scored four tries in seven Leinster starts that season, twenty-one-year-old St Mary's winger McWeeney was exactly who Ashton was looking for. Out with the hopeless and in with the hopefuls.

Reggie Corrigan, who started on the bench for the game, says, 'I was surprised by the call, but everything had been leading towards that. Ashton was picking on form, and Leinster had done well that year, beating Leicester in the Heineken Cup at Donnybrook. We were making a bit of noise. Our backline was exciting, and scoring tries the likes of which hadn't been seen before. There was a strong feeling that certain people would get in as it was a change-around with Ashton. He was looking for guys with strong skill-sets.'

Hickie says, 'John had an awesome, great year for Leinster, but was probably playing for them on a semi-professional contract. The expectations of people were completely unrealistic. There was no appreciation for the differences … you look back now and there was no parity back then.' St Mary's had four players in the Irish backline – Hickie, McWeeney, scrum half McGuinness and fullback Nowlan, completing a remarkable ascent that had taken him from St Mary's sixth team to the national side in less than four years.

The Templeville Road club had another debutant to cheer on in the Irish pack. Malcolm O'Kelly had played with Leinster during the first season of professionalism, but was part of the exodus to London Irish. The lock comments, 'It was a brilliant day for me. Keith Wood would have been the captain. We really got stuck into them. We might have even scored first, and it was just one of those amazing days in Lansdowne Road. It wouldn't have lasted very long. We were very much a sixty-minute side, which is what we were seen as at the time. We would run out of juice, or ideas. We would give it everything we had and just run out of steam. It is hard to know what it was down to. A lot of the time, I certainly felt tired going into matches, so the fitness regime wouldn't have been ideal either, in terms of looking after the players. But still, there was a certain amount of match fitness and match belief. If you don't have the belief that you are going to win; well, that affected us in those days.'

'Back then,' Hickie proclaims, 'there was zero parity. There was no area of the game where an Irish team could step up to New Zealand – fitness, skills, technical ability, game plan, defence. The skills and ability just weren't there, because the organisation – skills, fitness and conditioning coaches – wasn't there. Players had not been developed as much as they had in New Zealand. They were just behind in every manner.' Aged twenty-one, however, and in a glut of form, Hickie backed Ireland to push the All Blacks close. 'When you go out to play a game, you don't ever think you are going to lose. You always think you have a chance. If you don't think that, you shouldn't be playing.'

In the away dressing room, Marshall turned the air blue in a pre-match speech Wilson still laughs about: 'Short, sweet, lots of expletives.' Marshall comments, 'We had so many legends on the team that I didn't have to worry about captaining. I knew I could rely on that quality, experience and skill-set. We had a clear game plan and were in sync. What I had seen with Irish rugby teams, I knew they were going to rely on brute passion. They had a lot of new caps but, the way I saw it, they were an inexperienced side with nothing to lose. That's dangerous. We knew we had to match that intensity. We had to get our blood boiling. That was the basis of my speech, brief as it was.'

'That was probably the most physical game I have ever played in,' says Eddie Halvey, Ireland's open-side flanker. 'The hits in open play and in the contact areas were brutal. They were a different class back then. They are still the best in the world, but the games are closer now. Back then they were beating teams by thirty and forty points. Against the southern hemisphere teams, you either got it right or you got it very wrong.'

In a sold-out Lansdowne Road, Marshall remembers Ireland 'exploding out of the blocks'. After ten minutes of pressure they scored a try. 'It was just an onslaught. Standing under the posts for that conversion I remember thinking, "Holy shit, we are in for a war today". The crowd were feverish, ferocious and Ireland were throwing bodies into the breakdown. We knew we'd have to grind our teeth.'

Wood was strained by an increased workload – from Munster to Harlequins – in the English Premiership, but was immense in the first half. Two Andrew Mehrtens penalties tipped New Zealand ahead, but Wood wrested the lead back with his second try of the game. Miller hacked a loose ball ahead and the Irish hooker outsprinted Wilson to touch down. It was 15–14 after twenty-seven minutes. 'Keith Wood was special that day,' Wilson declares. 'His performance just added to the legend that is Keith Wood. It was a feisty start, but we were always confident that, over the course of eighty minutes, we'd get the job done. Ireland had the ability to throw everything at the All Blacks for forty, fifty, sixty minutes.'

Fired up but undisciplined, Ireland gave away penalties that Mehrtens continued to put away. 'You can have all the fire in your guts and be in the ascendancy, but you need to turn that into points,' Marshall says. 'We were slowly but surely accumulating points. For all of Ireland's aggression and dominance in that half, they didn't put scoreboard pressure on us.'

Nick Mallett, then coach of South Africa, was of the belief that unless his team scored thirty points against New Zealand, they would not stand a chance of winning. Fifteen was the peak of Ireland's powers as the first-half ticked down. The visitors were not finished yet. Their forwards gradually, brutally, worked their way into a scoring position. 'I remember coming across Zinzan Brooke and his ability to just dictate,' says O'Kelly. 'He seemed to be screaming and shouting at the players, telling them what to do and what have you. And I remember being in awe of the guy.'

Christian Cullen, scorer of eighteen tries in nineteen Test starts, had been earmarked as the All Blacks' biggest attacking threat. Black shirts streamed forward in search of a score to take to the dressing rooms. Cullen darted up the right wing and was set upon by three Irishmen. Osborne played scrum half and found his captain nearby. Marshall assessed options to his left and, deciding little was on, jinked inside Dawson and made for the line. Four strides in and he was at the Irish twenty-two and avoiding a tap-tackle from Wood. McWeeney pursued, but both he and Nowlan arrived too late to prevent the try. Mehrtens converted as the half ended with New Zealand 27–15 ahead. 'For all their pressure and courageous play,' says Marshall, 'Ireland went in twelve points down.'

Halfway there, but little else left in the tank. Paddy Johns and Popplewell, with London Irish and Newcastle, respectively, were familiar with frantic league matches in England. Both looked spent as they trudged towards the dressing-room steps. Popplewell glanced back at the East Stand scoreboard and shook his head. Back in the Irish dressing room, Wood was receiving treatment to a gammy ankle and wondering if he could go on. Rob Henderson, a one-Test veteran and survivor from that summer's developmental tour, was attempting to rouse his backline colleagues for the second forty. McWeeney was close to tears. Wilson had given him a rough ride in the opening forty minutes.

The game ran away from Ireland in the second half, with Wood forced to watch most of it on crutches in the dugout beneath the West Stand.

O'Kelly notes, 'There was a very distinct game change for them in terms of they just went right through us in the forwards. They just tightened things up. They had been throwing it around, and we had been knocking them back. There was a distinct game-plan change, and they just went right through the middle of us, and they just started scoring tries. No discredit to them, but we were just chasing shadows in the second half. They had so much artillery that you couldn't live with.'

Ian Jones remembers the tactical change as 'slight'. He adds, 'We trucked guys through the middle before and after the break. Through fatigue or lapses in concentration, the gaps started opening up and the backs scored all the tries. We could never go wide without going through the middle at the start. We had to earn the right to go wide. It was also about playing at the highest intensity for long periods. When you play at that level for eighty minutes you have the ability to put points on a team very quickly … We had some good depth coming off our bench too, so there was never a drop in our intensity or speed.'

Marshall continues, 'We had the calibre of players that, when we sniffed blood, were able to attack from all angles. All of a sudden it is up to the opposition to respond. If they don't, we go for the jugular.'

Reggie Corrigan looked on from the bench. Four days shy of his twenty-seventh birthday, the Leinster prop was combining provincial duties with second-division club rugby at Greystones. He had given up a full-time job for a three-month trial at Leinster, and form had elevated him to the national team. He would earn his first cap a week later against Canada. Ashton spared him as Popplewell and Wallace saw the game to the bitter end. He recalls, 'Although our skill levels weren't good, our fitness levels were nowhere near good enough to bring us through eighty minutes of a game. They would get us to maybe fifty, sixty minutes of a game, and then we fell apart out of fatigue, lack of organisation; and concentration goes when you're tired. That was always our failing. Against the bigger teams we would fade in the last twenty minutes. The challenge was to get up to a level of fitness where we could maintain it for eighty minutes.

'The phenomenal speed and the sheer physical size of the players did make you stop and think. New Zealand are not the biggest team in the world, compared to South Africa and England, but that black jersey and the speed at which the game was played was something else. They didn't make a mistake, and their skill levels were unreal. The ball moved through their hands lightning fast. They didn't make mistakes or drop balls. If you made a mistake they would punish you. It wasn't so much the physical size but the intensity and the way they played the game that stood out.'

The wheels came off for Ireland as the All Blacks ran in five tries. Wilson and Osborne crossed twice, and Mehrtens, who scored thirty-three points that afternoon, also dotted down. 'I did a lot of falling over the line,' a modest Wilson remarks. 'A lot of people were giving me good opportunities to score, so I was happy I could finish some of them off. I was the beneficiary, finishing off many great attacking moves.

'Once we got on a roll, our confidence grew. By the end, it looks as though we dominated from start to finish, but that was not necessarily the case. You think it was one-sided, but when you had someone like Mehrtens kicking at eighty-five per cent, you're scoring in sevens, so the score can go up quickly. We were a testament to pro footy, and our conditioning was way ahead of the game.'

The scoreline read 63–15 when Tony Spreadbury blew his whistle for full-time. Donald McRae, researching for his book *Winter Colours*, spoke with Ashton after the game. 'The All Blacks are now so good,' the coach proclaimed, 'they're running out of teams to play.' Certain nations had swan-dived into professionalism, while others closed their eyes and cannonballed. Ireland, it seemed, teetered to the edge in water wings and dipped a cautious toe.

'The success of the AIL in the 1990s proved to be no breeding ground for success in the national team,' states *The Sunday Times* reporter Peter

O'Reilly. 'It was all blood and thunder stuff, local derbies, hard-fought wins. The jump from club rugby to international was too great though. That is why we were so shit in the 1990s. Setting up the provinces as our professional representatives was like setting up a business. Give them a home, put structures and a professional support staff in place. Still, it was slow coming.'

One of the reasons Jones remembers Lansdowne Road fondly is for its proximity to Dublin city centre. 'Heck yeah, we had fun that night. I can't remember all of the details, of course. I was privileged to play in that game and to be part of a team that was so unique in nature and filled with special talents – Fitzy, Zinzan, Mehrtens and Jonah Lomu. You have to savour those Test wins and remember that it could always be your last.

'The post-match speech was nerve-racking,' admits Marshall. 'It was not so much getting up and saying a few words in front of the Irish team and dignitaries but my own teammates. These were guys I had looked up to and admired for so long. They were all watching me now and hoping I'd mess up, so they could have a laugh.

'Speaking of which, and I will apologise now in your book if I haven't before. I got confused and I called Keith Wood "Nick" in my speech. Must have mixed him up with Nick Popplewell. That was embarrassing.'

Ireland would be happy to spread the embarrassment out. Two years as professionals, yet light years behind the world-leading All Blacks. Amateurism was supposed to be a remnant of the past, but it hung over Ireland and would not encounter a meaningful gust until a dark night in Lens, France, two years on.

# 5

## MUNSTER PLANT A FLAG

Rags, who had been around the squad for a couple of seasons, stood up and said, 'We want to win the European Cup.' People burst out laughing – that was the general atmosphere.

*David Wallace*

By 1996 the Munster branch had six full-time contracts, eighteen part-time deals and developmental offers for the province's top eight prospects. While many of the younger players were in college, and delighted with a £2,000 stipend to play rugby, senior squad members parked jobs such as electrician, bank teller, carpenter and dairy farmer to pursue a new career path. Prop Peter Clohessy, who had earned fifteen Ireland caps upon the advent of professionalism, was managing a courier company, but took up his contract offer. 'I said I'd give it a lash for a couple of years and see what happened. A lot of the other lads felt the same way. It was a novelty. No one, then, saw it as a real career option. I kept my hand in with a couple of other jobs, to keep ticking over.'

Munster's first Heineken Cup campaign, in 1995, included the sum total of two games and lasted seven days. The province that had famously beaten the All Blacks in 1978, and Australia in 1981 and 1992, could draw on club rugby giants such as Shannon, Young Munster, Cork Constitution and Garryowen. Consistency had long been an issue in the Irish Interprovincial Championship, but they could beat all comers when their blood was up.

They trailed Swansea 13–10 going into the final minutes on 1 November 1995, before Paul Burke popped a pass to fullback Pat Murray, who broke a tackle before diving over. Little did the players know at the time, but Murray's score would spark a twelve-year unbeaten run for Munster, in Europe, at Thomond Park. Over the course of that run, the province's relationship with the Heineken would go from a passing interest to a full-blown love affair. Heartbreaks and adulation.

'What drove the Irish success story was Munster, and what drove Munster was the AIL,' Peter O'Reilly explains. 'Since 1990, up until St Mary's won it in 2000, and for a few years after that, Munster teams dominated the AIL. That fierce parochialism that existed within teams like Cork Constitution, Shannon and Garryowen – Munster harmonised that into one team and added some organisation to it. There was always something very parochial and small town about them. There was a proper training schedule in place at Munster, but divisions existed – the Garryowen lads and the Shannon lads would train in their own pods out at the University of Limerick. You were very much defined by your club when you came into training.'

The following season, 1996/97, saw an expanded Heineken Cup and, despite a heavy defeat by Cardiff, an opportunity to reach the knock-out stages. Toulouse waited at Les Sept Deniers stadium. Keith Wood had departed for Harlequins in London and Clohessy – serving a six-month ban for stamping – was heading to Australia for a season of Super 12 rugby. The Toulouse match got away from Munster early and midway through the second half, with his team haemorrhaging points, captain Mick Galwey gathered his colleagues into a huddle and pleaded, 'Let's keep it under fifty.' The final score was 60–19.

As one of the travelling press corps that day, O'Reilly recalls, 'We were on the same charter flight as the team the day after, and were picked up by the bus to the airport that morning. The Munster players were on the bus, and many were still pissed from the night before. One of the players was still sucking on the sly can down the back of the bus.

'Around that time, Munster would often be contacted by the IRFU to let them know their fitness coordinator would be down to perform the fitness and bleep tests. The club contacted the players, and that night, after the tests were done, would be when they would go on the lash. They knew the coordinator would not be down for another while.'

David Wallace went straight from school into Garryowen's senior set-up, and was there less than two seasons before Munster, then Ireland, came calling. Before he embarked on Ireland's 1997 summer tour, Wallace had taken part in his first meeting with Munster's senior squad. It would be the only time they would all meet John Bevan, their prospective coach. 'I was shocked to be there,' Wallace admits. 'I was in with the likes of Gaillimh and Claw. I was a fan of Munster growing up, and to be almost at the same level as those guys, and part of that conversation, really hit home. I was delighted to be there. The feeling must not have been mutual for Bevan, as he never took up the role. He probably saw us bunch of reprobates and said, "I'm out of here." I'm sure he regrets that decision.'

Following a failed attempt to secure the coaching services of Bevan, Munster installed a management trio of Declan Kidney, Jerry Holland and Niall O'Donovan, the latter of whom was in charge of logistics and contract negotiations. Ian Fleming was part-time physio, and there was an occasional kit-man. Kidney would, in time, subsume Holland's coaching duties. From the first day it was clear to the playing staff who would be calling the shots. It was up to the players if they obeyed or shot back. Clohessy proclaims, 'I was one of the senior lads at the team when I got back [from Australia]. Declan was still fresh from his schools background and had a certain way about him. Treating most of us like we were his pupils. He wanted to do things one way, but we didn't agree with it. We stood up for the young fellas too when we felt it was necessary. Eventually, we found a happy medium.'

One such compromise occurred when Kidney divided the Munster squad into five- and six-man groups, and sent them off orienteering. Clohessy and Galwey were teamed together with younger squad members.

Donncha O'Callaghan recalls the veterans' attitude as, 'Who thought we'd enjoy this shite?' The team marked their card at a couple of posts before skulking off for some pints. 'We definitely did some orienteering,' insists Clohessy, 'but the detour to the pub was great for bonding too. We were cute enough to finish up in time to get back at the same time as everyone else.'

Wallace says, 'Declan realised he was fighting a losing battle trying to discipline Gaillimh and Claw. He picked the battles he could win. We were young lads up to no good at the time. The senior guys took us under their wing and showed us what it would be like to be an old-school rugby player.'

A goal-setting meeting with Dave Mahedy at the University of Limerick training base, before the 1997/98 season, still resonates with Wallace. 'We were coming up with goals like beating Ulster, winning in France and winning the interpros. John "Rags" Kelly, who had been around the squad for a couple of seasons, stood up and said, "We want to win the European Cup." People burst out laughing – that was the general atmosphere. Dave said he thought we should put it up, and the response from a good few of us was "Ah, that's not realistic." There was a lot of debate about actually putting it up on the board. Rags had to argue his point, to convince us to put it up. That was the attitude at the time. We were a group that was thrown together who didn't back ourselves. We had no past history in the competition and thought Europe was a competition for the big teams. The year before we had been hammered by Toulouse. As far as many of us were concerned, there were the serious teams of Europe – then ourselves.'

Peter Stringer was nineteen when he made his debut for Munster, in October 1998. Six years previously Stringer had been an aspiring scrum half in Presentation Brothers College, Cork. World champions Australia arrived at Musgrave Park, Cork, to take on Munster, and the teenager was one of the ballboys. He says, 'I was given the bucket of sand and would come on when Charlie Haly was kicking at goal. Gaillimh and

Claw were playing that day. I still have a photo from the day – Gaillimh was sent off for fighting. The picture is of him walking off, and I'm on the sideline holding a bucket of sand. A few years later and we were in the same dressing room.'

Stringer had left school, where he had played under Kidney, in 1996 and stepped straight into the Munster environment. 'It was so alien for me,' he confesses. 'I was in with guys like Anthony Foley, Eddie Halvey, Claw and Gaillimh. It was quite daunting for a young fella, but you worked hard and learned your trade. You followed suit with what everyone else did.' The majority of the Munster squad required minimal arm-twisting to partake in drinking sessions after matches or – 'for bonding purposes' – early in the week of a big game. 'I went along on the nights out,' says Stringer, a tee-totaller, 'but as for the drinking parts, I held tough. I had been through school and college, and a big part of it had been about drinking. I had to withstand that peer pressure, so I was well able to handle myself by the time I joined up with Munster.'

***

Halvey, Foley and Alan Quinlan – three talented back rows in their mid-twenties – were already veterans of the Shannon RFC drinking crew. Shannon won the first of four consecutive AIL titles in 1995, so had plenty of reasons to celebrate. Halvey had just turned twenty-five when rugby was declared open. A talented Gaelic footballer, he found time to line out for both Treaty Sarsfields and his county. 'I remember one time,' says Halvey, 'when myself, Dan Larkin, Pat Murray and Phil Danaher all played for Shannon in the morning, and played for Limerick against Tipp in the Munster Championship that afternoon.'

Halvey played in Munster's first Heineken Cup match before, in January 1996, signing for Saracens on the same day as Michael Lynagh. 'Sarries had some very talented back rows then,' recalls Donal Lenihan. 'Tony Diprose, Ruan Pienaar and Richard Hill were on the books. Eddie found it difficult to adapt to that professional drive over there. You can say that for all professional sports – some guys react better to that regimented lifestyle than others.'

'I only lasted six months,' Halvey says, 'as my mother became terminally ill with cancer. I took back up with Munster and was offered a full-time deal. We would have trained twice a week – once in Cork and once in Limerick – and played on weekends. We did some training with our clubs too. Everyone was still trying to find their feet. The coaches were new to it as well, and everyone was trying to do their best for the team. There were no individual training programmes for players; it was one size fits all.'

Wallace remembers Halvey as an incredibly and naturally talented player in the amateur set-up. 'He was streets ahead of everyone else,' says Wallace. 'Once the game went professional it improved fitness, skill levels, power and the strength and conditioning of most guys. It gives guys such an added advantage.

'Guys like Eddie would have got by on that natural talent alone in the past, but times were changing. To be fair to the rest of the team, you can't have one guy doing his thing, as good as he is, and the rest of the team working hard. That doesn't lend itself to the professional game and that sense of team spirit. I was lucky to be coming through at a young age, but in a lot of ways you have to respect the likes of Gaillimh and Claw. For them to adapt and stay at the top level of the game, having come from a staunchly amateur background, is commendable.'

Wallace adds, 'To succeed today you need to have that work ethic. Natural talent will only get you so far, but you will be quickly exposed if you are not willing to put the work in. As time goes on, less guys get through the system without that mix of talent and the willingness to graft for the team.'

Malcolm O'Kelly came across the Limerick native in Irish training camps. 'Halvey was a disaster,' he states. 'He couldn't help himself, unfortunately. He didn't have the ethos that was going to make him a great player that he had the potential to possibly become. He just didn't have it. He didn't have any ambition. If you do, if you really want it, you do whatever it takes to do it. You're prepared to train and work hard.'

Lenihan became Ireland's team manager in 1998. The last of Halvey's eight international caps was in November 1997, but he was in and out of Irish squads for the next three years until he moved to London Irish. Lenihan comments, 'Eddie had a massive amount of talent, but found it difficult to give that same level of commitment. We were doing a fitness test with Ireland up in Dublin in 1999, and we had to get Anthony Foley to make sure Eddie got up, in the car, in time for it. Anthony showed up late and apologising, as he had waited for Eddie as long as he could but he never showed. We gave him plenty of chances.'

Halvey concedes, 'A lot of the time in those years, I wasn't fit enough, and that, to be brutally honest, was down to myself. I wasn't being a true professional as they might say. Having been an amateur, I enjoyed getting out there and playing for the love of the sport. When you're trying to justify it as a job it loses some of that … At times I could have done a bit more and I wasn't. I was just getting by. It was the background stuff that got to me. I just wanted to go out and play matches at the weekend.

'I could have given more, and I would have gotten an awful lot more out of it,' he adds. 'That was not from a lack of trying and pushing by the coaches and teammates. It took me quite a lot of time to get that message across to myself, but it was too late by the time you realise that and age is catching up with you. There were times when I wasn't at those peak levels, and other times when I was. It was definitely my own fault. Mental strength, not just physical strength, is so vital in players nowadays. That crossover to professionalism affected me.'

Hailing from Tipperary, Quinlan also divvied his sporting loyalties between Gaelic football, hurling and rugby. 'I had that sense of pride and passion for my club, Clanwilliam in Tipperary town. When I went to Shannon I really saw what it meant to the people in the community, local community, parish and all around that area. People devoted their lives to the club and volunteered for the club. It was their place to meet and place to go and socialise. There was something that gave them a bit of hope and inspiration around their own lives. That was brilliant, and it continued on to Munster.

'That whole tradition of guys from different clubs coming together and representing Munster. I suppose what happened with the All Blacks – beating them in 1978 – and defeating Australia in 1992. Before I ever got to play for the province, I knew all about their history, tradition and past players. I was lucky to come through at a time when there was a Heineken Cup – a European stage to perform on. Past guys who were as good or better didn't get that opportunity.

'It was a strange time,' says Quinlan. 'A little bit of the unknown, I think. My first contract was a part-time deal in 1996. The main feeling was one of excitement, because I had worked for five-and-a-half-years as a mechanic before that. For me, this was getting paid to do something I loved doing anyway, so there were no big expectations or thoughts that you were going to make a career out of it. And I say unknown, as there was nothing or no one to measure it against. We didn't really know what we were getting ourselves into.

'We were lucky that we had Declan, as he grounded us, tried to get us to understand what it meant to be a professional – the discipline and sacrifices that were required. It was something that was a work in progress for a number of years. We were trying to get our heads around the diet side of things, eating the right foods, pushing yourself, and how far could you go fitness-wise.

'Certainly in 1997, a lot of guys were part time, so we trained in the morning in the gym, and most guys would go to work and come back, and we would do a rugby or a fitness session in the evening. It was a strange scenario. Training sessions were all over the place, and most of them were in UL [University of Limerick], but we could be training in some of the clubs in the evenings. So we didn't really have any space as such, there were no offices or no particular gym, and we were using the facilities out of UL. It was kind of unstructured, and there were not enough support staff around. That was a learning curve for everyone.'

Quinlan was a Munster mainstay for fifteen seasons – earning 206 caps – but made just 27 Ireland appearances (11 starts) during a decade in and out of international favour. 'Look,' he says, 'I had to understand the whole disparate side of life away from the game, and what was required to push myself. I knew I had a bit of talent for sure, but just from a fitness point of view, from that diet point of view, it was very early days for me. I burst onto the scene, making line breaks up and down the field and thought everything was easy, but there was a lot more to the game than that.

'The higher you go up the levels you find that out. I played well for a couple of years for Munster and got into the Irish squad, but picked up a shoulder injury in 1998 and couldn't really force my way back in … There was a period there where I probably wasn't at the required level of fitness and mentality. I hadn't adapted and learned what was required to play at the level above Munster, but I was learning all the time. After 2001 I realised what was required. Again, experiences teach you stuff, and I got the best out of myself for a couple of years after that. I had some injuries along the way, which kind of hampered me, but I have no qualms really. I was relying on talent and skill, which, thankfully, I had naturally. But just some of the fundamentals and the principles of the game, I wasn't … I wasn't mentally tough enough either.'

Quinlan adds, 'I look back now, and I just wish I had known then what I know now. I think I would have got a lot more caps, and probably pushed myself on a little bit in the earlier days to be sure. But that's just the way it is.'

Anthony Foley had played interprovincials for Munster in the amateur era and was looked upon as a long-term prospect and future captain when, at the age of twenty-one, he lined out as open-side in the Heineken Cup victory over Swansea, in 1995. By that stage Foley had played six times for Ireland, and appeared against Japan in a World Cup. The amateur-to-professional switch had no immediate impact on him, but – for Munster and Ireland – increased fitness demands saw his career stall.

'It was very difficult,' he admits. 'And, at the time, we didn't have any sort of professional model to base it on. We were the first really professional sports teams within Ireland and were really finding our way in the dark for a lot of it. Look, once we got a handle on it and the competition that we were playing in grew, it became evident that there was a lot of excitement around it and you could earn a decent living from it, and fellas cottoned on and made the changeover.

'For me personally,' Foley adds, 'it was around physical development. When you're a big lad coming through, you really didn't need, in the amateur game at the time, much time in the gym. Your physical presence would get you through games. But then, a couple of years into the professional game, you were the same size, but you were relying on skill and durability. You needed to adjust to that and make sure you were able to play through seasons. I got into that. There were a few stumbling blocks along the way, but I got over that and never looked back. I feel it was important that I got to see both sides of the game.'

One of Foley's stumbling blocks included three years in the international wilderness, bookended by defeats by England. 'You talked to yourself; you figured it out,' he says of his renewed drive. 'There were a lot of good role models around the club at the time. Around that period when I was struggling to adjust, we [Shannon] won four AILs on the bounce, and Munster had won a few interprovincials. You might wonder how you were struggling, but you were because you wanted to be the best at the highest possible level. It all depends what standards you were holding yourself to. Mine would have been international standard.'

Any suggestion that Halvey and Foley's initial lack of drive for personal improvement hindered the team grates on Ronan O'Gara. 'That would be very inaccurate,' he declares. 'You can't say they didn't apply themselves. Fair enough, maybe the one issue might have been them coming from an amateur game and their body-fat percentage may have been higher, but what they brought to the party, to the pitch, to the environment was tenfold.

'They are two that probably stand out as big influences, you know, because you don't learn from a text book; you learn from people. That's really important. You learn how to play, but you learn how to cheat as well. There's a good way of cheating – and that's not unfair play. You learn how to do little things to get the job done. That's not in a ruck or anything, but it's in terms of if all the defensive line is nine yards back instead of ten yards back, the ref is not going to ping you. If one fella is eight yards back and another lad is twelve yards, there is a dog-leg and it is an easy decision. These are the things you pick up from players who've been there and know what they're talking about. You wouldn't read about that anywhere.'

Halvey says, 'I know for a fact that I could have got a whole lot more out of it. I know time passes by and you're too late, but … I thoroughly enjoyed what I was doing. I've got great friends and great memories out of the game. I don't think I ever let a team down – ever. I went out there and gave it everything.'

Foley was a virtual ever-present for Ireland upon his recall. He played fifty-three times over five years (taking his total to sixty-two), and scored five tries. He retired from Munster in 2008, having represented the province 188 times. Having acted as forwards coach at his province for four seasons, Foley was named head coach in 2014. Asked to sum up Munster's enduring appeal to Irish rugby supporters, and their ability to rouse themselves for European matches, he answers, 'Pride. It's pride in place, pride in parish, pride in your friends. It is understanding who you represent. It's not just yourself, it is the people connected to you going back to your underage coach, the school you came out of, the parish you came out of. A lot of people are connected to you, and it is how you hold yourself to that. That's the best you can do.'

***

The season of 1999/2000 saw Munster appoint a full-time fitness coach in Fergal O'Callaghan, import John Langford from Australia and entice Keith Wood back for a season. Wallace began to hold down a regular spot in the back row. It was also the season that Halvey turned down a full-time contract and went back to club rugby and working as a sales representative for a meat wholesalers.

'You can fall in love with a game,' Halvey reasons. 'Your diet, your life-style. You are being constantly monitored, measured and counted … I just fell out of love with it. I never stopped enjoying the game, but I fell out of love with everything around it. You had fellas there that would die for you at Munster, but I just didn't have the appetite. I still loved playing club rugby – it was a purer form of enjoyment.'

'Declan gave us a real sense of belief and drive,' says Wallace. 'Having someone like Langford arrive and seeing his work ethic helped immensely. That pre-season in 1999 you could see that we were turning into athletes, rather than just rugby players. Prior to that season, we had the talent, but never had the fitness levels the English and French sides had. We would stay with them for fifty or sixty minutes – then they would put us away. For the first time ever we were on an equal footing. It made a massive difference in terms of the jump we made that season. Added to that, we had O'Gara and Stringer coming through as regulars.'

'Myself, Frankie Sheahan, Wally [David Wallace], Anthony Horgan and ROG [Ronan O'Gara] all competed at the highest level in Munster schools and transitioned at the same time,' says Stringer. 'As halfbacks, myself and ROG knew what we wanted, and played to the team's strengths. The last thing the forwards want to see after getting up from a good scrum is the ball going nowhere.'

Stringer juggled a part-time rugby contract and a chemistry degree at University College Cork in his first season (1997/98) with Munster. By the time Munster embarked on their quest to reach the Heineken Cup final, in May 2000, Stringer and O'Gara had developed a 'professional connection and an incredible relationship'.

'We led completely different lives away from the pitch,' the scrum half says. 'He was a year ahead in school, so we both had our own set of friends. Only when we got to Munster did we start playing well together. It continued that way for many years. It was important, I feel, to live those separate lives away from the game. We're not that close, but we spent most of our careers together. I know that I needed the outlet of those friends and my family, as it was an escape from the squad environment. Still, you often found you were clinging onto old friends and a way of life the more the pro game took over.'

O'Gara credits Munster's older pros for instilling in him that pride in the jersey, the cause. 'I would've got a £7,500 a year full-time contract, and the established lads were on £25,000. It was more of a grant than a wage, and it was fine for most lads as they were still living at home. The one young lad that got a car was Brian O'Meara. He was the star.'

He adds, 'I'm very conscious of how the senior lads shaped me. That's something I'm very proud of – the fact that I always continued to represent them, because they are your mentors for all your years. I respected those players and placed huge value on the things I learned from them. Without them I'd be a tenth of the player I became. That environment at the time was special. Perhaps, trophywise, we didn't reach our optimum level … perhaps if we'd had a Joe Schmidt-type coach in the earlier years we could have won more.

'Keith Wood was obviously good, as he brought ideas from Harlequins,' O'Gara continues. 'Keith played one year with us, but he was involved in Ireland a good bit, so us Munster lads learned from him. Then we had a lot of intelligent players – Dominic Crotty, John Kelly, Killian Keane, Jason

Holland. Then you contrast that with fellas like Anthony Horgan, Mike Mullins, John O'Neill – direct and hard-running. You have Rhys Ellison and Trevor Halstead too.

'Munster have always had good backs, but the perception was the forwards were the dominant part. Yes they were, but that's because we always had such back-row options. Axel [Anthony Foley] was there, Jim Williams, Denis Leamy, Halvey, Quinlan. Colm McMahon was always sniping around; David Corkery, Greg Tuohy. Time will tell, but there were freakishly good players at Munster. Dave Wallace was a different class to most players. The Leinster equivalent [today] would be Sean O'Brien. These names feature on a world stage. That's how good they are.'

'Beating Saracens at Vicarage Road [their home ground, in November 1999] was the beginning of our turnaround,' Wallace adds. 'Pipping them at home gave us a lot of confidence. On our day, if we played to our ability, we could beat anyone. Woody [Keith Wood] coming back gave me so much confidence. He was a bit like Brian O'Driscoll with Leinster. He was world-class. So, when you saw he was on your team, you felt you could do anything. I came through the age grades with ROG, too, and I always felt confident playing behind him; he gave you the best percentages of winning, he controlled games, kicked to the corners and played to the strengths and advantages of the team. A lot of young out-halves now get too much spoon-feeding in the academies, and don't have the inherent game-management skills. ROG came from that club-rugby background where it was either sink or swim. With him in place, the veterans and Woody, who had returned that season, we developed an attitude of, "Why shouldn't we be beating these teams?"'

For Wallace, the memories of lashing back against Saracens, despite being 34–28 down in the final minutes, are vivid. 'We had a ruck on our twenty-two, and we marched them down the park from there. Jeremy Staunton got a try in the corner and ROG hit that conversion that went over the post to win it.

'We faced them the next weekend at Thomond Park. It had a 15,000 capacity back then, but there were well over 20,000 there. There was mist and fog about, and it seemed colder under the floodlights. It was an amazing experience – that game – and it showed our mentality at the time. Our view was that we could go out and score a try when we needed to, no matter where we were on the pitch. Mark Mapletoft scored with minutes to go, but Gaillimh told us all, very calmly, that we would go up their end and score the winner. Keith Wood got over, and ROG got the winning conversion that went over after hitting the right-hand post. Funnily enough, we replicated that exact final passage of play the following Monday morning in training at Thomond Park. We got over for a try and were in good spirits as ROG took a conversion from the same position. His kick came off the same post and went over. We fell about the place. I don't know whether he meant it or not, but it was certainly impressive. Those wins were two big steps on the way to developing that culture where we felt we could beat whoever we wanted.'

In 2001/02 Kidney introduced a twenty-one-year-old Young Munster lock, Paul O'Connell, as youthful foil to Galwey. The Limerick native had played on the same Ireland Schools team as Gordon D'Arcy, but elevation to the provincial senior team did not happen as rapidly as it did for the Leinster talent. Munster topped their Heineken Cup group, in January 2002, but had lost flanker Corkery to a leg injury. Kidney needed some athleticism, some brawn, in his back row, and called on a familiar face.

'Declan came to me,' Halvey recalls. 'We had a couple of conversations, and eventually worked out that I would train twice a week with them and play a few games. They paid my travel expenses and I got match fee, so it wasn't like I was this amateur, showing up on a Saturday. I was still working away, though, and getting in as many games as I could with Shannon. I was pay-per-view, in a way. The pressure was off, and I loved those games, that season. I got that appetite back again.' Kidney's men handed Stade Français a 27–10 beating at Thomond Park to set up a sweltering semi-final against Toulouse. Trailing 15–11 at the break, Munster ran in two second-half tries, including a length-of-the-pitch team effort finished off by O'Gara. A stunning 31–25 win set up a final against Northampton Saints at Twickenham.

Munster, Wallace feels, never came close to matching their true potential in that season's final. 'We played like underdogs all season, and always played like the better team,' he says. Declan had a great way of motivating us for games and finding angles about teams or players disrespecting us, taking us for granted. We didn't approach that final the way we had our other games. We had that team meeting the night before when things got emotional. We played with a different mentality that day and suffered because of it. We only played well in patches. It is one we will always regret as we left it behind. It hurt much more than [the Heineken Cup final against] Leicester in 2002, as they were a good team who played better than us on the day.'

Halvey says, 'We lost 9–8, but nobody let anybody down. Everybody gave their soul in that game. I've no regrets about it whatsoever. It was incredible to see the support we had that day: 40,000 screaming Munster supporters. That game unified us, as Munster supporters. Suddenly it all came together. From 500 people at Temple Hill [August 1999] to see us play Leinster, to tens of thousands making that Twickenham trip. The level of support – that sixteenth man – was born. Everyone was Club Munster after that, rather than individual clubs.'

***

In May 2006, Munster were in their third European Cup final in seven seasons. Clohessy and Galwey had retired, but both men were in attendance as part of a Munster horde that neared 50,000. Their opponents, Biarritz, boasted French internationals such as Imanol Harinordoquy, Dimitri Yachvili and Serge Betsen, but it was Sireli Bobo, their Fijian winger, who inflicted early damage with a try. Munster, however, were not leaving

Cardiff without the trophy they craved so much. On seventeen minutes, Halstead finished off a breathtaking counter that involved O'Gara, Horgan, O'Connell and Jerry Flannery. The French side seized up, yet Munster were struggling to turn pressure into points, until Stringer seared his name into Heineken Cup history. Munster heaved into a scrum, ten metres from the Biarritz line, and Stringer caught Yachvili on the hop by picking and sniping up the blindside. Betsen swabbed a paw in the scrum half's direction, but missed his mark. O'Gara converted, and Munster led 17–10. They would go on to see out a nervy finalé and win 23–19.

'In my mind and my career,' declares Stringer, 'that try is one that stands out. It was an incredible feeling, that day. We had lost a couple of finals before, and the emotions that came out after the game were overwhelming. The location, the history and the amount of Munster supporters all added to that. It was an incredible sensation, to run out onto that pitch and see that eighty per cent of the crowd were supporting us. It was really, really special.

'As we were in the dressing room I thought back to when we all started. I knew them all so well. Seven or eight years together. That one day happened as a result of a lot of hard work done by a hell of a lot of guys in the dressing room. There were guys who helped us along on the journey. Sitting down, I looked around at my buddies and reflected. These were the fellas I wanted to share that win with.'

O'Gara is of the view that close, gut-shredding calls helped forge a greater bond between Munster and the Heineken Cup. 'The romantic view is if we had walked out at Twickenham with the cup that day [in 2000], would that have been the peak of the Munster story?' he says. 'That was a phenomenal day of support and a learning experience, obviously. You wouldn't have liked it to be like that, but you have to take it on the chin, learn from it. That's what sport is all about. There are an incredible amount of things to learn from losing situations, but the easy thing to do is brush it under the carpet.'

Mick O'Driscoll concurs with O'Gara. 'Getting to the final in 2000, when we were beaten, then quarters and getting beaten in another final in 2002 – that made us who we are,' says the former lock and the province's current forwards coach. 'When that happens to you, one of two things usually happens – you either fall away or you keep going after it and eventually get it. Luckily enough, we eventually got there. It did take a long time, but certainly a lot of good players came through. I'm not saying that there weren't good players in the early days, but we got some of that outside influence coming through, and that focused us a little more. We realised that there was a core group that came through at the time, and that if we didn't do it soon, we were never going to do it. There was never anything said, but it kind of evolved and everybody understood where we were at.'

'We probably celebrated the Heineken Cup win more that year than 2008,' says Wallace. 'The overriding feeling amongst the team in 2006 was sheer relief. We got there, eventually. The fact that we had this unbelievable support in Wales was probably a big key for us. Just like Woody, or John Langford or ROG in the past, the Munster fans gave us the belief that day. They gave us the edge over our opponents all season. I remember running out of the tunnel at the Millennium Stadium and feeling this wall of noise. There was a real feeling of "We can't come off that pitch without that cup. We are going to do this." Losing was simply unfathomable.

'Beating Toulouse in the 2008 Heineken Cup final was a sense of pure achievement, rather than relief. Ever since they had beaten us so badly in 1996, we had this absolute respect for them and the way they played the game. To be up against them in the final was the pinnacle. What better way to win the Heineken Cup than by beating Toulouse. That was more satisfying for me.'

'There were only a few guys left that would have played in that first final,' says Marcus Horan, 'but it was great to see guys like Gaillimh and Claw after those wins in 2006 and 2008. They took just as much pleasure out of it as we did. We all knew that we would not have made it that far were it not for the guys that went before us. No one knew who we were or where we were from at the start. We were putting Irish rugby on the map, and we were proud to do so.'

***

Jerry Flannery sits in a meeting room at the Firgrove Hotel, Mitchelstown, in August 2014 and obliges each interview request. Retired from the game two years, the former Munster hooker is now part of the new coaching ticket led by Foley. Eighteen months had been spent honing strength-and-conditioning coaching with Arsenal Football Club, but one call from 'Axel' was all it took. Flannery left London life behind to rejoin Munster and their quest to scale European rugby heights again. As a player, Flannery achieved his trophy-winning goals. Now, as scrum coach, he is certain Munster will emulate the success he once basked in.

'It's weird,' he says, 'because I would have grown up and everyone would have talked about beating the All Blacks, beating the All Blacks. It would have made you feel that when you played for Munster, there was something special about that team – that they could literally do anything. Somehow that has been a part of it, but when I came into the squad we had come close in a couple of European and Challenge Cups. But we talked about, "We can't always be saying next year we'll get good … next year."

'In 2006 I was lucky enough to get in the team and we won. In a way I was like, "Thank God we don't have to talk about the fucking All Blacks any more," you know? I look at the current crop of players, and I think that they are probably sick of hearing about 2006 and 2008. They want it to be about them, but I'm lucky enough that I'm part of a coaching ticket where we can hopefully give the players that chance and that opportunity to go and make that happen.'

# 6

# ULSTER'S SHORT-LIVED DYNASTY

'My first game for Ulster was in 1991 against Cornwall,' says Gary Longwell. 'We played Yorkshire that season, the interpros and that was it. We played every other week, as the powers that be thought it'd be too physically demanding if we played every week.

'Whenever we went down to a game in the south, we were stopped at the border and some gardaí would board the bus. They were there to protect the Royal Ulster Constabulary policemen that were playing for Ulster at the time. They would shadow them all day before the match, sit with them during the post-game dinner and drinks, and see them back to the border. Thankfully the country has moved on. To give it a bit of perspective now, these guys were risking their lives to play rugby.'

Longwell arrived in an Ulster side dominating the interprovincial landscape. Jim Davidson had introduced a training set-up at the province that verged on professional. Queen's University, with Phillip Matthews, Trevor Ringland, David Irwin and Nigel Carr, provided the backbone of an Ulster team that beat the touring Australians in 1984 and won three interprovincial titles in the mid 1980s under Davidson. Davidson left to manage Ireland, but the titles kept coming. Ulster were unbeaten in the interprovincial championship between 1984 and their 1992 loss to Leinster, at Ravenhill. When Munster were setting their goals for the 1998/99 season, many players put 'beating Ulster in Belfast' at the top of their list.

'We had a fantastic set of players and coaches who knew how to get the best out of us,' Longwell declares. 'In one game we were down six points to

Leinster with five minutes to go. Keith Crossan scored in the corner with about a minute to go, and Ringland converted. On another day, Ian Brown knocked over a last-minute drop goal to beat Munster in Belfast. We just had that belief and always found a way to win. Had there been a European competition back then, I feel we would have claimed a few trophies.'

Longwell was twenty-four and into his fourth season with Ulster when rugby became open. Players such as Maurice Field, Denis McBride, Stephen Ritchie and James Topping were contracted by the IRFU as full-time with Ulster. Along with Longwell, they were part of a group of seven players who were the province's first professionals. Younger players such as Robin Morrow and Sheldon Coulter were on part-time deals. Longwell comments, 'I had worked a couple of jobs before the offer came along, but decided I would go for it. I was still living at home with my parents, so £25,000 for my first rugby wages did me nicely.

'We had a gym session in the morning and usually had enough around for a game of five-a-side after that. Then we would grab a bite to eat – a few would head home – and wait around until 7.00 p.m. or 7.30 p.m. when the other lads would come along for training after work. We would have some basic form of strength and conditioning, but some lads would miss sessions without remarks being made.'

Ulster missed out on the first Heineken Cup season, and failed to make it past the group stages in 1997 and 1998. Tony Russ brought in Dave Haslett to assist with the coaching, but the province were failing to make a mark against the bigger sides. In June 1998, Russ moved on, and Harry Williams, a former principal of Holywood Primary School, was asked back for a second coaching stint. Williams immediately implemented daytime training, and players who could not commit were dropped. Scrum half Andy Matchett and flanker Stephen McKinty were the exceptions. The full-time squad was extended to twenty players, who included Allied Dunbar Premiership returnees Jonny Bell, David Humphreys and club captain Mark McCall. A neck injury less than a month into his second spell at Ulster, and McCall's playing days were over. Humphreys took over the captaincy.

The season began poorly when they lost to Connacht for the first time since 1983. Heavy defeats by Leinster and Munster followed. Longwell continues, 'We had been abject failures in Europe up until that point. We played Edinburgh at Ravenhill first time out and were 14–0 down. Some lads were laughing. The attitude was "here we go again". We got the next score, stuck at it and were 38–35 going into the final minute, when Duncan Hodge got a drop goal to level it for them.

'The following night, Toulouse destroyed Ebbw Vale 108–16; we were due at theirs next. The chat among the lads was that if we didn't play well, the game could be very embarrassing for us. We lost 39–3 that night and the mood in the changing room was good. Harry came in and sent boots flying. He told us we were a disgrace, that we were Ulster, and how dare we laugh after a loss. We put Ebbw Vale away in the next game, and were fortunate that Toulouse did not send all of their top, top players to Belfast when we met again. We were down at half-time against Edinburgh, but Harry came and gave another great talk. Sheldon, with an intercept, and Mark Blair got over for tries in the second-half, and we won 23–21.

'We drew Toulouse in the quarters, and this time they sent over their crack squad. That was really the start of it. We had a massive crowd packed into Ravenhill, as it was coming up to Christmas.' Williams' Ulster did their basics right, won clean set-piece ball and had both Humphreys and goal-kicking fullback Simon Mason to pin sides back. The pair combined for all of the hosts' points as they won 15–13. 'There's no reason why we can't go all the way now,' Williams trumpeted after the final whistle.

Humphreys had injured his shoulder making a covering tap-tackle on Xavier Garbajosa in the closing stages of the Toulouse victory, but was able to return for the last-four clash on 9 January 1999. Longwell continues, '[Ulster chief executive] Mike Reid did a great job of getting 20,000 supporters into Ravenhill for the semi-final – temporary stands. Simon kept the scoreboard ticking over and Humphreys got a great try to swing it.'

Ulster decamped en masse to Lansdowne Road for the Heineken Cup final three weeks later. The demand for tickets was unprecedented. Reid relates that he was accosted by a man who told him he had queued for three hours at Ravenhill to secure two tickets. 'And', the man added, 'it took me forty minutes to find Ravenhill in the first place.'

Among the (conservatively estimated) 49,000 crowd that jammed into the national stadium were future Ulster players Chris Henry, Paddy Wallace and Darren Cave. 'Colomiers were beaten before they stepped on the pitch,' Longwell claims. 'They were shocked at the amount of Ulster fans inside the ground. We ran a lap of the pitch as we finished our warm-up, and Stuart Duncan stuck the shoulder on their hooker (Marc Dal Maso) as we jogged by the Colomiers boys. They actually left the pitch, jogged off, instead of standing and fighting. It was an intimidating atmosphere that day and a few of their lads gave up.'

As for the game itself, Ulster stuck to the script that had served them well during their run to the final. The game was played primarily in Colomiers' half, and Ulster's forwards earned the penalties for Mason to convert. 'Looking back,' says Longwell, 'it was a dull game. Simon Mason just kicked everything. With twenty minutes to go, we knew we had the game won. There was a big party up in the stands.'

The match ended 21–6, and Humphreys had to wade through a sea of pitch-invading Ulster supporters to climb the steps and raise the trophy. McCall was waiting for him when he arrived, and they hoisted the cup together. 'It felt like an absolutely massive moment,' says Longwell. 'Ireland was coming out of a really bad time, and that run to the final united a lot of people. A lot of Gaelic fans got along to that game, and we received letters and cards of support from all over the country.

'A huge regret I have is that we never built a dynasty off the back of that result,' Longwell admits. 'We lost focus and fell apart. Some of the players that might have got cut after that season may not have been the greatest, but they were fantastic in the dressing room. We got guys in from England and the southern hemisphere and, good as they may have been, they did not have the same allegiances to Ulster Rugby.'

The following season saw Ulster lose all of their six pool matches. Their next win in the Heineken Cup arrived on 6 October 2000 against Cardiff. It was their only victory of the campaign. They would not reach the knockout stages again until 2011.

# 7

## EXILES:
## PASTA, PARTIES AND GREEN ROVERS

There was a video released by the IRFU in 2000 where some of their old guard say they had an epiphany, a masterstroke. Where they realised the need to focus on the provinces – give them a competition. That masterstroke came about four years too late, as the moment the game went pro, everyone scarpered.

*Peter O'Reilly*

Saturday afternoon, 25 April 1998, and Clive Woodward's London Irish welcomed Harlequins to Surrey. A crowd of slightly over 4,200 wedged into The Avenue, expecting a toil between two of the Allied Dunbar Premiership's struggling sides. Home fans who vacated Fitzy's Bar vaguely in time for kick-off were rewarded when Justin Bishop raced over for The Exiles' first try. Seven more followed – Bishop completing a hat-trick in the process – as Quins were blasted 62–14.

Thierry Lacroix, Dan Luger and Jason Leonard were part of a Harlequins guard of honour for London Irish captain, Conor O'Shea, and his players. It was the club's biggest win in 100 years of rugby. Eleven of the victorious match-day squad were from Ireland: O'Shea, Bishop, Mark McCall, David Humphreys, Justin Fitzpatrick, Gary Halpin, Malcolm O'Kelly, Kevin Spicer, Kieron Dawson, Niall Hogan and Niall Woods (scorer of thirty-two points). The match was the highlight of a forgettable season. The Exiles finished eleventh, twenty-six points behind league champions Newcastle Falcons.

\*\*\*

Former Ireland lock Malcolm O'Kelly was twenty-one when he finished college, in 1996. His rugby training was spread between St Mary's (Tuesdays and Thursdays) and Leinster (Wednesdays out at Old Belvedere). 'I had played for Leinster – the season before – against North Transvaal, Connacht and a couple of Heineken matches against Milan and Pau,' remembers O'Kelly. 'I had a bit of experience with them but, when I finished college, it happened to coincide with the whole changing of the rugby world and the game going pro after the World Cup. I got offered a deal by London Irish. Provisionally, it was that I'd go to Oxford and play there, then play for London Irish. That fell through, so I hopped on a plane and went over to London Irish and took a deal that was unbelievable when compared to what everyone else had been offered.'

He was joined at the club by Niall Woods, three years his senior and established in the Ireland backline. 'The exchange rate at that stage [between British sterling and the Irish punt] was about one to one,' Woods says. 'For me, it wasn't necessarily about the money. I just wanted to go and play ... My last season here with Blackrock, seven of the ten AIL games were in the pouring rain, so when you are on the wing and you aren't getting much ball, well ... Woodward was a very good talker, so he sold it to me – himself and Conor [O'Shea]. Woodward was a big factor. Conor was at London Irish the previous year, and even came back and played for Leinster in the 1995/96 season in some of the games. During my first contract with the club, you were allowed to come home and play for Leinster in the Heineken Cup.'

Woods continues, 'A few others went to England. Paul and Richie Wallace went to Saracens, Keith Wood went to Quins, a few guys went to Mosley; Henry Hurley, Alain Rolland, Martin Ridge went up there. There were a few of us scattered. Jonny Bell came in with us. He was in Northampton, in college, anyway.'

Woodward had led the club into the Premiership and, with the IRFU slow to offer deals to top players, targeted Ireland's best young talents.

Added to the eleven players who handed the 48-point thrashing to Harlequins were Rob Henderson, Jeremy Davidson and Victor Costello. 'We had a really solid outfit, and a lot of young guys who had yet to make their names,' O'Kelly recalls. 'Only very few of the guys had been capped at that stage. Jeremy was. He went on to play for the Lions in 1997. He was our talisman, really, but it was a difficult time. We went over there with the amateur attitude, where we had only trained in the evening. Now we were training during the day. We didn't have to work; some of us were students just finished college. We had an ethos of just chilling out and not doing very much – doing as little as possible, really. It was very haphazard. Some guys trained at night, some guys trained in the day – we would be all over the place.'

The Irish recruits were given team cars upon arrival and sequestered in houses together. As many as five Irishmen would live together, and it was in one of the three main houses that the parties usually ignited. O'Kelly says, 'We had a "work hard, play hard" ethos. Post match, it was what you did. We all went out together; we bonded. We weren't the only people. Every club was doing it; that was the buzz – it was what you did. Win or lose, you did it. Everyone did it, but there were a lot of guys who came over from Ireland and were part of it. There was a great English crew as well, "Plastic Paddys" if you want to call them that. Kieran Campbell, Sean Burns and these guys all rolled in and it was really good fun.'

Woods says, 'You were getting paid to play, so there would have been a few nights out – a lot more than there are now – and you took the view that, if you came in with a hangover, the coaches got you, trained you hard and the hangover was gone. So you thought you were all right. They are a bit more scientific, nowadays.'

Peter O'Reilly recalls weekly trips to England for player interviews, as the country's best talents were operating across the Irish Sea. 'I flew over to London one week to interview Niall Woods,' he says. 'He picked me up at the airport in a green Rover, provided to London Irish by the sponsors. He was sharing a house with Victor Costello and Jeremy Davidson. You could tell it was their house as there were another three green, sponsored Rovers parked out the front. I remember, too, that they were all eating pasta. Now, pasta is a good meal to have four or five hours before a game, but that's all they were eating. They were loading the pasta into them as if it were the food of the professional.

'There was a suggestion, around that time, that the Irish players would come home to represent their provinces in the European Cup. There were some slanging matches between [national manager] Pa Whelan at the IRFU and Exiles' coach Clive Woodward. It was some gambit from the union – "I know you're paying them, but could we get our players to come back and play for their provinces?" It was a shit-fest, a complete mess.

'I remember asking Niall about his ambitions for playing on the Lions' tour to South Africa the following summer. He was angry, as he thought the IRFU would use the Lions as a fear factor. Players abroad were not guaranteed selection for Ireland, which would ruin their Lions chances. Here he was at a proper pro club, whereas the set-up at Leinster was a circus, and he was threatened with missing out on Ireland selection.'

Indeed, the Exiles allowed their Irish players to return to Munster and Leinster for the first season of Heineken Cup rugby. That stance hardened once Ulster entered in 1996/97 and the appeal of the competition grew. Woods was one of the players caught in the crossfire. 'Woodward said to me, "If you go back and play for Leinster, I'm not going to pick you again." I was over in Ireland because my girlfriend at the time, her father had a heart attack. So this is all over the phone. And I said, "Well what are all the other boys doing?" and he said, "They're all staying." In reality, they all told him they were going back, but I was none the wiser.

'The way I viewed it was they were my employer. I can't afford not to be getting picked by your man. He had a personality to probably do it. I remember talking to my dad and he said, "He's your employer, you need to stay there. Your primary employer." So I stayed there.' Woods suffered as a consequence. Refusing to return to play with Leinster was one thing. When Woods remained in London and missed Irish training sessions, which were outside agreed dates between club and country, Pa Whelan told him he was risking his Test career.

Woods played for Ireland only once again, in February 1999. 'Warren Gatland was coach. I was on the A team for Wales away. I got called in after Girvan Dempsey was injured and played. Gatland rang on the Monday saying, "You're not playing the next match, Girvan is." I said, "Right, okay." He said, "Look, you didn't do much wrong." I didn't get a huge amount of the ball – it was in Wembley against Wales – but he said Girvan hadn't done anything wrong. Gatland said, "If you were fifty–fifty I'm going to pick someone from here. Actually even if you're sixty–forty, I'm still going to pick someone from here."'

Back in 1996, Woods' next battle was against his club, six games into his first season at Sunbury, after the players were summoned to Woodward's house and asked to take a fifteen per cent pay cut. 'This,' he says, 'took place in Woodward's lovely, big house in the countryside in Surrey, with his convertible Beamer outside and his own banking job. I just took the view that I had just moved from Ireland and left training to be an accountant to come over here. I agreed to be paid X and I'm staying on it. Woodward was such a good talker that there were only three of us who didn't take it. We just said no, we are staying as is. All the others took a pay cut and waived their bonuses, match fees. There was a £500 match fee, win, lose or draw. I said, "It's in the contract."'

'The results weren't really going our way,' O'Kelly concedes, 'so by mid-October we looked to get a new forwards coach, who turned out to be Willie Anderson. He was great. All the guys knew him. He was really good at his job – very professional. He roped everyone in, started training a lot harder, started training at night and during the day. A lot of training. But everyone was happy with Willie.'

Anderson, a former Irish captain, introduced one of the Exiles' Plastic

Paddys to professional rugby the following season – 1997/98. 'My career with London Irish started at a train station when I was five,' recalls Adrian Flavin. 'My father was getting a London Irish ID for my older brother, and he asked, since I was there, if I would also like one. "Yeah, fair enough," I said. I turned up to Sunbury as a five-year-old and stayed on for twenty-one more years.

'London Irish was in our blood,' he adds. 'My two brothers, mum and dad were all involved. My parents held all sorts of positions in the junior rugby set-up, and my mum ran the first-ever kit shop for the juniors and seniors. That was back in the Umbro days.' Flavin, who played at hooker, appeared once for the club in his first senior season. He spent most of his time at the club's Foundation (academy) under the guidance of Ray Hennessey.

'It was pretty much a full Ireland team back then,' he says. 'I used to get paid, in crisps and Coke, to sit on the steps and retrieve balls during training sessions. You'd get a cushion, so it wasn't all bad. You would sit there until a ball came your way, then get it back to them. A couple of years later, and I was training with these guys. "Bloody hell, here I am." You had to get on with it quickly, as Davidson or Ken O'Connell would let you know about it. You'd hear all about it or get hurt.'

Flavin shared an older Rover with two academy teammates, but soon found himself in a newer model. He explains, 'After Jeremy Davidson did his cruciate they had to get him an automatic. I got his old one. Driving around uni in that car, you thought you were the bee's knees, which, of course, you were not. What a fantastic job it was – to get paid to play rugby. There were still one or two big nights out as the era passed over from amateur to professional, but I was still young enough so I missed out on half of the really crazy nights. I was still cleaning the boots for a hooker called "Psycho" at the time.'

Money issues clouded the club's existence, and, in 1999, O'Kelly remembers contractual wrangles hampering his return to Ireland. 'There had been a lot of contractual issues, either guys whose contracts were breached by London Irish, or other guys, like myself, who were forced to see out their contracts. There was another, difficult element to London Irish. It was to do with all the changes that were going on. The first year we nearly had fifteen guys get the chop and another fifteen brought in. The following year, something similar. It was quite brutal, volatile and not the way you want to go about filling a squad.'

Flavin comments, 'The money at the time was something that would never last. Teams like Richmond and Newcastle were paying players something like £200,000–300,000 a year. Nowadays a full-blown pro might do well to get that, and now there is more financial support from unions, greater ticket incomes, sales and merchandising. It was crazy, and it didn't work.'

By the time O'Kelly returned to Leinster, Richmond had been placed in administration, and a struggling London Irish merged with London Scottish, who were in worse shape. The club could not afford to keep on the likes of Davidson and Humphreys. In the second game of the 1999/2000 season, Woods was playing with a Premiership fifteen in a World Cup warm-up match for England. The English team, managed by Woodward, were coasting in the first half, when Woods was caught in a tackle and felt his knee go. Three of the Premiership team had already limped off, so he remained on the field. 'Just before half-time, I was chasing a chip, and my knee snapped,' he recalls. 'I thought I had been shot. Cruciate, the works, gone. Medial ligament, cartilage. I knew I was out for the rest of the season.'

Exiles broke off contract-extension negotiations when their versatile back damaged his anterior ligament in rehab. Harlequins entered the picture and signed him up for the following season as a goal-kicking fullback. Woods got a forty per cent contract bump, but the return for his new club was a mere six games. Further knee reconstruction was required in January 2001. 'The surgeon said the knee was completely arthritic; that

I would be limping for the rest of my life if I kept playing,' he says. 'I just said, "I need to stop." I had just turned thirty at that stage. I had been playing first team since eighteen, nineteen, so I had a good run.' Most English clubs, he explains, could terminate contracts if a player missed six cumulative months over the course of a season. He trained and rehabbed with Harlequins until his six months lapsed, in April 2001.

\*\*\*

Ten of the fifteen players who had started for Ireland against the United States, on 10 January 1996, were in the Premiership. They were earning full-time wages that dwarfed anything their union could, or chose to, offer. Victor Costello had sampled London life for an injury-curtailed season before returning to Leinster in 1997. The back-row had played his first senior, non-cap, Irish games in Australia in 1994. 'Gary Halpin, who I played with at London Irish, declared Australia "the last of the great, drinking tours",' says Costello. 'I remember we scored one great try, through Claw, against the Wallabies, but that was the height of it.'

O'Kelly did not make his Test debut until the All Blacks swept into Dublin in 1997, but was called in for training sessions in the Murray Kidd era. There were strained attempts, he remembers, at team bonding. 'The controlled pints thing on a Wednesday was literally that. It became such a farce. Half of this professional rugby vibe was the funniest feeling of creating a committed squad by having compulsory fun. Under Murray we'd have a compulsory fun night out: "We are all going out in our IRFU tracksuits and all having fun." It was so not fun.'

Costello earned five caps under Kidd, but found the new coach, Brian Ashton (appointed in January 1997) an equally hard man to please. 'Ashton was picking Plastic Paddys like Dylan O'Grady and David Erskine. Lads like myself, Eddie Halvey, Alan Quinlan and Anthony Foley were breaking their arses and achieving good results for their provinces, and not getting a look-in. It was the IRFU's version of the Jack Charlton era [with the Irish football team]. Maybe they thought they could win the World Cup with a team full of English accents.

'Dion O'Cuinneagan, that idiot, was a player with Ulster who then went and played for Munster in a Heineken Cup semi-final [in 2001]. How much more calculated or opportunistic can you get? Those lads took a lot of caps off people. Nobody is going to tell me that Matt Mostyn on the wing is ten per cent the player Denis Hickie is. Ashton's watching brief was the Premiership, so these guys were making the squads. It was fucking unbelievable.'

Fourteen players from the Irish squad dumped out of the 1999 World Cup before the quarter-final stage were earning their living abroad. Warren Gatland, their coach for the tournament, had complained beforehand about the lack of time he was getting with Premiership-based players, but it took failure on the world stage to make anyone in the union sit up and pay attention. Ireland needed its best players back home, but, to achieve that, the union needed to increase salaries and play a role in establishing a competitive league. David Humphreys (to Ulster in 1999) and Eric Miller (to Leinster in 2000) were two of the first established internationals lured back. The Celtic League – featuring sides from Ireland, Wales and Scotland – was formed in 2001. With the union offering sizeable, suck-it-and-see wages, established internationals – such as Keith Wood and Paul Wallace – returned home to see if there was any substance to the union's talk of finally taking this professionalism lark seriously.

# 8

## LEINSTER STRUGGLE TO KEEP UP

The greatest achievement of Brian Ashton's thirteen months in charge of the Irish national team was, in 1997, pressuring the IRFU into appointing full-time head coaches for the four provinces. The former Bath coach wanted each province, in time, producing thirty professional players all feeding into the cause of the national team. Fine in theory, tricky in practice.

Former Ireland out-half Paul Dean had coaching responsibility for the Leinster backs amid the advent of professionalism. 'There was no immediate change,' he comments. 'I was paid a token amount of £2,000, but I gave it back. I didn't want it. Everyone was new to professionalism. Certain people in the Leinster branch were of the opinion that if you paid someone, you could give them a right bollocking. Accepting that money would have been akin to taking the king's shilling. I gave the money back, as I wasn't taking abuse from anyone. Thankfully, professionalism has weeded out many of the amateurs that were involved in the running of the game around then.'

Shane Byrne had been in the Leinster team since 1992, and – four years on – was in Bolton Street, training to be an engineering draftsman, when he was offered his first professional contract. 'Myself, Denis Hickie, Richie Governey and [tight-head prop] Angus McKeen were some of the first to sign up. I got £25,000 and a Ford Mondeo. When I went in to tell them at Bolton Street it was a bit like the Simpsons, where Homer sprints off and there is just this mist left behind. They were very good, though, as they said they would hold a place for me if I wanted to come back.'

Team manager Jim Glennon had brought Leinster to the Heineken Cup semi-final, and led them to the 1995/96 interprovincial title. Premiership clubs scouted the club, and began to offer money that the branch, through the IRFU, struggled to match. It did not help that Glennon never password protected his mobile phone. A former Leinster player reveals, 'Jim had one of those old Nokia 3210 phones, where you could ring in from another line and check your voicemails. There was a password you had to enter, but Jim must have left it as "0000", the factory setting, because any time the boys wanted to know how their contract negotiations were going they just placed a call. Pop in the password and you could hear a message from the branch or union guys: "Well we can go to this much for his contract, but don't tell him that." The lads knew exactly where they stood. The union couldn't figure it out. The only trick was not to listen for too long, as if you got to the end of the voicemail, it would be recorded and Jim would know. All very *Mission: Impossible*. I don't think they ever figured it out.'

In 1997, Leinster thanked Dean, fellow coach Ciaran Callan and Glennon for their services, and brought in a man who had built up an impressive résumé in Wales. Mike Ruddock had coached Swansea to a Welsh Cup win, victory over a touring Wallabies side and two national championships.

One of Ruddock's first jobs was to stem the talent drain to England. He realised there was work to do before signing on. The extent of that work, and the resistance Ruddock met, left him stunned. 'I came over here and became the first full-time professional coach of Leinster,' he comments. 'But of course the players weren't full time; we had three or four of them. By the time I left it was just changing. It was an interesting time.

'Looking back, I gave a first contract to Gordon D'Arcy, who is still playing [in 2014/15]. It's amazing he is still delivering the quality that he is, this much further down the track. Leo Cullen was in one of the first group of players I had. Bob Casey, Brian O'Driscoll, Girvan Dempsey, all those guys. Shane Horgan was an eighteen-year-old kid I remember first seeing on the back pitch in Donnybrook. Irish rugby had lost a lot of guys, either through retirement or who had gone off to play in England.'

D'Arcy would arrive in the Leinster squad in 1998, Ruddock's second season, but he had already trained with the senior side at that stage. 'You would get a medium jersey and it's down to your knees,' D'Arcy recalls. 'You were given a jersey and you were told to wear it and it was usually massive, and you were usually getting tackled by somebody grabbing your jersey and dragging you and pulling you to the ground.

'We trained in St Andrews, and we trained out of a Portakabin,' D'Arcy adds. 'Only the Irish contract guys did weights. Everybody else trained three nights a week, and we played probably twelve games a season. It's pretty much apples and oranges to how it is now.'

Ruddock likens the weight room/cabin to a telephone booth. He adds, 'The majority of teams were doing the same thing as we did as amateurs. They were getting paid now to stop them jumping ship and going to play for another club. It was a big learning curve, being professional, in terms of how it all came about.

'No one had a template initially, no one had professional conditioning staff, video analysts – there was none of that stuff going on. We obviously did our own analysis, but it would just be off the Betamax recorder back in those days. It took a while for us to put all our systems in place, and for the governing bodies to put their systems in place and to generate the revenue to put it in place through the leagues, certainly the Celtic League, because initially when I came over we only played the interpros, and we played in Europe, and then the team would play club rugby in the AIL otherwise.'

Dempsey was in the Leinster set-up from the age of nineteen after catching Glennon's eye in the AIL with Terenure. His first full season was 1995, with training on Tuesdays and Thursdays at Old Belvedere and eight matches in the calendar. Now director of the Leinster Academy, Dempsey laughs when reminded of Ruddock and his Betamax recordings.

He adds, 'We were in St Andrew's school in Booterstown for training; then we moved to Belvedere. Pre-season was in Donnybrook. We didn't have a focal point or a home training ground. We were moving around between different clubs and fields, wherever we could get a bit of space. Sandy Heffernan was the honorary secretary at the time and basically ran the show. The branch worked out of a small Portakabin at the Wesley end [of Donnybrook].'

Byrne declares, 'The facilities and planning structures at Leinster were still dire. Nothing changed overnight. Mike, as coach, gave the province their first real drive, but he was still answerable to the committee – the powers that be. He had no real say in the selection process. The training for the full-time lads began at 9 a.m., and you were often scheduled to start in the gym under no supervision. It would be at University College Dublin or over at Belvedere, where it was so cold sometimes that you would spend your morning in the bar, trying to keep warm.'

'We still look back and laugh at those old days, and what we were given,' says Dempsey. 'There were Mars bars and cans of Coke handed out for recovery after sessions. Now you have the recovery drinks, a science behind everything and an education, for the players, of their dietary and training needs … Looking back to those first few years, and the social element was very much part of the game. You look at it now and see how dedicated the players are, and how alcohol is not really part of their diet or programme. We'd be going out on big nights out and getting bags of chips on the way home.'

On the rare occasions when Ruddock assembled enough players to run proper drills, he ran into trouble with the neighbours. He recalls, 'My first-ever training session was on the back pitch at Donnybrook with Leinster. Here I am, I had signed up to coach the elite crop of Leinster rugby, and the next thing is one of the committee guys came over and gave out yards to me because I was using the twenty-two nearest the tennis club. We were making a bit too much noise, especially some of my expletives, so we were told to move. There ensued a bit of debate over this. The point of the story is, we are a professional team about to produce a number of internationals, and we didn't even have a full pitch. We only had three-quarters of a pitch. We couldn't go into the far twenty-two.'

The best result of an otherwise forgettable 1997/98 was a Heineken Cup home win on 12 September over a Leicester Tigers side containing Martin Johnson, Neil Back, Martin Corry and Eric Miller, who had joined from Leinster that summer. The home side were buoyed by strong performances from the in-form St Mary's duo of Kevin Nowlan and John McWeeney, and Victor Costello, who had returned to Dublin after an unhappy spell with London Irish. Costello declares, 'I didn't enjoy the experience and I didn't like the club. It was very disjointed. We were getting our arses handed to us every weekend. It was not what I was used to. I made a decision that I wasn't sticking around.'

A glimpse of Leinster's future was on offer to the Irish journalists who headed out to France for the Under-19 World Cup. Problem is, not one journalist made the trip over from Ireland. Led by Munster coach Declan Kidney, the Irish squad contained Donncha O'Callaghan, Paddy Wallace, Adrian Flavin, Kieran Campbell, Shane Moore and UCD back Brian O'Driscoll.

'You could definitely tell there was something special about Brian,' Flavin proclaims. 'He wasn't playing thirteen back then and was an out-half in schools rugby, but they accommodated him at twelve. I would have played [England] underage with Jonny Wilkinson, and he had that same attitude and skill level as Brian. A lot of us were delighted to be getting paid to play rugby, but Jonny's attitude was "I'm a rugby player; that's what I do. I'm going to give every waking second of my time to making myself the best rugby player possible." It was clear at that age that Brian and Jonny had big futures in the game.'

Television cameras were waiting for O'Driscoll and the Irish team as they returned home with the World Cup trophy. He was called in by

Ruddock to train with the seniors, but run-outs were limited to A matches. Peter O'Reilly, writing for the *Sunday Tribune* at the time, recounts his first sighting of the player who would prove so crucial in Leinster's future success story. 'At the start of the [1998] season, Leinster played Munster in Dooradoyle on a Friday night. The crowd was considerably smaller than what you would have expected at the time for St Mary's versus Garryowen. There was a bigger crowd the morning after for the Leinster and Munster A game. People wanted to get a look at this O'Driscoll lad. Warren Gatland was there too, and, like the rest of us, he was there to see the new star. During the game, Cian Mahony, who was an Ireland Under 21, absolutely shredded O'Driscoll on the outside to score.'

Ruddock was pleased, at the outset of 1998/99, when the Irish Interprovincial Championship was extended to home and away fixtures. Leinster looked on course for a fine season after obliterating Ulster 35–11 at Ravenhill, and winning two of their opening three pool fixtures in Europe. They failed to take 1998/99 into the New Year, however, after losing their final four matches of the season, including a 25–10 reverse to a Killian Keane-inspired Munster at Donnybrook.

Fresh from Test-match appearances one and two, O'Driscoll joined Leinster for pre-season training in July 1999. 'I was in a strange situation of having earned my first cap for Ireland before I played for Leinster,' he says. 'I played a few Leinster A games and got injured. It was a very different set-up to what it is now. There was no league then, and we didn't have a great history of getting out of the pool stages of the Heineken Cup.'

The team's existence remained nomadic. O'Driscoll comments, 'I remember getting text messages as to where certain training sessions were going to be held. It could be in St Andrews, Old Belvedere or UCD. It was very hard to get any kind of stability when you are bouncing around like that.' O'Driscoll and his new teammates at Leinster would often arrive in their training gear and use an open car boot or driver's seat to change into their socks and boots.

The upcoming season would feature interprovincials, a break during the World Cup, and the Heineken Cup. O'Driscoll and fellow Blackrock College alumnus Ciaran Scally started the opening match away to Munster at Temple Hill in Cork. Denis Hickie scored twice for Leinster, but Munster possessed too much forward power and cruised to a 31–20 win. 'There is huge pride in wearing the jersey, but then you lose a game against a province that becomes one of your biggest rivals – the [competition] probably started building from that very first game. It's why I've always enjoyed playing against Munster, and always enjoyed winning,' says O'Driscoll.

Leinster went three from six in the interprovincial championship, and, in between, helped Argentina to warm up for the World Cup by hosting them at Donnybrook on 24 August. Los Pumas ran in seven tries in a 51–22 blowout, including a brace from twenty-two-year-old out-half Felipe Contepomi. Leinster had seven players in a World Cup squad that were dumped out of the World Cup at least a week too soon for the nation's liking. Munster kicked them several times when they were down in the first game back, but shards of confidence were pieced back together with a stirring 23–22 victory over Ulster at Ravenhill. They defeated Leicester 27–20 in the Heineken Cup, but losses to Glasgow and Stade Français ensured they would not follow Munster into the knock-out stages. Leinster's final match of the season saw them hound Leicester again: 32–10 was the remarkable scoreline from Welford Road, as Casey and McWeeney crossed for tries, and Emmet Farrell kicked twenty-two points.

'We always knew Leinster had the potential,' says Ruddock. 'I remember talking to people about the massive potential Dublin had, but the point being a lot of the Irish lads had never even done weights. I was the coach, and I was picking the heaviest weights up at the time. It was a culture that had to emerge in Irish rugby. I can't honestly say I was sitting there thinking Irish rugby, and Leinster in particular, were going to dominate

Europe over the next ten, fifteen, twenty years. It seemed quite a way off at that time.'

***

Reggie Corrigan was twenty-five years old, and flitting between the front and second row for his club, Greystones, in 1995. Noel McQuilkin arrived at the AIL second-division club, took two looks at Corrigan and set him straight. Corrigan explains, 'Noel and I had a long chat where he said, "Look, you need to concentrate on propping. That's where you're good at." Under his guidance, that's where I played.' Corrigan settled into the front row, and began to enjoy his rugby. When Leinster announced an open trial in June 1997, Greystones clubman Ken Ging secured Corrigan an invite.

'I went along to the trial, grossly unfit,' continues Corrigan. I would have been two stone overweight, and not fit enough by any means. Mike Ruddock saw in me, though, that I could scrum. Props were, and still are, difficult to come by, so he thought I was worth the effort. He came to me with the proposal of a three-month trial with Leinster, where I would train with them professionally and see where I was at the end of that. It was a difficult decision, as I had just bought a house; I had a job in sales and all that went along with that. I had always worked. The choice was to give up that work, take a gamble for three months and see what happened. It took a lot of soul searching because of the house thing, but, in the end, I said, "This might never come up again." I gave it a go for the three months. I gave up the job, went for it and literally just trained every day for three months. At the end of that, I had shed the two stone and put on quite a bit of muscle.

'Mike just went around and looked at everybody on the Leinster scene, and the clubs had a big bearing on that. He dragged people in. Some made it and some fell by the wayside. Victor Costello was another guy having fitness issues. He had fallen out of favour with Leinster, but came back in at the time of the trials. He and I were propping up the back on the three-kilometre runs.'

Corrigan adds, 'I remember in the early days at Leinster, and under Brian Ashton with Ireland, the attitude was, "Well you're getting paid so you have to do four, five hours training on the rugby pitch." You were exhausted by the time the end of the week comes, and when you had to go play a match. The training wasn't tailored to that power, explosive game. It was general fitness stuff – weights, endurance, aerobics, cardio. Very general. In fairness to the medics and staff involved with it, they didn't have a lot to work with, and they had first to get people to a base level of fitness where they could then progress them to the next stage. The early days were very amateur, really.

'Professionalism had just started, but it wasn't at the level it is now. It was purely about training and training. Long, long and very tiring sessions. I committed to that, and then got my debut against Ulster in Donnybrook three months later. From there, my part-time contract, all £7,500 of it, got increased to a semi full-time contract. From that, I was on the bench that November for the internationals against New Zealand and Canada. It was an unbelievable run, from June to November, where I had gone from a two-stone overweight club player to an international.'

Canada were defeated 33–11, but it took Corrigan eleven further Test matches, five years and two coaches before he was to end on the winning side again. In between, he had suffered a broken back – four fractured transverse processes [vertebrae] – on tour against South Africa, and featured in Ireland's ignominious 1999 World Cup exit at the hands of Argentina, in Lens. 'We then came up against a team that might not have had the greatest players in the world but who were very physical and with a huge desire to win,' he says. 'We didn't have a game plan to beat them and we ended up floundering around a bit. A number of us, after that game, were dropped off the squad entirely by Warren Gatland – five or six of us.'

'I'll never forget', he adds, 'when I was let go after the World Cup and wasn't picked for the next squad, I was pretty low about it – pretty down. I was probably feeling a little sorry for myself and saying, "Why me? Everyone else messed up too." I had a great chat with [Leinster coach] Matt Williams about it. We went off, sat down for a coffee, and I was telling him how I was pissed off with the whole situation. Matt was brilliant. He said, "Look, here's the deal. You need to focus on your rugby." This happens when people get capped, get involved quickly. All of a sudden it is a roller coaster. You're staying in great hotels, everything is looked after for you, you're getting interviewed for papers. Sometimes you lose a bit of focus on your training. That could well have been the case for me. Whereas in the past, when I had nothing, I was training my arse off. That's all I was focused on as I had no distractions. I accepted all of that.

'So, what Matt said is, "We're going to focus on Leinster. We're going to make Leinster a powerhouse and we're going to make it something they can't ignore. You're going to be a part of that. I'm going to name you as captain. You'll take on the roles and responsibilities of captain and will be seen as a leader, playing games and training hard. Forget about Ireland. Don't even think of it." Initially, I doubted whether I could do it, before I thought, "Yeah, I'm going to make Leinster my focus." The only distraction was Ireland squads being announced, but I ignored it. What happened was that I started to play well and we won that Celtic League final against Munster. All of a sudden, as captain, you're part of a culture of change at an organisation. That can't be ignored, and it wasn't ignored. Eddie called me up, and I was basically first choice loose-head from that [2002] tour to New Zealand on.'

Injury in the 2003 Six Nations looked set to cost Corrigan a place in the Leinster team for their Heineken Cup quarter-final – the second season in succession the province had reached the knock-out stages. 'I had fractured the arm in thirteen places,' explains Corrigan, 'but the surgeon did an amazing job and stuck me back together with a steel bar. I was back in seven weeks, and the quarter-final was against Biarritz. We played terribly, but we got there.

'The draw came out for the semis, and it was a home semi-final. The final would be against Munster or Toulouse. We had Perpignan. It was just a lesson in life. The coaching staff, when the draw was made, probably started thinking about the final, because Perpignan were a team that we should have been able to beat in our sleep. We should. We lost focus ahead of that semi-final. We were brilliant at the time. Our backline was electric and we had a great set of forwards, the line-out was exceptionally good. We should have won that game, but were already thinking Heineken Cup final. We lost focus, things went wrong in the game and we didn't have an answer to it. I'll never forget it; it was the most deflating, disappointing experience I've ever had in rugby. We were literally grieving for two or three weeks after, as we knew we had blown a massive chance.

'I remember,' he continues, 'three years prior to that, a psychologist was talking about our ambitions and what we wanted in sport. We'd say, "Oh it would be nice to win a Triple Crown, this that or the other." He pointed out that we were not saying we wanted to win the European Cup, a competition we were taking part in every year. The reality was like us saying we were going to win the World Cup. We didn't think it was a possibility. Three years later it was a very distinct possibility, but we didn't grasp it. It was very disappointing. I always see that as an opportunity lost to win a Heineken Cup.'

Williams was named Scotland's coach at the end of that season, but spoke with his captain before moving on. Corrigan remembers, 'I said, "Look Matt, it's an international role. You can't turn that down. Nobody would hold it against you for leaving." We knew we would suffer in Leinster as a result of him leaving. Matt was brilliant in terms of driving us forward and demanding things off the branch in terms of training facilities and all that. He was very good. He was at the forefront of a lot of those new ideas. He had us doing yoga, recovery sessions, ice baths. After that came Gary Ella, and it just wasn't the right fit. On paper he seemed to have the credentials and the Leinster branch appointed him. Players didn't have the confidence in him to do the job he was supposed to do.

'After that, of course, came Declan Kidney, and there was a lot of excitement about him coming in. He had been successful with Munster, and had gone over to Dragons. There was a bit of messing around, given that he had already signed a contract with Dragons. It was up in the air, but he eventually came here and it seemed to be working well. Then, and he was very honest about it, Declan said he needed to move home (to Cork) and couldn't see out his contract. I was amazed at the timing of it, though, as it was just before the Heineken Cup quarter-final against a very strong Leicester team. Myself and [Leinster director of rugby] Paul McNaughton were in the loop, but it didn't come out until after our exit. So he left on that note, and we had to start all over again.'

# 9

# GATLAND GIVES IRELAND
# A FIGHTING CHANCE

It was February 1998, two-and-a-half years into the professional era, and Ireland were seeking their third national coach. Stung from their costly pay-off to outgoing Brian Ashton, the IRFU looked west to a coach making interprovincial waves with Connacht.

'I was thirty-eight and not finished playing that long when I became Ireland manager,' Donal Lenihan recalls. 'Warren Gatland was only thirty-four, but had seriously impressed with Connacht. We were both there by default. Ashton had been signed up to coach for six years, and barely lasted twelve months. Pa Whelan stepped aside as team manager for well-publicised reasons [an altercation with a Sunday newspaper journalist]. I stated my position as a players' manager early on, and remember getting pulled aside by an IRFU suit soon after and asked what exactly I meant by that.'

The summer of 1998 was bleak for the Five Nations countries. Shorn of several frontliners, England had been walloped 76–0 and 45–3 by Australia. Scotland had lost to Fiji and Australia, while South Africa branded a 101–13 throttling into the Welsh record books. France lost a mid-week match to Buenos Aires, but defeated Argentina and Fiji to claw back some European respectability. Ireland won one of four warm-up games in South Africa before the real fun began.

The Springboks, led by Gary Teichmann, were world champions, and possessed a litany of attacking talent. Ireland went into the matches with a clear tactic of physically imposing themselves on their hosts. Victor Costello, who played both Tests against South Africa, states, 'We were not going to roll over for them, but things got ugly, quickly. I've a theory that if you start throwing punches, (a) you're not fit enough and (b) you don't believe in yourself.'

Ireland lost the first Test 37–13, and did not fare much better in the second. They went down with literal, lusty swings as the 'Boks won 33–0. Donald McRae summed up the grizzly spectacle in *Winter Colours*: 'It was filthy stuff in Pretoria, grim bare-knuckle violence laced with boots and flying elbows. Mass brawls broke out in a drunken convoy as lines of players weaved across the pitch in fist-throwing tow. It was the most dispiriting rugby match I had ever seen.'

South Africa's then press officer, Alex Broun, recalls, 'The Battle of Pretoria was the first time I met Donal, and there were some very fiery scenes there. I remember I got into a nasty situation after that Test and I was in the Irish dressing room. I was a bit upset too, as it has been a very, very violent Test. It was one of the most violent I ever remember. I went in to get a couple of Irish players for a press conference. I was pretty bullish when I barged into the Irish dressing room and said, "C'mon, this player has to come now." Donal certainly put me in my place. He said "You fuck off. What are you fucking doing in here?"

'A few of the Irish players were like, "What's going on here?" and calmed us down. But they were battered and bruised, the Irish. My God, they were battered and bruised. They were bleeding from all over the place. They tried to give as good as they got, but the South African boys were a lot bigger and a lot stronger.'

For England back-row Lawrence Dallaglio, it was clear that his country needed to shake the Celtic Nations loose to progress in the professional era. He told Donald McRae, 'It's no coincidence that the Australians improved so much in the late 1980s when they popped across the Tasman and played the All Blacks two or three times a season. I really believe that, if we get the chance to meet that quality of opposition on a regular basis, we can eventually conquer the world.'

Broun feels there was 'a huge possibility' of England and France forming a breakaway tournament with New Zealand, Australia and South Africa. 'The Springboks beat Wales by over a hundred points and nearly put a hundred on Italy. There was a lot of talk about a new competition with those five nations … People were asking, "What is wrong with Wales, with Italy? What is wrong with Ireland? They're so poor."'

Hope came, nine months later, in the shape of a spry twenty-year-old from Clontarf, Dublin, called Brian O'Driscoll.

Ireland had swatted Georgia and Romania aside, in November 1998, to qualify for the following year's World Cup. The 1999 Five Nations brought just one victory, as Wales continued to show benevolence to their Celtic cousins. Italy, one year away from entering an expanded Six Nations, arrived in Dublin in April 1999. Gatland named O'Driscoll on the bench, and Ireland won 39–30 to end their season in better spirits.

Irish fans would not see O'Driscoll in Test action until the summer tour to Australia, but the players had already encountered the Leinster back and his colleague Gordon D'Arcy the previous year. Lenihan comments, 'I remember the first training session we got O'Driscoll and D'Arcy along to. It was down in Cork and it was lashing rain. We brought in two young players for the session, but didn't honestly think they would make the World Cup. We had two injuries in the backline, so slotted them in. Conor O'Shea came up to me at the end of the session and asked me who in the name of God O'Driscoll was. "Who was that thirteen?" He was blown away by him. Still, we couldn't have anticipated back then that he'd become the player he was.'

Two weeks after the Italian win, Brendan Fanning of the *Sunday Independent* got his hands on a squad report from national fitness advisor Craig White. The report was not entirely bleak, but several Munster players did not come out well. White noted that he could not carry out leg-strength tests as only two players were able to perform them. Ulster's Gary Longwell did not cover himself in glory during White's tests. He says, 'I was in my comfort zone and way off international standard. Up to that point I had been coasting. They had a phrase at the time – campers or climbers. Campers got halfway up a mountain and stopped to enjoy the view. Climbers say, "How do I get to the next level?" I was in full-on camping mode – out on the town, enjoying the lifestyle – but that report was a wake-up call.'

Longwell adds, 'Times have certainly changed over the past couple of decades. Davy Irwin at Ulster would tell you that the Irish forwards, in the 1980s, would have eight or nine pints before a match. That was still going on when I first came onto the provincial scene in the early 1990s. Nowadays, Paul O'Connell would deck somebody for drinking out of his water bottle, as he might pick up a cold.'

O'Driscoll would receive his first Ireland starts against Australia in Brisbane and Perth. The *Irish Independent* reported, 'It is an indication of the state of Irish rugby that the great white hope of the game is a twenty-year-old who has yet to win his first provincial cap or play a league game. Brian O'Driscoll was the only player in a green shirt that stood in comparison with his opponents in the art of passing, running and evasion.' Ireland delivered their customary 'big performance' at the Subiaco Oval, but fell to a 32–26 scoreline. They followed that series defeat by edging Argentina at Lansdowne Road in a World Cup warm-up.

Malcolm O'Kelly, who was firmly established in the Irish second row, reflects on another encounter between an earnest psychologist and sceptical rugby players: 'The psychologist coined this phrase, "Dream it, believe it, see it, do it". It was four of them. The process ended at "dream it" as we, of course, just started laughing. What the hell were they talking about? Dream about winning a World Cup? Stupid! We all just giggled and laughed. There was certainly no way you were going to win a World Cup if you didn't dream it and actually believe it. It was only later on, years to come, that we got to a stage where we could actually believe, and honestly think, that you might actually win a World Cup. We have come a long way from back then, where it would have been a giggle and a laugh at the thought of a psychologist suggesting you just need to dream it and it will happen. Yeah, right.'

On 2 October O'Driscoll scored his first try for Ireland, while Keith Wood scored four, as the United States were beaten 53–8. Australia had too much class, pace and power as they cantered to a 23–3 victory in the next match. Gatland's men dealt easily with Romania in the next outing and set up a quarter-final play-off with Argentina. Ireland hit the front as early as the third minute, but with David Humphreys trading kicks with Gonzalo Quesada, they could not shake their opponents off. A converted Diego Albanese try, on 72 minutes, edged Argentina ahead for the first time all night.

The lasting memory of a game wrung dry of quality was Ireland committing fourteen players to a line-out before tossing their hooker, Wood, into the mix for countless, repelled heaves at the Pumas' line. The ploy failed and Ireland's World Cup was over. The favourites, devoid of attacking zest or risk-taking, were jeered off the pitch, and had a long night in Lens to wallow in their misery.

'After the World Cup,' Lenihan reflects, 'the future was in the hands of those young fellas. You look at the five players that played against Scotland in February 2000 – Ronan O'Gara, John Hayes, Peter Stringer, Shane Horgan and Simon Easterby – they would go on to play with distinction for the next decade.'

***

'I watched that match in a pub in Cardiff,' says Simon Easterby as he harks his mind back to Ireland's 50–18 Six Nations hammering by England at Twickenham on 5 February 2000. 'It was pretty horrific. I had played with the A side against England the night before, at Franklin's Gardens, and we had got by them. I was with my brother, Guy, and we had both played reasonably well. We went back to Cardiff to watch the main game. It didn't go particularly well.'

Following that Twickenham throttling, Simon Easterby was named in an Ireland team that included five new caps. Gatland's selection may have had the appearance of a roulette spin, but, as opposed to Ashton in 1997, he was choosing players who were punching in impressive Heineken Cup performances. The flanker was joined by Leinster winger Horgan and the Munster trio of Hayes, Stringer and O'Gara. Mick Galwey clutched his halfbacks close during the national anthems. Easterby says, 'I won a few line-outs and would have been blowing out of my back-end a bit for most of the game. The speed, that was the biggest thing – the noise, speed and intensity.'

There was scant indication at half-time, when Ireland led 13–10, that the hosts would blow the Scots away. David Humphreys replaced O'Gara in the second half – sparking eight seasons of jersey-tugging – and his try proved the catalyst for a rousing 44–22 win. The five debutants would go on to make 461 appearances for Ireland over the following fourteen seasons.

O'Gara kicked twenty points, and Horgan scored a brace of tries in a 60–13 stroll against Italy. The squad travelled to Paris in confident mood. 'One of my greatest Ireland memories,' Stringer reveals, 'was the win over in France in 2000. We hadn't won in Paris in twenty-eight years before that. I would have watched Ireland over the years on TV, and they would have started well for the first twenty minutes before France ran riot. We got there and there were a lot of new faces. There was no fear for us going there. Drico [Brian O'Driscoll] got his hat-trick, and we built from those foundations. That win gave guys massive confidence.'

The wooden-spoon spectre had departed and Ireland were now looking up rather than cautiously padding around looking for trapdoors. Marcus Horan got his first start against the United States on a summer tour. He credits Keith Wood for guiding Irish rugby towards a period of prosperity. 'He was a total leader in what he did on the pitch, and he was proactive off it. He was always challenging people in the IRFU off the pitch, and demanding higher standards from all concerned,' says Horan.

Gatland and IRFU Director of Fitness Liam Hennessy began a trend of bringing the Irish players over to Spala in Poland for intense training camps and cryotherapy recovery sessions. Munster strength-and-conditioning coach Aidan O'Connell says, 'You talk to any of the older players and that defined them in the early stages. It was a three-week camp and an infamous one, because it went on for so long … The stories I heard back from the guys – people were crying going back into it. They would have them train during the week, then leave them in the city, Krakow, at the weekend. They would relax slightly or might have a night out, but then they'd go back into the camp. Apparently, after that second weekend leading into the third week, the bus was so quiet. There were guys crying; they were that upset because they were being pushed so hard. They visited the Auschwitz concentration camp, too, when they were there. It all led to the sense of "Oh, I'm in hell here" and that mood. But, those training camps served Ireland well over the years.'

The outbreak of foot-and-mouth in Ireland did few favours when it came to squad selection for the 2001 British & Irish Lions tour to Australia. Just six Irishmen – Wood, O'Driscoll, O'Gara, O'Kelly, Jeremy Davidson and Tyrone Howe – were chosen to travel, despite the team winning their two outings in that year's fragmented Six Nations. Shane Horgan noticed a marked difference in O'Driscoll upon his return. He comments, '2001 was the tour that Brian took his game to a new level. When the lads came back from Australia, you could see that the tour had left an indelible mark on them. It raised their expectations of themselves, training methods and what they had to do to beat the best.'

Lenihan left Ireland, following their 22–15 win over France in February, to manage the Lions. One of his first calls was to ask Broun to be the Lions' media manager. 'He knew I was a stubborn bastard that would be handy in a battle,' quips Broun. He believes the tour was the single biggest contributor to Ireland's Triple Crown glories in the coming years. He says, 'Ronan O'Gara, for example, was six months younger than Jonny

Wilkinson, but was blown away by him. His jaw hit the ground. It was like a light bulb going on – that is what professionalism is all about. The players returned to Ireland and wanted to instil that drive and purpose into the Irish squad. England was about three years ahead of the Celtic nations in terms of being professional. You would pass the gym after a morning training session, and about eight or ten of the English guys would be in there doing extra work. It was that old adage – the more I practise, the luckier I get. Before a game, Jonny always wanted people to tackle – six on his right shoulder and six on his left. After a while you couldn't get a volunteer for him.'

Lenihan had the enjoyable task of informing O'Driscoll he would be touring with the Lions, but warned the young centre 'he still had to get the coaches behind him'. Lenihan comments, 'We played him at fullback in our first game. At the time you had Will Greenwood and Mike Catt as centre options. He scored a try against Western Australia, but so did everyone else. Some on the tour were still asking, "What's with the hype about this guy?" He then started at outside centre against Queensland Reds, who were leading the Super 12 at the time, a week before the first Test. We put forty-five points on them, and Brian got a superb solo try. It was the first day he really stood up and sold himself to the tour management. He played in three more Lions series over the next twelve years, but if you were to ask for his one stand-out moment it would be that intercept try, leaving gold shirts in his wake, in the first Test in 2001.'

Lenihan adds, 'The likes of Richard Hill, Neil Back, Martin Johnson, they opened O'Driscoll's eyes. Wood was that bit older and was the one clamouring for Ireland to make the change, but he had been the lone voice. He had been over at Harlequins and had seen how we should be approaching professionalism. Brian and Ronan were exposed to that, and soon became Wood's two willing allies. Paul O'Connell came on the Irish scene a year after that, but Wood's role in making the change deserves a huge amount of credit. Claw and Gaillimh had a different mind-set, but they still had a role to play in Irish rugby. Once you had Wood, O'Driscoll and O'Gara coming back from Australia and the likes of John Langford down at Munster, they started driving through to the Ireland players what was needed to compete with the top nations.'

A 32–10 no-show against Scotland ended Ireland's Grand Slam dream following the Lions tour. They thumped Wales in Cardiff, and denied England a Slam of their own, but not the championship, with a 20–14 victory at Lansdowne Road.

By the time New Zealand arrived back in Ireland, in November 2001, the hosts' mind-set had been transformed, and they were targeting victory. Kevin Maggs and Eric Miller scored tries to give Ireland a 16–7 half-time lead. David Wallace says, 'We scored just after the break, through Hickie, and were 21–7 up, but capitulated in the second half. We started with such intensity and purpose, but could not carry it for eighty minutes. New Zealand did all the damage in the second half.'

The All Blacks breached Ireland five times to win 40–29. It would be Gatland's last game in charge. On 28 November 2001 a five-man IRFU committee thanked him for his services to the national team and told him his time was up. As Gatland left the Berkeley Court hotel, in Dublin, his assistant Eddie O'Sullivan arrived through the main gates. O'Sullivan accepted the union's job offer that same day.

# 10

## MIXING IT WITH THE BEST:
## IRELAND 2002–2009

Eddie O'Sullivan's Ireland hit the ground sprinting in the 2002 Six Nations, with a stunning 54–10 disposal of Wales at Lansdowne Road. Paul O'Connell, rapidly established at Munster, steamed over for one of his team's six tries to cap a fine debut. A middling Six Nations campaign was followed by another close call against New Zealand, at Carrisbrook, and a 40–8 swatting at Eden Park.

Later that year Ireland defeated Georgia and Russia to qualify for the 2003 World Cup. The victories were numbers two and three in a remarkable ten-game winning streak. Australia were beaten 18–9 at Lansdowne Road, and in the 2003 Six Nations France were seen off 15–12. A Grand Slam decider awaited in Dublin, but Martin Johnson and his belligerent England blew Ireland away to capture all the controversy – making Irish President Mary McAleese leave the red carpet to walk on the grass – and glory. Ireland were dismantled, losing 42–6 in the painful process.

Simon Easterby, Ronan O'Gara, O'Connell and Donncha O'Callaghan proved themselves as valuable squad members by ensuring Ireland went unbeaten on a summer tour to Samoa and Tonga. All were included in O'Sullivan's World Cup squad, and pool-stage cruises against Romania and Namibia kicked off the campaign. 'We were a group that didn't go off past history. We were young and naive, but didn't have a lot of baggage. A lot of that stuff washed over our heads,' says former Munster prop Marcus Horan. Alan Quinlan bagged a crucial try at the Adelaide Oval, as Ireland avenged their 1999 World Cup defeat by Argentina. Next up were the hosts, Australia. 'We were very confident,' continues Horan. 'There were a lot of Munster players in that squad, and we were coming off the back of some good Heineken Cup campaigns. We took on the Aussies in their back yard and gave them a real scare. It was an enjoyable World Cup, but we could've done more. We threw everything at the Aussies and had nothing left for France.'

Malcolm O'Kelly recalls an enjoyable tradition that began in the hotel room of kit-man Patrick 'Rala' O'Reilly during O'Sullivan's tenure: 'We certainly used to have pizza and Coke the night before a game. That was our tradition under Eddie. We would have pizza and Coke. If anyone ever spiked our pizza, it would have been one way to get rid of us. We would send out for it, Four Star Pizza up in Rala's room. It was part of a social-building thing.'

Ireland achieved a series of fantastic results in the O'Sullivan era – defeating the Springboks and Australia twice at Lansdowne Road, beating France, reasserting their dominance over Argentina, and scoring handsome wins over Wales, Scotland and Italy. Triple Crowns were claimed in 2004, 2006 and 2007. The Six Nations championship was denied them in agonising fashion in the last of those years, when French No. 8 Elvis Vermeulen scored a last-minute try against Scotland. Ireland also formed a happy habit of knocking England over each time their teams met. Of the four consecutive successes against England, 2004 and 2007 stand out as favourites for many players of that generation.

Girvan Dempsey started at fullback against England on 6 March 2004 for what would be the official homecoming for the team that had won the World Cup four months earlier in Australia. 'We were very fired up that day, and what fuelled that fire was the press beforehand,' says Dempsey. 'From our own perspective, there was a little bit of trepidation going into the game, measured with a quiet confidence. We were still in that stage of being the underdog, and we fed off that. It was coming from that amateur era – being the little guys, heading to Twickenham. England were world champs, unbeaten at Twickenham in four years, and everybody had written us off going into the game.

'In fairness to Eddie, Mervyn Murphy [video analyst] and the management team, we'd prepped really well. We had a good game plan and had spotted some potential weaknesses in the English defence – they got quite soft in the wide channels, so we were looking to play that wide–wide pattern and test them down those channels. That's where I was fortunate to get on the end of that try in the second half. It stemmed from that linebreak from D'Arcy, and we fed back out, played that wide–wide, the ball came out, and I was lucky to be on the end of it to score. For us to still have the composure to see the game out [and win 19–13] after that was hugely satisfying.

'When you come into Twickenham through that concourse with all the fans, the visiting dressing room is to the left and the pitch is straight ahead and the English dressing room is on the right. There was a wall, on the way out, that was covered with plaques of all their victories at Fortress Twickenham – all the dates and scorelines of these wins. I remember after the game, Kevin Maggs was dying to put his own plaque up on the wall. He settled for a marker, and put the scoreline from that day right beside. To see what it meant to Maggs and Simon Easterby – guys that were playing their rugby in the United Kingdom – was remarkable. Maggsy was like a Cheshire cat. He was saying, "I can't wait to walk into training on Monday."'

The Ireland team that met England on 24 February 2007 was chasing greater feats than Triple Crowns. O'Sullivan's starting fifteen would invariably include seven Munster forwards, halfbacks Peter Stringer and O'Gara, the bulk of Leinster's backline, and the likes of Rory Best, Simon Easterby and Andrew Trimble. O'Driscoll had missed the opening game of the Six Nations, against France at Croke Park. Lansdowne Road was getting the wrecking-ball treatment, and the Gaelic Athletic Association's (GAA's) members had amended rule forty-two in their constitution to allow Test-match rugby to cross the River Liffey. French winger Vincent Clerc had gutted his generous hosts by streaking through to score a seventy-ninth minute try and clinch the game. 'That game is still hard to watch back,' admits Horan. 'I would love to have those few seconds back near the end. We had been fighting so hard for a championship for years, and gave it up then and there. That's the nature of the Six Nations though. The games you lose are the ones you remember.'

England were due eleven days later, and national focus turned to the reception Johnson's men – and their 'God Save the Queen' anthem – would get. Conor O'Shea was called in to impress upon the English players the white-hot reception they would get at Croke Park. The match would be played in the same venue that, in 1920, the Black and Tans – a mercenary force working for the Royal Irish Constabulary during the War of Independence – opened fire on a GAA-watching crowd and killed fourteen people. O'Shea left the players in little doubt that they would be at the centre of a storm. It followed precisely five minutes after their anthem played out to a pitched silence at a sold-out Croker.

Adding another layer of intrigue to the match were the October 2006 comments made by O'Gara ahead of Munster's Heineken Cup clash with Leicester. The out-half had remarked, 'I honestly think that both for Munster and Ireland, we've got more talented players than the English in many positions.' To this day, O'Gara is unrepentant. He says, 'If you talk honestly there's no need to cover your tracks. You see players and coaches that are trying to duck and dive things and it comes back to bite them. Sometimes the media can make sensational headlines out of what you say, but you learn that; it goes with the territory. The big example was what I said before the Leicester game. I one-hundred per cent stand over it, and I was proved right. I was most definitely proved right. In saying some Irish players were better in certain positions, it meant I was saying England had a few better players in other positions. I don't see what the big deal was about.'

Dempsey comments, 'For me, it was the best sporting occasion, as a professional sportsman, to be fortunate enough to be involved in. The magnitude of the whole occasion and the build-up really hit home. To have lost in that gut-wrenching manner to France – having scored that penalty to go four points ahead, lose that kick-off and see that move evolve in slow motion, with Clerc getting the outside break and score – the deflation after that game was awful. Brian came back into the side as captain and Peter was back at scrum half. All that week, in the lead-up to the England game, Brian was saying, "We do not leave Croke Park without a victory. What you do as a player is you prep and we, as a team, leave with a victory. We cannot leave Croke Park after our stint is over and have the history books stating that we have lost our first two rugby matches here."'

'We were slightly cocooned from the media hype,' Dempsey continues. 'We were conscious it was there and were slightly apprehensive about how the whole thing, the anthem, would be received. That was spine-tingling – hairs-standing-on-the-back-of-your-neck kind of stuff. The eerie silence. I've only looked back on footage, and saw we did leave England out there a long time at the start, to savour the atmosphere before we came out. The deathly silence for the English anthem and then how enthusiastic and vocal everyone was for "Amhrán n bhFiann" and "Ireland's Call". From there, it was a dream match. It was our day.

'Everything clicked and fed into our scores. I was fortunate enough to be on the score sheet, and then, very fittingly, Horgan scored after that overhead catch from ROG's cross-field kick. It was befitting of the occasion and the setting. Brian stated at half-time that we do not give up. We show respect to every opposition we play by not stopping. We do not stop, we do not sit back, we play and score, and score as many points as we can. We did that and Isaac Boss put the icing on the cake.'

The crowd were up, and singing 'Olé, Olé, Olé', before Boss, the Ulster scrum half, intercepted a lazy Shaun Perry pass and raced away for a converted try that made it 43–13 – Ireland's biggest-ever win over England. 'The whole occasion was immense, superb,' says Dempsey. 'It was a pleasure and an honour to be involved in.'

Simon Easterby recalls, 'My daughter, Soffia, was born the day after, my first child. It was a weekend I would never forget, for many reasons. The build-up for that game, everything about it, was different. For myself, having been brought up in England and schooled there, I always knew I wanted to play for Ireland. I went through the Under-21s system to get there. To get a chance to play in that game – with the history of Croke Park and everything that had gone on before – and then to produce that kind of performance was very special. That would live long in the memory, that Saturday.'

*** 

O'Sullivan spared the likes of O'Driscoll, O'Gara, Easterby, Dempsey and O'Connell the two-Test tour of Argentina in the summer of 2007. He determined that a rigorous pre-season followed by warm-ups against Scotland, Italy and a French club side would suffice ahead of the World Cup. Dempsey says, 'We had that infamous game against Bayonne that descended into a brawl, and Brian nearly got his head knocked off. We were slightly undercooked going into the tournament and were nearly trying to get our warm-up in the pool stages against teams that were match ready, match hardened, and we were caught on the back foot. The pressure was on us, as a squad and collective group, and we were trying to force things to make a performance. It was bitterly disappointing, as there was a huge amount of effort from everyone involved. Looking at the team we had, we massively underachieved.'

Having flailed in unconvincing wins over Namibia and Georgia, Ireland were soldered to the starting blocks against France, and lost 25–3. Argentina delivered the last rites again as they opened up an Irish side pushing for tries to pip them to a quarter-final. Juan-Martin Hernandez excelled as Ireland were beaten 30–15 at Parc des Princes. 'We just didn't perform, and were perhaps looking to live off the back of what we had done in the previous nine or ten months,' says Easterby. 'We had a steady decline in our performances, and got what we deserved in those two big group games.

'Coming off the back of a good autumn and good Six Nations does not mean you are going to cruise into a World Cup and expect things to happen … That's a trap we fell into, and it cost us dearly. It cost us a period of rugby too, because we were knocked back, mentally, after that as a team. We took a bit of a beating. We didn't do well in the Six Nations after that, and there were a few changes – new players came in and, of course, Declan Kidney.'

Many senior figures within the IRFU were content with the concept of giving O'Sullivan another year in which to reinvigorate Ireland. The timing, however, was perfect for a new man and a fresh direction. Kidney had led Munster to Heineken Cup success in 2006, and was on course to emulate the achievement in 2008 when he was approached by the union. Kidney would be afforded a summer off, and would take up 'the pinnacle of my career' from October 2008. Fittingly, his reign began at Thomond Park with a 55–0 saunter against Canada. Ireland failed to lay a glove on the All Blacks before rounding out the year with a 17–3 grind over Argentina. A team get-together at Johnstown House in Enfield, one month after the Pumas win, would prove fractious and cathartic in equal measure.

Six years on, Rob Kearney relives the moment when he stood up in front of Munster men such as John Hayes, Horan and O'Connell and suggested they were underperforming for their country. 'It was obviously a big moment,' he says, 'but I think had we got the wooden spoon that season, I would have been the villain of Irish rugby, banished out never to play again. The fact that we won and slammed, it was "Oh, something must have happened here." That has been overtalked a little bit, but it maybe was a big moment that aided the national team.

'Did we come to blows? No. I wish we had come to blows, because what was said was more awkward. I'd have preferred to have been in a fight.' Kearney explains how the December afternoon unfolded. 'We went out into pods. ROG was taking our group, and I just questioned … I didn't question the Munster guys' commitment to the national jersey, but just said there was something very different when they were playing for Munster than when they were playing for Ireland. Then we went into the big group and ROG read out the findings of our study, and Marcus said, "Listen, I have to stop you there. There's a big elephant in the room and something is really wrong here." To which there was a ten-second silence that felt like an eternity. So I had to back it up and say to the group what I had in the backs group.'

Kearney survived the session, and the Munster players – pride stung – tore into their training sessions. France were the first team to feel the force of a revved Irish team, with Jamie Heaslip scoring a stunning try in a 30–21 win. Italy were beaten before Ireland welcomed Johnson's England to Croke Park. They led 6–3 after fifty-six minutes, only for O'Driscoll to come through again with a pick and dive at the back of an Irish ruck. The visitors piled into Ireland in the closing stages, and gave themselves a glimpse of victory with a late try. Each player was required to put their body on the line. The Irish players made 116 tackles that afternoon and only three were missed. Paddy Wallace racked up fifteen hits for a winning cause, as Ireland held on for a 13–11 win. 'The [Grand Slam] question had been out there the moment we beat France,' says David Wallace. 'It just got louder after England.'

'All the players were familiar with each other,' says O'Gara. 'Obviously the big story was the four changes for the Scottish game. People have their own ideas about that. I don't know, but from a selfish point of view you just want to hear your name called out.' Paddy Wallace, Jerry Flannery, Heaslip and Tomás O'Leary were dropped to the bench as Kidney sought to freshen his line-up and keep players on their toes. In his book *Joking Apart*, Donncha O'Callaghan describes being knotted in fear that he would also miss out. 'It was the old Deccie strategy,' he said, 'designed to put the wind up everyone in the squad. It worked, as usual.'

Ireland edged the Scots at Murrayfield, and faced a seven-day wait until the championship decider against Wales in Cardiff. They had a superior points difference to Warren Gatland's side, so could still claim the title with a close defeat. Capturing a first Grand Slam in sixty-one years, however, occupied each and every Irish mind.

'Ah yeah, you would talk about it, of course,' O'Gara reveals. 'It's there but there's no point in speaking too much about it, because it could be gone in one instant. Definitely it is there in the back of your mind – how do you go about this – but talking about it isn't going to do much for you.

'I think the fact that it hadn't been won for so long in Ireland, no one had any experience of what it was like. That's why for us, or me at least, the build-up felt quite calm ... That's no good, having the championship in the bag. I don't know what it's like in golf, losing a Major but winning the FedEx championship on points. It's almost like the consolation prize.'

Ireland lost blindside flanker Stephen Ferris to a broken finger after nine minutes, and trailed 6–0 at the break. 'We didn't lose the run of ourselves. We were very controlled,' says Horan. O'Driscoll came up with another pick and dive to get his team into the match, and O'Gara converted for the lead. Kidney had pinpointed Welsh winger Shane Williams as a defensive weak-spot and, almost immediately from the restart, O'Gara chipped a kick in behind him that bounced up like a dream for Tommy Bowe to charge onto and score.

Ireland had the momentum, at 14–6, but failed to press it home. Two Stephen Jones penalties narrowed the gap, before the out-half landed a drop goal with six minutes to spare – 14–15 down, but Ireland were not done yet. 'You could just see the focus on everyone's face,' Horan recalls. 'We had a lineout on their twenty-two and knew it would be our last attack, and to get ROG into position. Everyone did their job perfectly. We were so used to each other, and everyone knew their role. You trusted the guy beside you and knew he felt the same.'

Looking back on his successful drop on seventy-seven minutes, O'Gara says, 'There are one or two big plays, minimum, in every game. If you look at the bigger picture, that's ten big moments. If one of them slips off, you're gone. People don't realise that. It's easy to take the global picture after, when it's in the bag.' There was still time for Ireland, leading 17–15, to concede an eightieth-minute penalty, and for Jones to leave his kick agonisingly short. Geordan Murphy screamed at glory-hunting interlopers to clear off as he pouched the ball and dispatched it into the crowd.

'We had come so close to championships over the years,' says Stringer. 'To get over the line in Cardiff, again, in that fantastic stadium and in the final, nerve-racking moments, made it so memorable.'

The party stretched on for two days, but one of the Irish heroes was satisfied with his night out in Cardiff. Gary Longwell played six seasons of Test rugby with Irish tight-head Hayes, and puts most of his caps down to the Cappaghmore native. 'Hayes scrummed in front of me and lifted me in the line. He was so selfless. We used to room together, as we were the squad's two big snorers. Professional rugby never changed him. He was exactly the same man when he finished up as when he started. One of the stand-out stories about "The Bull" was that he drove straight back to his farm the day after Ireland won the Grand Slam. The boys are all partying and singing at the Mansion House, and he's back to work. A lot of Ireland's success back then was built on John Hayes.'

# 11

# TREE-HUGGERS:
# IRISH CLUB RUGBY ON ITS KNEES

Ireland, Ireland, Munster, All Blacks, Lions, Munster, Ireland, Munster,
Lions, Lions, Munster. Now tell me that side couldn't hold their own in
the Heineken Cup.

*Ian Barry*

Dressed in jeans and a club blazer, Ian Barry takes me behind the bar and into
a back office that hosts a pool table and features four large, framed collages of
Garryowen's glory days in the 1990s. A twenty-year-old Keith Wood goes on
the charge with a full head of hair. Phil Danaher spins a pass to the backline.
The Wallace brothers, Richard and David, grimace in separate team photos,
and Brent Anderson's glowering, folded-arm stance follows you around the
room. Having met me for the first time three minutes ago, the Garryowen
chairman wisely takes me away from the post-match analysis and pints in
the clubhouse bar. My intentions are barely masked – I have travelled to
Dooradoyle to watch two of Limerick's former giants do battle. While rivalry
remains, the halcyon hue is fading. In the past quarter-century, Garryowen
and Shannon have shared thirteen All-Ireland League titles. During that
same period, however, crowds have dwindled from spiking highs of 12,000
and 'lads hanging out of trees to see games' to an average of 700.

When the IRFU announced the opening round of Ulster Bank League
(AIL) fixtures in July 2014, one game stood out. While reigning champions Clontarf began their title defence against Young Munster at home,
Castle Avenue, Limerick's two other titans would meet in Division 1B. The
top dogs had found themselves in a rickety kennel. I arrive early enough to

catch the Under-11s hurtling back and forth on the main pitch, and to chat with Síofra Scanlan, Shannon's PRO. She introduces me to former players and speaks fondly of her grandfather, Stephen Fitzgerald, who played in the late 1930s and early 1940s when the club mixed in junior rugby circles. Fitzgerald, who passed away aged ninety-eight in August 2014, held just about every position at Shannon, but Síofra's fondest memories are selling club raffle tickets with her grandfather beneath the stands at Thomond Park before heading up for a warming meal and a cushioned seat near Len Dineen in the press shack.

The AIL was at its zenith in the 1990s, and – along with Cork Constitution – Garryowen and Shannon were the main protagonists. Matches between the sides featured players such as Wood, Danaher, New Zealanders Anderson and John Mitchell, the Wallace brothers, Dominic Crotty, Eddie Halvey, Alan Quinlan, Peter Stringer, Anthony Foley, Mick Galwey, John Hayes and Trevor Hogan. It was not until 2000/01 that Munster began to restrict club appearances. The names and faces, now, are less familiar. A handful are involved in the Munster set-up.

Injured Garryowen and Munster hooker Mike Sherry pitches up just in time for kick-off, and takes his place on the mound behind the dugouts. His team are led out by fellow dart-thrower Ed Rossiter, and soon followed by Shannon. Their forwards imbibe last-minute instructions from assistant coach Marcus Horan, the former Munster and Ireland loose-head. Shannon start brightly, and should be further ahead than 3–0 before Garryowen hit back. Blindside Shane Buckley had made his first start for Munster, against Edinburgh, the previous week and is brimming. He heaves through two tackles to give the hosts a lead they will not relinquish. I wander the perimeter and note casual scenes I convince myself would make for a fine chapter – cleared kicks bouncing off car bonnets, octogenarians in Shannon scarves scowling at poor handling from the fullback in pink boots, a Jack Russell tied to a floodlight post, and the never-ending queue for burgers and help-yourself garnish.

Rossiter and Garryowen scrum half Neil Cronin add further tries, but there is still room for bluster as the referee denies a late push-over score that would have secured the bonus point. Shaking hands with Garryowen's PRO Tony O'Rourke at the final whistle, I remark on the fine conditions in which the match was played. 'It's always good to take a skinful from Shannon, no matter the weather,' he responds.

I am introduced to Neil Prendergast and Vinny Ryan inside the clubhouse. Ryan, a former Shannon chairman, is sipping a consolation pint from club rival Prendergast. Having enjoyed battles on and off the pitch for the past three decades, both men are comfortable in their mutual company. They relive some of the match's stand-out moments before talk quickly turns to the league's demise. 'The gap is widening between the AIL and Munster,' laments Prendergast. 'Munster are only interested in taking in schoolboys, and – when they don't work out – buying in from abroad. You used to cut your teeth in this league, but that rarely happens any more. The gulf is widening and there is no way back.'

Passing on a rapidly diminishing basket of chips, Ryan recalls, 'When Shannon played Garryowen in the 1990s we had 10,000 or 12,000 in for the games. All the papers, radio stations and pirate radio stations would cover it for weeks beforehand and interview the players. It was all anybody talked about. Now we play games, and our top players are never available for us.' Prendergast chips in, 'We have a game on a Saturday, and a Munster guy who isn't in their match-day squad is in the gym. He's not out on the field with his club. It's lunacy.'

The current state of the economy, they insist, has not helped matters. Young rugby players from the area have moved abroad or relocated to Dublin in search of work. I tell them of Donal Lenihan's declaration that a team of Cork exiles, based in Dublin, would prosper in the top division. Ryan and Prendergast nod in agreement. While the complaints of the club men are too many to count on two hands, they stress that their multiple bones of contention are not with Munster, but rather the IRFU. 'Look at the latest attendances at Thomond Park too,' says Prendergast. 'Numbers are dropping and I feel that is because of the disconnect between the club and the top level of the game.'

Ryan is confident that both clubs are not slipping off into the long, dark night yet, but predicts further marginalisation. His view is fuelled by a dictat for the new season that prevents Shannon from playing at Thomond Park on the same day that Munster have home games at the storied ground. A previous agreement had seen Shannon line out for Saturday afternoon matches, with Munster taking to the field later that evening. 'We've been told to stay away,' Ryan exclaims. 'So, we can't play at our home ground, as is our God-given right, because Munster are worried about parking for an extra thousand people for a Pro12 game against a lowly team that didn't exist ten years ago. We've been bloody well subjugated.' (I later follow up on Ryan's claims, and they are strenuously denied by Munster chief executive Garret Fitzgerald. He comments, 'Shannon and ULBohs [University of Limerick Bohemians] were given permission to play on the back pitch prior to [Munster's] Pro12 games provided the dressing rooms in the West Stand were vacated by an agreed time to allow proper preparation for the game and to comply with all Health and Safety regulations.')

Ten minutes later, and I am in the midst of Garryowen's AIL-winning run-in of 1992. Ian Barry and his brother, Neil, were part of a team coached by New Zealander Murray Kidd that captured the league after coming agonisingly close the season before. Not long after the celebrations sated, many of the Garryowen team were in Munster red for the 22–19 triumph over Australia at Musgrave Park, Cork. The likes of Danaher and Galwey (Garryowen and Shannon) teamed up to turn over the reigning world champions. Bob Dwyer's team knew they were in for a scrap as soon as the first kick-off was in flight. Brian Walsh, who played centre that day, jokes that Richard Wallace even resorted to a throw-down with the Wallabies' mascot.

Upon the opening of their new clubhouse, which must have looked swanky over twenty years ago, Garryowen invited Jack Rowell's Bath over for an exhibition game. The hosts put out a strong team and were matched by their English visitors. Mike Catt, Jon Callard, Andy Robinson and Ben Clarke were part of the Bath team that won 38–7 in Limerick that day. A strong bond was formed between the sides as the clubhouse had its head wetted into the early hours. The following season saw Bath host Garryowen at The Recreation Ground (The Rec). The early incarnation of the Heineken Cup soon followed after the game turned professional in August 1995. Many of the clubs demanded to be included as Ireland's representatives, but the union had slid its chips behind the provinces. Garryowen's friendship with Bath was all well and good, but they would not be contesting the same cup.

With the benefit of hindsight, I tell Barry that the IRFU made the right call when plumping for the newly professional provinces over the clubs. Affording 120 professional players at four provinces was a tough enough ask. Allowing Ireland's top eight, ten or twelve clubs to battle it out for a top-three place and European qualification would have ruled out more than half the country's best players. Barry regards his Garryowen club tie, and then tells me he would have been happy for the city of Limerick to be represented in Europe, as clubs/towns like Leicester and Toulouse are. 'Imagine it,' he invokes. 'The best of Garryowen, Shannon, Crescent, Young Munster, Bohs representing Limerick in Europe.'

That dream has long since passed, and with provincially contracted players rarely sighted in club colours and constantly changing league format, the clubs have suffered badly in the past fifteen years. Barry never believed he would somehow end up as Garryowen chairman, but, when his name was put forward, said he would take on the challenge as long as he did not have to pander to union administrators and 'all that committee stuff'. He declares, 'The IRFU employ the least-talented people on their staff to look after the domestic game, pay them an awful lot of money, and they haven't a clue. They're … let's just say that they are not fit for purpose.' Barry longs for a scenario where the IRFU concentrate on the provincial and international teams, leaving an entirely new body to oversee the amateur game.

He adds, 'We get a grant of around €20,000 a year off them but, for that, they impose an awful lot of restrictive rules and sanctions. You have to be eternally grateful. Now I'm not saying that the €20,000 isn't very useful, but if we lost it, it would not be the end of the world. We would move on and at least be free of all the restrictions and rules.' Barry is in favour of a competition departure that appeals to many across the domestic game. 'We should go back to the local and provincial games against our old rivals. Whoever gets through that goes on to an All-Ireland competition. A knock-out [format]. We could play Young Munster next week here, under the lights, and easily get in 2,000. That's all you want at this stage: that local rivalry. Lads walking down the street on a Monday and saying, "Ah you were shite, I was shite, whatever."

'We could get promoted to Division 1A next year and win it, and would anybody care? Would anybody report on it? It would be good for the club, the morale, but it is meaningless now. When we won in the 1990s it meant something, because you were competing against the best of the best.'

The clubhouse bar is busy again, but will echo for most of the season. Conor Murray and Damien Varley, smiling unsteadily for the camera in Ireland jerseys, have graduated to framed pictures. The likes of Sherry and Buckley may soon join them in green and be added to the wall. Both sets of players are sharing a post-match drink at one end of the bar as Barry and I emerge. Lost in his stories, Barry has left his wife to fend capably for herself. Before making his way back to her, he says, 'We're interested now in becoming the best amateur club we can be. Setting up the best underage structures and providing players that can one day progress to play for Munster and Ireland. Garryowen has a proud tradition of providing players for Ireland.'

I take my leave of the cross-town rivals, and pass through the blue gates with their bisected white star. At one of the first roundabouts I come to, I spy three directional arrows with rugby-ball motifs: Garryowen, Young Munster and Old Crescent. They spark the idea of Limerick – featuring Murray, Paul O'Connell, Keith Earls, Felix Jones and J. J. Hanrahan – doing battle with Toulouse at Thomond Park. It makes for a pleasant distraction on the late-night commute home.

# 12

## 'PURE JOY':
## ROB KEARNEY

My first exchange of words with Rob Kearney came outside the Old Wellington Inn in Manchester, on 29 August 2009. The twenty-three-year-old fullback was on his final weekend off before returning to Leinster for a tapered start to pre-season. It had been eight weeks since he had lined out for the British & Irish Lions against South Africa as Ellis Park, Johannesburg, hosted the third Test. Kearney had begun the first Test as backup to Lee Byrne, but an injury to the Welshman meant Kearney was in the thick of it from the thirty-sixth minute. The Lions lost the Test series 2–1, but the fullback was a sensation. Coming on the back of Ireland's Grand Slam success, in March of that year, this gave Kearney a strong claim as world rugby's best No. 15.

We were in England on separate jaunts, but for the same reason. Manchester United were hosting Arsenal at Old Trafford that afternoon. Kearney, I am sure, was as curious as I to see if Cristiano Ronaldo could really be replaced by the likes of Gabriel Obertan and free transfer drop-in Michael Owen. As a conspicuous, proud Irishman, I prefer to leave celebrities and sports stars to their free time, especially when I am enjoying mine. I was a couple of pints into my day, however, and Kearney's imperious performances compelled me to have my say. As we finished up our round and contemplated a fast-food lunch, I took leave of my friends and approached his beer-garden table – 'Rob, just wanted to say you were world-class against South Africa during the summer.' One hopes it was a nice moment on his trip to Manchester, but I suspect Kearney's highlight mirrored mine – that of Arsène Wenger getting dismissed from the sidelines for kicking a water bottle as United emerged 2–1 victors over the Gunners.

Kearney and I met in a professional capacity in Dunedin, during the 2011 World Cup. A large chunk of 2010/11 had been written off after Kearney sustained a wretched knee injury. He had returned in time for Ireland's warm-up games, but had been spared the home fixtures against France and England. The 15–6 win over Australia had been his first competitive match in 10 months. He followed that assured performance with a try in the handy dismissal of Russia. There was a moment of worry in the first half as he was wrong-footed by Vasily Artemyev and collapsed to the turf. The knee was spared any further trauma, and Kearney vowed to brush up on his defence. The final group-stage game against Italy was drawing near, but there was still time to marvel over Alex Ferguson's longevity as United manager. The wily Scot had led his side to their nineteenth league title and was eyeing number twenty. 'He might just go on forever,' Kearney remarked.

The fullback returned to Ireland a few weeks ahead of me. On the same weekend New Zealand overcame France to win the World Cup, Kearney was helping Leinster to an away win over Edinburgh. The setting was Murrayfield. The crowd was a shade over 3,500. He finished the season with a Heineken Cup winners' medal and was named European Player of the Year. He was back in New Zealand for the summer tour of 2012, and the All Blacks had another Irish player – other than Brian O'Driscoll – to rave about. He would be up against Israel Dagg, and the Crusaders' bolter created a speculation frenzy when suggesting the Irishman would thrive in Super Rugby. As so frequently happens with the All Blacks, kind words are followed by performances of ruthless intensity. I spoke in hushed tones with Kearney under the main stand at Waikato Stadium following Ireland's 60–0 thumping. What stayed with me was his openness, and his yearning to compete with the very best. 'As a national team it probably hasn't been that great a season for us …,' he said. 'We know against New Zealand that they like to offload. We knew that, didn't stop it, and they got a lot of, lot of tries from it.'

Italy were next on the fixture list, in March 2013, when I sat down, as part of a media pod, with Kearney again. Niggling injuries had prevented him from getting a clear run of games, and opposing teams had learned not to send up steeplers for the fullback to claim and attack from. The form of Welsh fullback Leigh Halfpenny had moved him onto the predicted Lions starting line-ups of most pundits. I asked Kearney about the flying form of his rival for the Lions' No. 15 jersey, and his honest response made for good headlines. 'Leigh Halfpenny winning our Lions duel' read the *Irish Daily Star*. We met again, six weeks later, as part of the Cooley man's role as brand ambassador for Kellogg's. We shook hands, and, as I took my seat, Kearney remarked, 'Any leading questions for me this time?' I prepared for a bumpy interview, but found him as interesting and accommodating as ever.

As soon as I got the go-ahead for this book, I put Kearney's name on an interview wishlist. He had taken over as Irish Rugby Union Players' Association (IRUPA) chairman from Johnny Sexton after the out-half's move to Racing Métro. He was a season into the job by the time we eventually caught up; I was advised it would be best to confine my questions to his role and responsibilities. 'You ask the questions, I'll answer,' he proclaimed after we had swapped summer-of-2014 niceties over the phone line. We began with his entry into provincial rugby.

'I first came into Leinster for an Under-15 camp, just after third year in school and my Junior Cert,' he said. 'The camp was at Old Belvedere and Kurt McQuilkin was in charge. Rugby was always in my family. My dad, granddad and older brother all played at Clongowes; that was something I always wanted to do. Up to fourteen or fifteen, though, Gaelic football was the major sport. I trained and played three or four nights a week, and would have had matches, in both sports, each weekend. When it came time to make a decision on which sport to pursue, rugby being professional swung it. I knew that you could make a much better life for yourself as a rugby professional than as an amateur GAA player.

'I was so lucky coming in as I was offered a one-year deal and, within that first season, I was playing. There were very few young guys playing for their provinces at the time, so the academy lads – myself included – got a chance early on. I was eighteen when I first came in, and by nineteen I was playing with the first team. I remember for my first weights session in the gym, with the senior team, I looked at the timetable, and I was in with Brian O'Driscoll and Shane Horgan. Your first inclination is to be awestruck, and I was a bit as I had grown up watching them on TV, men I had admired and respected. I knew I was in there for a reason and vowed to myself that I would not hold back. You have to get to grips with it pretty quickly and push yourself so it becomes a level playing field. I scored a hat-trick [against Parma] in a pre-season game that summer, so that helped me settle in.

'I got my chance early as Denis Hickie got injured, so I was put in on the left wing for around six months. It is different now. A lot of lads go through the academy process for three seasons before taking the step up, or not, to the senior team. Lads may get a chance now, but if they don't perform they go right to the back of the queue. It might be months before they get a look-in again.

'When Michael Cheika came in and offered me the developmental contract, he was very matter-of-fact about it – made it seem like my natural progression. What took me aback, though, were my first couple of calls about Ireland. One was on the same day I was playing for Leinster. I got a call from Eddie O'Sullivan, who let me know I was doing well. I was just nineteen at the time. I thought, a hundred per cent, that it was a piss-take. The following season, I got a call about coming in for training camp with the senior team. Again, my first thought was, "Someone's taking the piss."'

Kearney scored three tries in his first three senior games. He was narrowly denied a fourth against Ulster as James Topping and Andrew

Trimble ushered him over the touchline before he could touch down in the left-hand corner. He was soon put forward for interviews alongside Cheika, tearing home for Heineken Cup tries and training with the Irish senior set-up. For six months his feet hardly touched the ground.

'One of the strongest attributes that any team possesses is players looking out for one another,' he told me. 'When a young lad of twenty or twenty-one gets his first big contract, his teammates often take it upon themselves to make sure he does not get carried away with himself. Our academy system is so strong as the competition for places is so high, and it is full of lads with huge talent and ambitions. One of the first things many academy graduates think when they make the senior team is, "This is great, but I want more." That means holding down a regular spot, but aiming for Ireland, the Lions. That is encouraged, but that ambition has to be matched by hard work and dedication. That is where the senior professionals come in and keep the younger lads in line – remind them of their responsibilities. That team culture is strong at Leinster, and has been one of the main reasons for our success in recent years.'

Kearney can be bracketed in the second coming of professional rugby in Ireland. The academy system was not as multifaceted as it is today. Still, thanks to the likes of O'Driscoll and Horgan, the path to a professional rugby career was clearer. The second generation were vital in helping the province pull clear of the also-rans and become a winning entity. 'I can't believe the changes that have happened at Leinster since I first arrived,' he admitted. 'I was there for the Heineken Cup games at Donnybrook when it was not near full. Going to away games with thirty or forty fans in our section, cheering for us. The change has been enormous, and the most satisfying thing is that the trend has not reversed. Our support keeps growing. That is not just down to the players but the backroom staff that are needed in any professional organisation and the fans – the ones that were there from the start and the ones that have started to follow us. It all helps in building a huge project and a successful one, too.'

The players' union and its work with professionals away from the field, he commented, was a side of the game that always interested him. 'We're taking small steps in what is a big work in progress,' he explained. 'Some of the issues we tackled in 2014 revolved around sick pay and leave, guys getting injured and the player-development programme. Because, when they retire, it is all about easing a player back into the big, bad world out there.

'As professional players, we live in a bubble. Landing back in that real-world environment can prove a sticky situation for some guys. Our job, at IRUPA, is to ease that transition and provide career options and pathways. One such step in the developmental programme is the mentor scheme – teaming a player up with an entrepreneur or businessperson for guidance; giving them someone to bounce ideas off.

'The IRFU has done a reasonable job of running the game as professional now, and ensuring that each of the provinces are in good shape – competitive. They deserve a huge amount of credit for that. The end of season [2013/14] accounts look very healthy. The success of the national team feeds into that, so there is a vested interest in making sure Joe Schmidt and his coaching staff get what they're after. Rugby is a business now, and if you do not run it accordingly, everyone suffers.'

As rugby is a business, Kearney sees first-hand how players are commodities, but warns against heaping on further physical and mental demands. 'Players are training and playing now for eleven months of the year,' he said. 'We get four weeks of holidays, and we use that time to unwind a bit. Some lads might spend a good few quid here and there, but you are always conscious of not getting too carried away, or letting yourself go, or it will be harder on you in pre-season. Once you're back, you're back. No messing about. I can tell you exactly where I'm going to be every day for the next eleven months. Everything is mapped out for us – diet plans, training, extra gym and weight sessions, matches, club commitments and appearances. It is that regimented.

'The spectre of injuries is never far away, and is a pretty frightening one too. Anyone can succumb to a career-ending injury at any stage. There are fears about the next contract, too. It will happen to us all eventually; we won't be offered a new contract. Only the rare few get to walk off on their own terms.'

Concussion has become a red-flag issue since 2012, but Kearney is surprised it was not to the forefront decades before. He said, 'Concussion is now prioritised as a key factor in player welfare, whereas in the past it was looked on as a taboo subject. This is something that will affect you for the rest of your life – it is that serious. The IRB and IRFU have really stepped up their game in making sure the right information is available. When you look at where the game was in early 2013 to where it is now, everyone is a lot more educated. You have the ten-minute concussion check protocols, and the decisions are left with the medical staff, rather than the coaches interfering. You still have the odd case that occurs – a clearly concussed player continuing on – but they are now the exception.

'I have had two proper, bad concussions in my professional career. The full-on ones, where you are knocked out, are the easy ones to deal with. The knocks that are not full on – when you take a hit and have to give your head a rock to shake it off – they are the ones you must be careful about.

'I was knocked out cold once, playing for Leinster. That was my first concussion. The second was the game against France in 2009, the year we won the Grand Slam. It happened pretty early on, about ten minutes into the game. I pressed up for a tackle and took a hefty knock. I was back up quickly, but I collapsed twice getting back behind the chip line. I nursed the knock for a while and thought I had shaken it off. Geordan Murphy replaced me with two minutes to go. I can just remember not feeling too great afterwards, having a couple of early nights. I watched the game back during the week, and there were large parts I could not remember.

'That situation, with me falling twice and being so unsteady, that would not happen today. You would be straight off if the medical staff saw that.

It has become more of an open topic among the players, and it has been addressed by the IRFU. At our [summer 2014] national camp we had a brain specialist come in to talk to the players about concussion – how to spot signs, long-lasting impact, the dangers.'

Bernard Jackman, Kearney's former Leinster and Ireland teammate, wrote about his personal struggles coping with concussion in his 2010 autobiography *Blue Blood*. Four years on, and retired England centre Shontayne Hape spoke with the *New Zealand Herald*'s Steve Deane for a stark, gripping article entitled 'My battle with concussion'. In the piece, Hape details a career in rugby league and union that included at least twenty concussions. Hape commented, 'Players are just pieces of meat. When the meat gets too old and past its use-by date, the club just buys some more ... I sat out for a week, but I wasn't right. I was back to having constant migraines. I was pretty much in a daze. Things had got so bad I couldn't even remember my PIN number. My card got swallowed up twice. My memory was shot. Dosing up on smelling salts, Panadol, high-caffeine sports drinks and any medical drugs like that to try and stop the dizziness, fatigue and migraines was the only way I could get through trainings and matches.'

The Hape article, Kearney conceded, gave him several moments' pause. 'It is good for guys in the game to see and read that kind of personal account by a fellow pro,' he reasoned. 'The more accounts that come out like that, the more frightened guys will be. That's a good thing. The idea of, "Oh no, it's just a knock, I'll be fine" – those days are gone. Injuries are part of what we do. Part of our job, on a day-to-day basis, is committing to tackles that could very well end your career, but that does not stop you for a moment from pitching in.'

To that reckless end, the majority of rugby fans side with players as the never-ending rounds of contract negotiations spin to a blur. Kearney's latest contract was due to expire by summer 2015 and, by August 2014, Leinster coach Matt O'Connor was already fielding questions on his fullback's future. 'The lure of money, and the big-spending clubs, is not uncommon in rugby,' Kearney noted. 'It happens in most sports. Even the wealthy footballer will go to the club where he can get more money. Rugby players need to have that opportunity to maximise on their earning potential. At no point of our career, though, will one contract set us up for the rest of our lives.

'We are getting into dangerous territory now, as Irish provinces will never be able to compete with France. The Canal Plus television deal (€355 million for five years' broadcasting rights) is going to elevate their game even further. Ireland will never be able to repel all of their advances. There has been talk of bringing in private investors, but, the way our game is run, it will not be like France with entrepreneurs and billionaires throwing money out here and there. It won't be a case of an investor going, "Here's a million. Off you go and spend it as you please."

'The IRFU's job is to make it as attractive as possible for a player to remain in Ireland. Of course, money will come into it, but there are other aspects that they hope will make up for the financial differences. That in-cludes the best medical care and support, world-class facilities, provinces competing at the very top end of the European game.

'Speaking for myself, I have a huge allegiance to Irish rugby and to Leinster. I have been in the Leinster set-up since I was fourteen. At the same time, if a player feels he is doing a job and is not getting the recognition for that, or feels devalued, that is a major factor in looking to move on. No one likes feeling undervalued. That's not just in sport. The same, I'm sure, applies in banks, offices, businesses. It's human nature. Once that value reflects in how much they are getting paid, most players will stay and set about proving themselves all over again. There are one-offs, though, where players are valued at clubs, but simply move on as an offer is too good to refuse. Players are well aware of the ruthless and fickle nature of sport – they see talented teammates not offered new deals, injuries taking their toll – and that influences their decisions when contract talks come about.'

Our discussion had bled past the hour mark, so, conscious of his regimented schedule, I attempted to extract Kearney's reason for being: eleven months of a season, seeking to take the final bend at enough pace to edge home ahead of the rest; when you do, the clock is re-set and you go again; when you fail, the clock is re-set and you go again.

There was silence on the other end of the line. Then he said, 'The highs in rugby are unbelievable. When you win, there is no better feeling in the world. Walking out in front of 80,000 people for your country and hearing your national anthem – it's a high you can't describe, a feeling of pride that infuses your whole body. When you win a trophy and you're back in that dressing room, surrounded by your friends and you're all so spent – there is a feeling of such intense joy.

'And the lows are unbelievably low. If you have a bad day at the office, you can often leave it behind at 5.30 p.m. If you have lost a match or are in a rut of bad form, that stays with you for weeks, twenty-four hours a day. Then you have times when you are out of favour, the injuries and the times where you can't see the light at the end of the tunnel. I was lucky, in a way, to have some injuries early in my career, so I knew how to cope with that feeling of frustration – helplessness.

'But you will go through months and months of the setbacks, the crushing disappointments, the lows. You will go through it all just to feel those one or two moments of pure joy again.'

# 13

## LEINSTER COME OF AGE

We got sick of playing second fiddle to other teams, other provinces who had won the Heineken Cup and we wanted a little bit for ourselves.

*Brian O'Driscoll, Leinster*

Malcolm O'Kelly had arrived back from London Irish in 1999. Happy as he was to see a playing structure taking shape, a sense of Leinster's identity was lost in their constantly shifting training schedules. 'Mike Ruddock changed the attitude and drive at Leinster, but it wasn't until Matt Williams and Alan Gaffney arrived that we first challenged in the Heineken Cup,' he says. 'We came on leaps and bounds under them. In Australia, where the guys had arrived from, their union had voted themselves out of existence to make room for the new pro set-up, but there was no chance of that happening in Ireland.'

O'Kelly continues, 'Matt brought more of an on-field change. He would have changed up our defensive intentions, our tackle play, the way we trained. He brought Willie Anderson back on board. That was great, to have Willie back again. But we were still training in Belvedere. We trained there full time, but it was still changing in cars, not bothering to have a shower, zipping off home instead. It was a very part-time attitude, even though we did so much training. We trained really hard, loads of meetings. The ability to relax and socialise with each other wasn't there. When it was, it helped build the side. Williams and Gaffney looked at the bigger picture, and – for the first time in years – sought to develop Leinster's backline play. The backline that began to make Leinster's name would still have been fantastic, but they all came in as professionals from day one. That certainly aided in their development as a unit to be feared.'

Denis Hickie and Girvan Dempsey were established members of the Leinster backline when the Australian coaching ticket arrived. Shane Horgan had arrived via the club-rugby route (Boyne RFC) and, having convinced all concerned by his playing abilities and sheer physicality, was being trialled across the line. Williams' arrival, however, coincided with breakthroughs for two players who would eventually form a record-breaking midfield partnership for club and country.

'I would have first seen O'Driscoll and D'Arcy from the first moment they started; when they were kids, out of school,' says Reggie Corrigan. 'They came onto the scene in 1999. Drico's first Ireland cap was that game in Brisbane. He was with Leinster before that, and had gone away on team-bonding trips, pre-season games and I got to know him. A very quiet lad at the beginning – didn't have a whole lot to say. He was taking everything in, observing, being involved. Then, when he got onto the pitch, he brought an intensity and a different level.

'It was the same with Darce. He was at a period [in 1999] where he got injured, and he got really unfit and overweight. We went on tour to Australia – must have been 1999 – and we saw him and thought, "This lad is unfit," but he had been injured and was a young kid, not long out of school. Then, a bit like myself, he turned things around and really dedicated himself to the game.

'They were very young and there were older lads around,' Corrigan adds, 'so they listened to things from a senior point of view. They were very driven at that age and very ambitious. When they established themselves in that squad, which was very quickly, they weren't afraid to give their opinion on things and say what was needed to be said. They certainly didn't look at the time that they would develop into the world-class centre partnership that they did become, but there was massive potential there.'

\*\*\*

It merely adds to the Leinster stereotype that Reggie Corrigan is in confessional mode as he stirs his Americano in Starbucks. 'I'm at an age now,' he begins, 'where I can be as honest as I like, and I don't really give a shit. I was jealous of what Munster had. I was jealous of the fact that they were winning games, being successful, getting to Heineken Cup finals and all that momentum was building around them. They were playing a game that was considered to be pretty standard, but they were brilliant at it. That maul of theirs was something else. Then you'd look at us, and we'd create incredible tries out of nothing. The question was asked though, "Why can't we get it over the line?" A lot of blame was laid at our door as forwards, about us being bottlers and all that. It was so insulting you wouldn't believe it at the time, but you had to live with it. People only judge you on results. It was why the 2001 Celtic League final against Munster was so sweet, as our fourteen men [Eric Miller had been sent off] beat them. Where was the bottling there? Essentially, it was the same group of forwards.'

Shane Byrne, who started as Leinster hooker, recalls, 'After fifteen minutes of the match, Eric was sent off. We didn't panic and stuck to the game plan set out by Alan and Matt. We were going up against them, seven versus eight, in the scrum, and it was some battle. Paul Wallace, with his gammy ankle, was a Trojan in the scrum that day.'

Corrigan was Leinster captain in 2001 when they defeated Munster 24–20 to claim the inaugural Celtic League title. The prop was an instant acolyte of Williams, who had arrived from Super Rugby's Waratahs the season before.

Leinster had some silverware to decorate their Donnybrook Portakabins, but, when Williams left to coach Scotland in June 2003, the province veered off course. Gary Ella and Declan Kidney had a season apiece. Victor Costello recalls the province's transition period as never-ending. 'We went through a good few years where we had guys coming in with dodgy CVs,' he remarks.

O'Kelly recalls the period as one of tumult, during which many good players were cast aside. 'It is very hard to manage a team of thirty-five people, especially thirty-five people who are all prima donnas who all want to be on the team … You need to have honesty. You need to be able to tell a guy to his face that he's not good enough to be selected because of X or Y, or you need to believe in him and play him in enough games so he is developing and learning. That is what really good coaches do. Maybe there weren't enough games. There are now. We had big squads – thirty-five players and some may never have played. And they were good players. These guys played AIL, and they suddenly go off to England and have good careers. A lot of guys were shafted. Felipe Contepomi, for the first two, three years – the beginning of his career in Ireland – hardly played. He was behind Nathan Spooner and didn't get a look in. He was made to look like a duck and then turned out to be a genius.

'There were a load of guys in a similar position to Felipe. They were known as the balloon corps: Trevor Brennan, Bob Casey, David Quinlan, Aidan McCullen, Christian Warner. There were loads of these guys. No disrespect to Williams, Ella and Kidney, but that's what happened. Guys got shafted. Liam Toland was Leinster captain one minute and then got shafted, no contract, the next.'

Following Kidney's departure, Michael Cheika was given the top job. The Australian's coaching CV included stints with Padova and club side Randwick, but he impressed the Leinster branch sufficiently to be handed over some branded tracksuits and the keys to a cramped office. Cheika remarks, 'No one would have given a hobo like me the opportunity to come and coach. Leinster took a gamble on me.' One of his first meetings was with Brian O'Driscoll. Cheika offered the captaincy to his star player, who was still recovering from a shoulder dislocation on the British & Irish Lions tour to New Zealand. Frustrated at Leinster's lack of direction, O'Driscoll gave it to his new coach straight. He wanted to see real progress by the end of the season or he would move on. 'Fine,' Cheika replied. 'Let's go. We've got a lot of work to do.'

Cheika gave a young St Mary's out-half, Johnny Sexton, his Leinster debut in 2006. Eight years on, ahead of a Test match with Cheika's Australia, Sexton reflects, 'He was instrumental in changing our mindset, changing our culture in the organisation and then allowing Joe [Schmidt] to come in and take the organisation on the way he did. Without Cheiks, that wouldn't have been as seamless as it was, and he takes a lot of credit for that.'

Bernard Jackman played five seasons at Leinster and all of them were under the abrasive Aussie. 'With Cheika,' he recalls, 'the pre-seasons were ridiculously hard. They were meant to break you. We used to go to Killiney hill three times a week and the sessions up there were long, gruelling sessions. It was good though.

'As a squad,' Jackman continues, 'we probably weren't mentally strong enough. In our first year we played great rugby with him and [David] Knox, but we didn't have that set-piece. We didn't have the forward domination. Mike Brewer came in for year two as a breakdown coach, and eventually he was taking over the forwards. He brought a hard edge. He brought the understanding that, even though we had Felipe Contepomi, Shane Horgan, Gordon D'Arcy, Brian O'Driscoll, Denis Hickie, Girvan Dempsey, we needed to have a balance.

'The forwards needed to be given an opportunity to get themselves in the game. Sometimes as a forward pack, if you are just creating ball, getting ball to the backs … backs … backs …, you don't really get a chance to get a foothold in the game. As the team evolved you saw Leinster creating a driving maul, Leinster creating an attacking scrum. Leinster forwards getting in and picking and going, and really outworking teams. That was important. Maybe the rugby wasn't as pretty, but it was more successful. We became harder to beat and were able to win cup-final rugby. That was a big change. The forwards realised we needed to dominate teams for us to win, but we needed to change the game plan a little bit to give us a chance to do that. There was a bit more responsibility. We took on our responsibility and got better. That was the big change.'

\*\*\*

'I remember the August after the Lions tour to Australia, 2001,' begins Munster strength-and-conditioning coach Aidan O'Connell. 'Brian [O'Driscoll] had to go in and speak to the academy players, who would have been under the Irish umbrella at the time – the likes of Denis Leamy, Rory Best and Niall Treston. He was so nervous. He was still such a young man – only twenty-two. He was saying, "These are my peers. They're nineteen and twenty and I have to go in and talk to them about my experiences as a rugby player."'

O'Driscoll and Leamy would meet again, five years later, at a sold-out Lansdowne Road in the biggest Leinster versus Munster clash since the game had turned professional.

It seemed highly unlikely that Munster and Leinster would meet in the Heineken Cup semi-finals in 2005/06 after both sides lost their opening pool games. With Kidney back for his second coaching stint, Munster rallied to win their five remaining matches, while Leinster squeaked through as eighth seeds. On April Fool's Day, 2006, Leinster took on Toulouse on the French side's home patch. Faced with the daunting prospect of a torrid afternoon in the hostile abode of the three-time Heineken Cup champions, Leinster were immense. They tore into Toulouse and led 41–21 going into the last minute, before two late tries gave the scoreline a tinge of respectability. Later that day, Paul O'Connell and Ronan O'Gara excelled as Munster downed Perpignan 19–10. The semi-final would pit Ireland's strongest provinces against each other.

Corrigan packed down in the front row with Brian Blaney and Will Green. On 23 April the two sides met at Lansdowne Road, with Biarritz awaiting in a Millennium Stadium final. Corrigan says, 'We were teammates for Ireland, but the rivalry was huge. If it wasn't, there would be something wrong. We were well beaten on the day.

'The one thing that stands out from that day was the running out onto the pitch. That was the winning of the game right there. We ran out, and it was a sea of red everywhere and no blue. It was a case of "Hold on a second, we're in Dublin here, what's happening?" The Munster supporters were amazing. They got tickets from everywhere and got their colours. We gave them a good start too.' Munster were leading 3–0 after ten minutes when Paul O'Connell snatched a Leinster line-out. A rolling maul ensued, and it was Leamy who crashed over for the statement-making try. His team were 16–3 up after thirty-two minutes and sealed a crushing win after two late tries from O'Gara and Trevor Halstead. 'That was a real bad day for us as a province,' Jackman confesses, 'but we used the result, the hurt, to learn from that. The fans learned from it too.'

Say what you want about flag-waving fans and the nostril-flaring passion of the Munster players, the simple fact was that Leinster were still not good enough. They were harried and bullied from the start, and were already back in the dressing room long before O'Gara scored the killer try and ran to embrace the red-clad masses in the North Terrace. Cheika had brought the club to the brink of European glory in his first season, but Munster shoved them off a cliff.

The following seasons saw Leinster eliminated in the quarter-final. Shane Jennings and Leo Cullen returned from Leicester Tigers in 2007/08. The team did not make it past the pool stages in Europe, but another league title (with Magners now sponsoring the shindig) arrived at the season's conclusion. Contepomi was flourishing under Cheika, and had an able deputy, that season, in the form of twenty-two-year-old Sexton. O'Driscoll had long since seen the progress and committed himself to bringing greater success to his province. Cheika believed Leinster were on the verge of toppling Europe's finest. Isa Nacewa and Rocky Elsom arrived from Auckland Blues and Waratahs. A new generation of talents, such as Jamie Heaslip, Rob Kearney and Luke Fitzgerald, were filtering through. The pieces were in place.

***

'It kind of pisses me off when people say that game was my breakthrough,' says Sexton. 'I had played a full season before that – seventeen or eighteen games between the Magners [Celtic] League and Heineken Cup. They moved Felipe out to No. 12 for a lot of the league games. That annoyed me a bit. The people who thought that hadn't watched a lot of Leinster the season before.'

While the out-half is correct about his impact in Leinster's league-winning 2007/08 season, he had started only two Heineken Cup matches coming into the 2009 semi-final against Munster. With Lansdowne Road on its reconstructed way to becoming the Aviva Stadium, 82,208 supporters filled Croke Park. Munster fans travelled in numbers, but on this occasion blue matched red and no one side could claim victory. That matter was left to the Irish rivals. Sixteen of the players taking part had won the Six Nations Grand Slam a month previously, but provincial pride, and a place in a Heineken Cup final, took precedence. Leinster hit the front after fifteen minutes when Contepomi crisply struck a drop goal. He was out of the game with a bad knee injury eleven minutes later. Sexton was on for the biggest game of his life and his first task was to take a forty-two-metre penalty. He stepped up and sent it straight down the middle.

Sexton says, 'I'd had a slow start to the season and was back playing club rugby [with St Mary's] for a while. It was a big comedown, especially after I had done well in the [pool games] against Castres. I got my chance against Munster and that game probably changed my career.'

D'Arcy scored a first-half try, and Fitzgerald stretched Leinster's lead after the break. Munster's final undoing arrived on sixty-two minutes as O'Gara threw a pass intended for O'Connell but intercepted by O'Driscoll. The match finished 25–6 in Leinster's favour. Speaking after the match, Cheika said, 'We weren't given much of a chance, and it is hard when you're told that you're not good enough, but I thought the players showed how much it means to them to play for Leinster.'

Sexton was afforded only thirty minutes of game time before the final against Leicester Tigers at Murrayfield. In a back-and-forth battle, Sexton landed eleven points, O'Driscoll dispatched a drop goal, Heaslip barged over for a try, and Elsom clocked in an astonishing performance of grit and drive. In 2000, the Leinster squad had met with a sports psychologist and sketched out goals that included beating Munster, making the 2001 Lions tour and winning a Triple Crown. Not one player, according to Corrigan, wrote 'Win the Heineken Cup'. He says, 'We didn't think it was a possibility.'

Possibility became champagne-soaked reality. Leinster, however, were not done. Cheika departed for Stade Français in 2010, and Joe Schmidt, Clermont Auvergne's backs coach, took over. Leinster reached a Heineken Cup final in the New Zealander's first season, yet required a Sexton-inspired comeback to see off a stunned Northampton Saints. Twelve months on, and the Blues surpassed their great southern rivals when they claimed their third Heineken Cup. Their victims were an Ulster side that had defeated Munster at Thomond Park on their way to the final at Twickenham. They fell short, 42–14, to Schmidt's side, and looked on as Leo Cullen asked Shane Jennings to help him lift Leinster's third Heineken Cup in four seasons.

In April 2014, Cullen reflected – with his understated, dulcet demeanour – on his trophy-laden second coming at Leinster: 'When we won in 2009, there was a sense of relief that the organisation and squad had, after we had been striving for so long to get to that point. 2011 was a feeling of euphoria after coming from behind in the manner that we did; 2012 was about reaffirming the ambitions of the team, and about us wanting to be successful … We've had some great times in recent years.' O'Driscoll may have had his doubts during Leinster's years in the [training and trophy] wilderness, but his take on eventually getting over the line is similar to O'Gara's. 'I am a big believer that the lows happen for a reason, to drive the desire,' he comments. 'If you look back at the semi-final of 2003 in Lansdowne Road, when we should have been in a Heineken Cup final against Toulouse, we lost to Perpignan. You look to 2006, when we got beaten out the gate by Munster – that fuelled the desire, and you had to rely on that in subsequent games to be able to get yourself up to go the extra yard, push yourself that extra couple of per cent.

'I wouldn't go back and change a whole lot. I'm glad the transition took its time and I had to live those early years. We won the first Celtic League, but didn't win another one until 2008. Going without any success in that period of time definitely drove the desire to go on and win a few Heineken Cups, and constantly strive for excellence.'

# 14

## 'EVERYONE THAT COULD JUMP SHIP, DID': CONNACHT'S REFUSAL TO LIE DOWN

'This time last year I was chasing my tail,' laments Pat Lam as he sits in a spacious gym at The Sportsground with Mils Muliaina five metres away. 'It was only me and Dan McFarland, which is ridiculous at this level.' It is not the first time I have heard a Connacht coach complain, but hearing griping Galwegian linen aired in the presence of a one-hundred-times capped All Blacks legend is a new experience. Times are changing out west, but many still wish the pendulum could pick up the pace.

Lam, a New Zealander who appeared in two World Cups with Samoa, arrived in Galway in 2013 with lofty ambitions for the province. He spoke with infectious enthusiasm upon touchdown, but, by the end of October (and a 16–13 loss to Leinster), the enormity of his task was beginning to dawn. Connacht achieved their greatest-ever rugby result two months later, by stunning four-times European Cup champions Toulouse at Stade Ernest-Wallon, their imposing home ground. It was the high-water-mark of a season that saw them finish tenth in the league and miss out on the new Champions Cup by a considerable distance.

Undeterred from his long-term project, Lam continued to utilise his Super Rugby contacts. Tom McCartney and Bundee Aki were signed up for the new season, along with fullback Muliaina. The captures took the Kiwi playing contingent into double figures and added a genuine air of excitement around the province. 'I came here purely on the vision and the basis of the cause,' says Lam. 'When I talked to these guys I said, "Listen, this isn't about playing for just another club and we'll have the craic."

'This,' Lam continues, and he pats a meaty left hand above his heart, 'is Connacht. This is where they have come from, this is where they are and this is where they aspire to go. This is what we're going to do, and this is what I'd like you guys to do as part of it. That's why I came here. If [the board] had said to me, "Oh, become coach of Connacht, win some games and enjoy life in the west of Ireland," I'd have said, "No thanks." They said, "This is where we're at and this is where we're going …" Woah, really gets you going. That's why you play the game – to have that cause.

'When I first arrived,' Lam recalls, 'I didn't expect we'd have no chief executive for a long period of time; I didn't expect it'd just be me and Dan for a long time. I didn't expect a lot of that. What I did do is spend a lot of time with the people on the board and the key people in the IRFU, because there's a Plan Ireland document. I read that strategic plan. The biggest thing for me is I love this game and want to see it grow. What I read and understood from that document is that the game will only grow if the Irish team is strong. We've got our goals, but it is not about the provinces. We've got a part to play in growing the game in Ireland. If we can provide another avenue for young, Irish players to come through and play for the national side – because that funds the game and pays the bills – great. A kid in Castlebar or Clifden is not interested in rugby because Leinster, Munster or Toulon win the European Cup. He gets interested in the game because of the Six Nations or Ireland winning the World Cup.'

Lam won the Heineken Cup as a player with Northampton in 2000, when they beat Munster at Twickenham. Sitting in Galway, fourteen years on, Lam still uses top teams as a reference point when referring to his young squad of players: 'Other teams can replace that international with that international. Look at Toulon. If you look at our squad last year. I asked a few people, even on the [Connacht] board, to name their best fifteen. They did, and then I threw down facts. I said "Do you know that not once in twenty-eight games did that fifteen play together?" It didn't happen once. That's not a problem for teams like Leinster. If Jamie Heaslip's not playing, Jordi Murphy plays. If Sean O'Brien is missing, Shane Jennings plays. We get Willie Faloon injured, and get Jake Heenan, who is playing his first year of rugby at this level, in. He gets injured, and we bring in a young academy boy, a nineteen-year-old. See the difference?'

Before I can nod in agreement, Lam reaches out and grabs my shoulder. 'People might see that and say, "That's terrible," but I look at it as a total positive. It's a chance to give a young guy the exposure. He's in the academy, but he has played seven [senior] games. People from the outside may look at it and ask, "What's going on?" but I look at it as this young kid from Ireland has now achieved that, and will get better and better.'

What stands out from my chat with Lam is the fact that there were open lines of communication with the IRFU, and that money was finally funnelling its way out west. In Paul Bunce, Connacht had finally joined the other three Irish provinces in having a dedicated head of fitness. Aki, signed from Waikato Chiefs, and a two-time Super Rugby champion, would have easily slotted into the Leinster and Munster midfields, while if ever there was a marquee signing to lace up and run out onto Thomond Park, it would have been Mils Muliaina – former teammate and surfing buddy of Doug Howlett. Mils, however, was in Galway, and settling into west-coast life. It all seemed miles away from the union's previous dealings with the western province.

***

Back in 1995, Nigel Carolan, Connacht's academy director, was playing centre for the province. Eddie O'Sullivan was double-jobbing as Carolan's coach at Galwegians RFC and Connacht. He was also in charge of the Ireland Under-21 side. When the game turned professional, O'Sullivan spied a perfect opportunity to take on more work hours at Connacht in return for remuneration and added job security. He threw a demanding dice in the IRFU's direction – a two-year contract or he would be moving on. It was a risk that backfired. O'Sullivan was also turfed out of his

Galwegians job. 'We were due to go on a tour of Sweden in August 1996,' says Carolan. 'Eddie pulled back, because he couldn't agree a two-year deal, which was madness. As it happened, Warren Gatland was flown into Stockholm to carry us through to the new era.'

Gatland took over a squad that contained thirteen players on part-time contracts, star out-half Eric Elwood on his national full-time contract and players sourced from the province's main clubs. Buccaneers, Corinthians and Galwegians were the main providers. The New Zealander made a good impression during his two years at the helm, guiding Connacht to interprovincial wins over Leinster and Ulster, and reaching the quarter-final of the European Shield. Fellow Kiwi Glenn Ross endured two forgettable seasons in charge, while South Africa's Steph Nel took the province to the quarter-finals of the inaugural Celtic League in 2001/02. There were signs of on-field improvements the following season, as Nel built his team around the likes of Gavin Duffy, Johnny O'Connor and Damian Browne.

As Brendan Fanning expertly details in *From There to Here*, the IRFU were facing a deficit of €4 million by the end of 2002/03, and €6.9 million the following year. The late-autumn scheduling of the 2003 World Cup meant the usual home Tests in November were off the table, while the foot-and-mouth outbreak of 2001 had led to the cancellation and rescheduling of Six Nations games. The setbacks had not been kind on the union's coffers. Seeking to redress the balance, Philip Browne declared that a major issue for the IRFU was the number of professional players the country could afford to pay. By this stage, Connacht had a number of full-time pros on its books. As they were the weakest of the four provinces, the union zeroed in, and an almighty fight for survival – carried out in public and in print – began.

John Muldoon, tasked with captaining Connacht in 2014/15, was just breaking into the senior team as it faced the threat of being snuffed out. 'You're hearing all these rumours coming towards the end of the season,' he says. 'I was playing with the Irish Under-21s at the time, which was coached by Michael Bradley. There were all these rumours about Connacht being disbanded. I was training with these fellas at the time – Duffy, O'Connor, Colin Rigney, Rowan Frost, Ronnie McCormack – and they all start jumping ship. You start going, "Hold on. What's going on here?" I don't want to sound cruel here, but everyone that could jump ship, did. At the same time, you had all these people going to Dublin and marching [on the IRFU offices].

'At the time, as they say, one man's misfortune is another man's fortune. I have no qualms about saying that I certainly wasn't good enough, back then, to be on a full-time contract. But the fact that all these people left suddenly opened up opportunities for other people to come in. Thankfully, I was one of those people … For someone who, at twenty, would have usually been on an academy contract, to get a full-time contract was huge.'

The march Muldoon referred to included the crowd of more than 2,000 supporters and 'Friends of Connacht Rugby' on 24 January 2003. Club captain Eric Elwood was part of the group that strode towards 62 Lansdowne Road to let the union know what they made of their plans to cut Connacht loose. With a banner with the words 'Connacht Fans Say I.R.F. Off' fluttering outside the union's front gates, Danno Heaslip was accompanied by young rugby fans Cassandra Deegan, Michael Farrell and Mark Rapple into its headquarters to deliver a letter of protest. The IRFU backed down six days later.

Muldoon says, 'All those people that walked and put up a fight against the IRFU – at the time I probably didn't realise how significant it was – Connacht has to be eternally grateful to them. When you look back at footage, it is not just people from Connacht that walked. There were a lot of people from outside Connacht that got involved and showed their support. They'll have to be remembered.'

Muldoon's route into rugby is typically winding in a province that provides eight per cent of the Irish population. 'I played hurling in Portumna up until I was about fourteen. My brother had picked up rugby and would play in the school during the winter, when it would be too wet and cold to go out and play hurling. The way it went was that if you got twenty names to start up a team, you had a team. If you couldn't, there was no team. In first year there was no team, but we got a team together when I was in second year. I was particularly poor at the start and didn't know what I was doing.'

The flanker credits a growth spurt for his sudden ascendancy to team captain of the school's Junior Cup team. He played with Nenagh RFC, but it was not until he moved to Galway for college, at Galway Mayo Institute of Technology (GMIT), that he fell under the purview of the provincial set-up. Once again, it was a numbers game. 'When I was with Ireland Under-19s,' Muldoon comments, 'I went along to training with GMIT and only five people showed up. The other lads went off to the pub while I started some fitness with one of my mates [John Burke] in the corner of the pitch.' The Galwegians Under-20s invited the duo over to train and both were asked to turn out for the club's senior team. Over a decade on, Muldoon has more than 200 appearances for the club.

Bradley, a former Munster and Ireland scrum half, was appointed Connacht coach for 2003/04, and took the team to the brink of the Challenge Cup final. Harlequins' Will Greenwood denied them with a late try in the closing stages of their semi-final second leg, and Gavin Duffy, who had departed eighteen months previously, left the pitch in tears after helping his new team conquer his former club. League form was patchy, but, in the words of Muldoon, Connacht were proving to be 'a good FA Cup side' capable of knocking over top teams on their day.

With London Irish from the age of five, hooker Adrian Flavin was lured to Connacht in 2006 after a discussion with the head coach. 'I met Brads on the Wednesday, but the day before I had been in a contact session at London Irish,' he says. 'I got in a punch-up with Nick Kennedy, and he caught me flush on the nose, breaking it instantly. He hasn't got the nickname "Razor Knuckles" for no reason. Brads got in touch with me and said he'd be the one in the Connacht trackie top. I told him I'd be the one with a broken nose and two black eyes.

'To see Brads' passion for Connacht and his belief that he could get the province on the up was enough to convince me to make the move. The club was in a similar position to where London Irish was when I started, and I could see they were at their turning point. My first game was against Glasgow at home, and the attendance was about 700 or 800. To compare that to the place they are now is remarkable. They would now get four or five thousand for the less-attractive Heineken Cup games, and sell out for the big games and interpros. Brads, Eric Elwood and Jerry Kelly would all have to get a mention. Jerry fought tooth and nail for Connacht over the years.'

The idea of Connacht being used as both a feeder province and staging post for young talents from Leinster, Munster and Ulster was suggested almost as soon as the IRFU officials arrived back from Paris in 1995. With each province trying to grow their own player bases over the early years of professional rugby, the concept was stagnant. That began to change when Bradley was in charge, and continued during Elwood's tenure.

'Every player that came and played well obviously bought into what we were doing out at Connacht,' says Flavin. 'If you came in with a chip on your shoulder or felt you were better than other lads, you were soon fucked out, to be honest. With the likes of Michael Swift, Johnny O'Connor and John Muldoon you had guys with high standards. If anyone thought, "Bloody hell, I'm here at Connacht," they didn't last long. You can see the lads that did embrace it. Sean Cronin, Jamie Hagan, Ian Keatley, Fionn Carr – they all added to the environment and bought into the Connacht spirit. We tried to create an environment where guys didn't want to go back. If that was the case, and they did, then they would be richer for the experience and so would Connacht.'

Flavin adds, 'Nigel Carolan and Johnny Duffy have done a great job in the academy – bringing through the likes of Kieran Marmion, Ronan Loughney, Jack Carty, Robbie Henshaw, Darragh Leader and Eoghan McKeon. Doing that means you can add in the likes of a Muliaina to add experience and excite the fans. It would be great if you could fill the starting fifteen with local boys, but that is not always going to happen. As long as the guys coming in buy into the spirit at the club, then everyone benefits. Look at Jason Harris-Wright – he's an Australian who came to Connacht via Leinster and Bristol, and he is a mainstay, a guy who has captained the club in big games.'

The big games became huge affairs for Connacht, starting in 2011/12, when the sustained success of the Irish provinces in Europe allowed for a fourth Heineken Cup slot. The men from the west were in the big time. Pool six contained Toulouse, Gloucester and a Harlequins side ably guided by Conor O'Shea. Quins were stunned by the ferocity of Connacht's assault at their home ground, The Stoop, that November, but twenty points from Nick Evans saw them shade the tie. If Connacht felt they should have won that game, they were damned certain of it as they squandered countless chances in a 14–10 slip to Gloucester. By that mid-December stage, the province was in the grips of a pitiful losing streak. The poor run of league and cup form would plague the side until Quins made the trip to Galway in late January 2012.

'It is not the result, who we were playing or the fact that we knocked Harlequins out,' declares Flavin when asked for his finest hour in Connacht colours. 'It was the fact that we had lost fifteen games in a row before that, and that no one dropped their heads. There was no bitching, no in-fighting. Everyone stood up on the Monday and – through sheer desire or stupidity – said, "We can turn this around." Fifteen losses, some shitty times when we thought, "Jesus, what can we do?" Some days we were blown away, whereas others we lost in the last minute. Quins at home, and John Muldoon stands up and says, "Tonight we are going to win." It was not the best game in the world to watch, but we had come through four months of losses. We weren't coming off that pitch that night without a win, and we got there.'

The 9–8 nail-gnawer against Harlequins delivered Connacht's only Heineken Cup win that season. Three arrived in 2012/13, courtesy of a poor Zebre side and a memorable home triumph over a Biarritz side containing Dimitri Yachvili and Imanol Harinordoquy. At the end of the season, after twenty-eight years of wringing himself dry for the cause, Elwood stepped down from his coaching role. Lam arrived from Auckland, via a short stint with the Samoan national team. Fortune played a rare hand in an injury-showered season by dropping Zebre in Connacht's Heineken Cup pool. They started with a win on Italian soil, but league form was wretched, and a carpeting by Edinburgh in Murrayfield – the week before an away encounter with Toulouse – saw Connacht fly out of Ireland to zero fanfare and fewer expectations.

'Proving to teams we belonged at the top table was our first major achievement,' says Muldoon. 'One memory that stands out from our first season in the Heineken Cup was that the standing ovation we got from Toulouse after losing 24–3 showed us we deserved to be there. A lot of their fans wouldn't have known too much about us, and would have turned up expecting their team to trounce us. For them to give us a standing ovation long after their players had left the pitch meant so much to us.'

Just under two years on from that night, Connacht were back at Stade Ernest-Wallon. The French side was captained by Thierry Dusautoir and was infested with world-class talent. The likes of Louis Picamoles, Hosea Gear, Clément Poitrenaud and Yoann Huget – part of a €13-million squad – took to the pitch on 8 December 2013, with talk in Toulouse revolving around the time the home side would claim their try-scoring bonus point. The hosts 'started with a bang', but were repulsed by white jerseys. Veteran Connacht out-half Dan Parks kicked two penalties to make it 6–0 before Jean-Pascal Barraque's try and conversion, right on half-time, made it 7–6.

The second half onslaught never materialised; instead, Marmion sniped over from close range after Carr went close in the right-hand corner. Dusautoir's converted try put Toulouse right back in the contest, but the westerners held firm in a fraught closing period. Never had the Sky Sports red button been pressed so much in such a short period of time on the island of Ireland. Most came late to the party, but were eager to catch up. They were rewarded with a 16–14 win.

Toulouse gained revenge the following weekend in Galway, but that loss did nothing to cheapen a weekend Muldoon will never forget. 'A few days before the game, a friend told me Toulouse were 1/200 [to win]. I asked what we were, and it was twenty or twenty-five to one. I remember thinking, "Jesus, in a two-horse race that is ridiculous." I told a couple of people that we were quietly confident, and there were a few quotes from Pat that were quite bullish. I think that's the beauty and the frustration of Connacht Rugby – we always believe we can beat anyone on our day. We did well to get through that fast Toulouse start, and they were very fortunate when Robbie Henshaw's score was called back. I was talking to Michael Corcoran [of RTÉ] recently, and he told me he thought we were going to lose it. The way we had played and the way it was going, I didn't think at any stage we would lose.'

In a rare occasion of largesse, the players flew back to Galway that evening on a charter flight. Beers were sipped from plastic cups as the match was replayed during the journey. There were some bleary eyes at the Monday morning video-review session, but no one wanted to miss the playback. 'It was a nice moment,' says Muldoon. 'A lot of people were looking around that room, taking it in. The feeling was that we didn't want to be the whipping boys of Irish rugby any longer.'

On 1 January 2015, Muldoon led Connacht to their first win over Munster in six years at a howling, rain-whipped Sportsground. They lost, eight days later, at home to Edinburgh. The heart is there, the performances are improving, but maintaining consistently high levels remains elusive.

Lam is contracted until June 2018, and can see genuine progress. For the first time since Warren Gatland left in 1998, however, Connacht are heading in the right direction.

# 15

## DOUBT:
## O'GARA, HART AND SEXTON

'The mentality is different for players,' says Ronan O'Gara. 'I can remember being in camp and it used to do my fucking head in. You're just thinking, "Game, game, game." It's just a weird bubble you live in. It's only when you stop that you think, "Fucking hell, was I like that?"'

Ronan O'Gara traded the thrill of clinching matches with drop goals for Top 14 coaching in 2013. Honest to a fault, he remains an interviewer's dream. One needs simply to place a Dictaphone in his vicinity and utter 'Well?', and he is off. I sit opposite the Racing Métro defence coach with a notepad full of questions and a miniature coffee. He answers most in his blinking, honest way, but wonderful tangents and recollections are best teased with the occasional word or steer.

His final game, fittingly, came in Munster red as the province fell short against Clermont Auvergne in the 2013 Heineken Cup semi-final. Beaten by a hairline fracture at Stade de la Mosson, Montpellier, O'Gara took in the acclaim of the travelling Munster hordes. He led Rua, his young son, off the pitch, but gave nothing away in a post-match interview with Sky Sports. 'I wasn't thinking of next season, and I certainly wasn't thinking of stopping. It's just, something clicked inside me at the end of that final whistle and I just knew it was time to go. It was very weird, difficult to describe, but I have always trusted my instincts and that was what I felt. That was my mind made up.'

'I got good advice,' he tells me. 'Don't announce you're retiring; announce what you're doing next. It immediately brings the attention to what you're doing as opposed to what you've done. In Ireland we're very good at overdoing things and farewell parties and whatever. I think when you know what you're doing next it makes it easier to move on, but it isn't easy. The people you've probably talked to – Brian O'Driscoll, Stephen Ferris, myself – have had very successful careers, so it's only natural to be sad to leave that behind.

'It's that test you miss, you know, that weekly test of you against yourself – never mind the opponent – that's a good mental challenge that you miss. Then you snap yourself out of it and say, "Well I've had a good career," so you get on with it.'

O'Gara continues, 'That's the thing about sport. It's ruthless. It's a quick death. One day, you're going in there with your gear-bag, and the next pre-season you're not. That is very hard to accept. It's good advice for the younger fella who's playing – just appreciate it now, you know. That's a cliché, but it's very, very hard to get that buzz again in anything you do.'

I ask O'Gara about the lows that rugby players, even ones who captured Heineken Cups and Grand Slams, go through during their career span. 'Jesus, yeah,' he says, 'and especially if you're a kicker, and especially if you are lucky enough to play in an awful lot of pressurised games. I make the point that the ten position, the kicker position, is unlike any other. It's a team game, but I often say to Johnny [Sexton] and the other players, "Every time you take to the pitch, you will be judged and read inside out." That's a great responsibility to have, but you have a direct influence on the results. If you kick poorly you're probably going to lose, unless the [other] team are also very poor. At the highest level, in professional Test matches, that isn't the case. That's something you have to embrace and go for.

'There are incredibly good lessons to learn from negative situations,' he continues, 'but the easiest thing to do is brush it under the carpet. You become mentally strong by adapting the lessons learned from bad days and making your resolve stronger. So, the next time that situation comes, you're going to perform. And I've had that every second season of my career, and – by the end – I was good at the pressure moments. I craved that. I could see this day was coming and I'd say, "Bring it on. Let's go."

'Quite early in my playing days, if we were 21–15 down I'd think, "Jesus, please don't score, please don't score," because I'd have to kick the conversion to win it. Or, if it was a penalty at 14–12 [down], for a while I'd be half hoping the penalty went against us. I suppose I just didn't believe in myself, you know. That was me at the start, and that's the way it was.

'That's another interesting argument in terms of goal-kickers. How many of them always [talk] in terms of a technical breakdown when something goes wrong. No one's going to say, when they're standing over a ball, "I actually shat myself." I know because that's what happens at times. It's the honest, brutal truth. For a second, you probably let the occasion – "There are 80,000 people watching me here now" – [get to you] and you're gone. You've lost it. It's very hard to get it back. You think you get it back and you're in the zone, but you nearly have to be robotic. And then, if you're robotic, is that the right technique? You just have to blot everything out, but are you human then? You have to realise where you are. That's why it's a fascinating subject.'

O'Gara admits to many trials and errors before he finally settled on a goal-kicking technique that served him best. 'The best bit of advice I got was,' he points to a circle on a TV screen, 'you see that hoop there? You have that as your target. I'd have it in the middle of the posts, so if I hit right or left of that a little bit, I'd still get the flag. I have three or four metres either side of my little hoop; that's the imagery I use ... Some days it's so easy, whereas other days you feel you are doing the same things and say, "Jesus, what's happening here?" It just goes to show you that if you practise and practise and practise, with the right technique you get the results.'

The flow is briefly interrupted by a 'call me' text from O'Gara's wife, Jessica. He responds before contemplating when his kicking game was imbued with a sense of laissez-faire: 'It was in the very latter years. It's hard, because, when you're in the player zone, there is no release valve. Even when you're off, you're never off. Be it three months off, you've still got a big game. "I've a big season ahead of me." It's never-ending. It's only when you stop … You know, the biggest thing I enjoy in coaching is the pre-match meal with Racing, because it was torture for fifteen, sixteen years. Now I have a nice bowl of rice pudding. I have about five or six cups of coffee, and if there is a newspaper there, I could pick it up. Obviously I take the coaching very seriously, but the work is done and you have a little bit of a lull before you play.'

***

'Really? He said that?' asks an astounded James Hart when informed of O'Gara's early hatred for the late penalties and drop goals that crafted his legend. 'That's the best part for me. I love that pressure – the whole match coming down to you, your nerve and technique. Nothing better.' Hart pauses a moment. 'I suppose he had all that extra pressure, being from Munster. I'd do anything for us [Grenoble] to win, but I wasn't born here, I didn't grow up here. This isn't my hometown club.'

The Captain's Run officially ended well over an hour ago, and only now does Hart collect the balls strewn across Stade des Alpes. Philippe Doussy, Grenoble's skills-and-kicking coach, assists in the task, and shares some brief thoughts when the deed is done. '*Merci*, Philippe,' says Hart, as he makes his way towards the dressing room. Walking alongside, I observe that, for someone who is not starting the next day, Hart has put in a shift and a half. 'When you're not playing,' he answers, 'these sessions are the only chance you get to sharpen up and run lines with the team.'

With the rest of the Grenoble squad engrossed in the President's Lunch, the scrum half and I have the playing field to ourselves. Racing Métro are down from Paris, and looking to replicate their away win here last season. For the second match in a row, the Dubliner has been named on the bench as backup to Charl McLeod. Arriving from Super Rugby's Sharks, the former Springbok hit the ground running. Injury had forced Hart out of the opening league fixtures, and now he was playing the waiting game. Three schoolmates from his Belvedere College days are over for the Top 14 match, and I remark that the 20,000-seater stadium should be pulsating by kick-off. 'A football team plays here, but it's still the best pitch I've ever played on – great for place-kicking.' A touch over two years into a professional rugby career, Hart's awe at his surroundings is fading. Stade des Alpes is his place of work and the watching brief is a source of frustration.

Hart was twenty-two when he came to the attention of most rugby followers in Ireland. Impressive showings off the bench led to a start at scrum half away to Racing. Irish eyes were on Sexton, who was slowly feeling his way into French rugby, but Hart stole the show. Ably abetted by the Grenoble pack, he slotted over eleven points in a dicey 22–20 win. A new, three-year contract was signed soon after, and his stock continued to rise as he contributed twenty points in an imperious win over heavyweight Toulouse. By the season's end, Hart was being tipped for a senior Ireland call-up and a return to his home province of Leinster. His rise forged a giddy template for young Irish players who had found themselves surplus to requirements in the provincial academy system. Grenoble had signed both Chris Farrell and Denis Coulson in summer 2014 as they targeted Champions Cup rugby.

Taking a seat on the away team bench, Hart recounts his reluctant introduction to rugby. 'I didn't like it at the start, but my dad, Don, brought me down to Clontarf minis. I had a load of mates that played soccer, so I started playing with them. We had a green out the front of our house, so we used to knock around the whole day out there; back from school, drop the bag in and you're out playing. No messing about. In for dinner, quickly eaten and back out. I suppose that's the same for any kid. I was lucky enough to have mates who had the same interests. GAA or rugby, if the

Six Nations was on, but mainly playing Liverpool and Manchester United matches. Everyone with their own jersey and favourite player. Mine was Michael Owen.'

Don Hart was eager for his son to enrol in Belvedere once secondary school came along. He happily succumbed to the 'brainwashing' of Schools Cup rugby in first year and, seeing the euphoria of a double-winning season (Junior and Senior), signed up for playing duty. Hart played with the Juniors in third year before a transition year trip to Toulouse – from where his mother, Patricia, hails – stoked his fires. 'I had some classes off during the day, so I used to go to the grounds early, just to watch the first team train,' continues Hart. 'I remember Byron Kelleher and Jean-Baptiste Elissalde at the time and loving them. Really, from watching those sessions, I decided that this was something I'd really like to do.'

By the time Hart had set a rugby-playing goal for himself, he had lost his father to a brain haemorrhage. 'My dad had a brain tumour when he was around twenty-four. The doctors eventually told him he was better, and he was fine for fifteen, sixteen years before it came back. He passed away, after having chemo and treatments, about three years after it came back. I was ten when it came back, and thirteen, going on fourteen, when he died. That was tough in a lot of ways, but my dad used to bring me to all my games and soccer training. He was mad for bringing me to all my games and watching all my games. Like any dad who's interested in his son, we'd chat every evening before I went to bed. Even if I'd scored a goal, we'd talk about how I could have done something better.

'My mam has given me great support, and has been there for me and my sisters. It's still not the same, especially as I'm the only boy in the family, not to have your dad around. Even now, I wonder what it would be like if my old man could come to the game or what would he think of what I've done now, because, clearly, it hasn't been an easy road. I've got to look at it in other ways; maybe if he hadn't have passed away I wouldn't have been so determined to do what I've done to get where I am now.'

The uneasy road that Hart refers to was the teenage heartache of being rejected by his first love – Leinster. As soon as fifth year began at Belvedere, the young scrum half was plotting a course to the Leinster Academy. His first roadblock was Hugo Nolan, who had moved into sixth year, taken up the captaincy and retained the No. 9 jersey. 'You know how it works in Ireland,' says Hart. 'If you want to make Leinster [academy] you've got to be making schools teams in fifth and sixth year. You need to be the main lad, so I was raging.' A run of form with the Belvedere seconds led to Hart's coach, former Ireland lock Gabriel Fulcher, putting him forward for Leinster trials. 'I had a trial game at Donnybrook and had a stormer. I then played Leinster Under-19s, and didn't look back once I hit sixth year.'

During his stint with the Leinster Under-20s, Hart missed a home romp due to an eye infection [sleeping with his contact lenses in], but was pitched in from the start against the Clontarf seniors. 'The game went fine,' he says. 'I didn't do much wrong, didn't make a break and was told after that the coaches were happy with how I had done.' Hart's rugby career went off-road three days later. 'We were going to find out who made the cut for the Leicester trip. That would basically be the team that would play the interpros. I remember I got my Leaving Cert results on the Wednesday, and we had a gym, stretching session that day, too. I had got my results and was on my way to that session on the bus – we were just going by St Stephen's Green – when I got a call from Gabriel Fulcher. He was my coach at school but also of the Leinster Under-20s. I honestly thought he was asking me how I had got on with my results. He said, "We're making the cuts for the Under-20s," and when I heard that it hit home. I can just remember my heart sinking. I picked up my bag, pressed the bell and got off around the [Grand] canal. I walked back to Belvedere with Gabriel talking to me all the way. At the time I was so devastated that I wasn't even hearing him. I was just thinking, "Oh God, what do I do now?" It was massive for me. If you don't get into Leinster Under-20s, you don't have much chance with the Irish 20s, then getting into the sub academies with the provinces.'

Hart skipped the post-Leaving Cert revelries that night and sought solace at the club he was not altogether sure of when his father had first brought him as an eight-year-old. Former Leinster and Ireland hooker Bernard Jackman was earning his coaching stripes with the club, following his playing retirement in 2010. Jackman once stated, 'James would come down to the club every evening, bringing a bag of balls along with him, practising penalties and kicks. Lots of players want to be great, but not many are willing to put in the hours and hours of practice that it takes. I've never seen anybody train as hard as James Hart. He has made himself an unbelievably good, technical player.'

After a spell of distance coaching back in Ireland, Jackman was recruited by Grenoble on a full-time basis in 2012. He was asked if he knew of any talented, young players that might be suited to the team's *Espoirs* (academy side), and Hart was on his way. He settled into life in the Isère region, and appeared eight times for the senior team in 2012/13. Turning twenty-two just as the first of the pre-season matches came into view, Hart suffered another setback. 'I had just come back from my summer break in Ireland and, on my first day back, the head coach [Fabrice Landreau] said, "Okay, we're thinking of loaning you out to a side in Pro D2 or Fédérale 1 [third division]." It knocked the wind out of me. I was thinking, "What the hell! I've just signed a two-year deal."'

An ankle injury to French scrum half Nicolas Bézy saw the loan move put on hold. His pre-season run included a twenty-minute run-out on the wing against Biarritz and not making the squad for a friendly against Montpellier. Reprieve came in the form of injury to Mathieu Lorée and a middling performance by Valentin Courrent against Oyonnax, a week before the Top 14 kicked off. 'I came on and did a job,' says Hart. 'Got the ball in, got it out and kicked a couple of penalties. We scored a couple of tries in that week too, and, from there, it took off.'

McLeod, recruited on an expensive pay packet from South Africa, is Hart's latest challenge. Extremely vocal and instructive to his backline in the two training runs I witnessed, the thirty-one-year-old did not lack confidence. The following evening against Racing would see him snipe through the blue-and white line to score a crucial try. Hart would come on with ninety seconds to go, as Jackman – who had taken over from Landreau as head coach – sought to wind down the clock. Sitting on the bench, surrounded by 20,000 empty seats, Hart envisions a greater role in an early season triumph. 'McLeod deserves the jersey,' he reasons, 'but I just need my chance.

'Mentally, there are ways where you've got to be able to motivate yourself, even though it can be tough sometimes. I'm not going to lie, and even though I love rugby, sometimes I get sick of it. I get sick of training hard, working hard and not getting the benefit straight away. You've got to be persistent, that's the main thing … Sometimes, and I know it does sound ridiculous, but when I see my mates working or in college and they're just enjoying life, I feel like saying, "I'd love to hang up the boots and try that for a while."' Hart laughs as I remind him he is only twenty-three.

'You want to change the atmosphere,' he continues, 'where you're always training, always working. There is sometimes that feeling that you'd like to see different things, do different things. That comes with the territory though. I'm definitely one of those people that is hugely persistent. I'm stubborn, and I've got that tunnel vision. A loss always motivates me more than anything else, or being told you can't do something or "This guy is ahead of you." That drives me. Someone saying I'm not good enough or that this guy is better than me – all the work I do is constantly to prove those people wrong.

'If anyone asked me now, or any kid came up and said, "I want to do this," I honestly believe that, if you put the work into whatever it is and believe it a hundred per cent, you can do almost anything you want. You just have to give yourself the opportunity. My being here now proves that.

I've had to come a huge way to get where I am. I think of all those hours, the practising and going to the club [Clontarf] when I didn't have to. Those are the hours that pay at the end of the day.'

Landreau, promoted to the club's director of rugby, calls Hart to scold him for running extremely late for the team lunch. The club fine is five euro, so I offer to split the damage. Zipping his boots away in a Grenoble-emblazoned kit-bag, Hart reasons, 'It feels like I'm never going to get that nice run at this stage. It just hasn't been easy, and it has definitely been a bumpy aul' ride. Lots of ups and downs. Sometimes I do wish that things would get stable, but I don't expect it to get easier. It has always been that way.

'I'd love to be a Johnny Sexton, where, every week you're fit, you know you're going to be playing. You know you're the main man there. He's clearly worked hard to get that status and has played great, but I don't know if that's something I will ever have. It just reminds me of being back in school. A guy like Sexton must feel like the guy in sixth year, who knows he is going to be playing.'

***

'Everything happens for a reason,' Sexton tells me as he drives through Paris. 'At times I've had really good runs as first choice. I made Leinster schools when I was in fifth year, but missed out on Irish Schools [team] and the Under-19s when I was in sixth year. I played Ireland Under-21s during my first year out of school, and started with Leinster the year after. There have been times when I've had it tough. I had to sit behind Felipe Contepomi, and would have been quite ambitious at the time. I had to learn patience and, looking back, I learned so much from him and from biding my time.'

Sexton and O'Gara tussled over the Ireland No. 10 jersey for two seasons before Declan Kidney opted for the younger out-half. Few doubted O'Gara's kicking capabilities, but Sexton brought an incisive, running dynamic to the backline and got the nod. That season saw him claim his third Heineken Cup with Leinster, but the following twelve months changed everything. By July 2013 he was still Ireland's starting out-half, but he was also a Test-series winner with the British & Irish Lions and a member of Racing Métro's Top 14 squad. In hindsight, it seemed as though Sexton would always be Warren Gatland's Lions out-half in Australia. The Irishman was not so sure.

'I had just signed the Racing contract, and had a bad hamstring injury against England. I had only played one full game, against Wales, in the Six Nations. I was happy with that performance, but in my head I thought I had to get back for the final games. I worked my arse off to get my hamstring right. I worked with Mike Carswell, my physio in Dublin, every day, and made some trips down to Limerick to Ger Hartmann. I needed to tick all the boxes to get back, and I did. Then, the day before the Italy game I twisted my foot in training. It was a big blow. I thought my Lions chances were gone.

'I got back for Leinster and we won the Amlin Cup and the league, but not once before that squad was announced did I think I was a certainty. Owen Farrell was doing well, and Jonny Wilkinson was having another great season in France. It was a great feeling to get the call-up, and a dream come true to head off with the Lions. There was a lot of chopping and changing with the team, but I played all three Tests of a successful Lions tour. Not many people can say that. Still, I always want more. I didn't get the place-kicking duties. Every minute I played, Leigh Halfpenny played. I hope to be the first-choice place-kicker for the next Lions tour to New Zealand.'

While some supporters may suggest Sexton's best chance to defeat the All Blacks may arise in a red jersey, he is bitterly aware of the two opportunities that Ireland let slip against the world champions. His fifty-metre penalty had dropped a metre short in Christchurch in June 2012, allowing Dan Carter to drop goal New Zealand to a 22–19 win they barely deserved. Eighteen months on and Sexton had a simpler penalty attempt on the All Blacks twenty-two, ten metres to the right of the posts, that would have put Ireland eight points clear with six minutes to play. Between his placing the ball and sending it towards the uprights, seventy seconds passed. The Kiwis at the Aviva Stadium crowd could only be hushed so long, and a clamour of booing broke out as the kick veered right and wide. Ryan Crotty daggered in an injury-time try and Aaron Cruden's conversion completed a stunning turnaround.

'The way we lost the game was pretty heartbreaking. To be ahead going into injury time and lose … it still hurts thinking about it now. I will get another chance down the line. In the World Cup we can only meet them in the quarter-final or final, depending on results. There is no better place to beat them. Hopefully we can learn from that loss and take their scalp.'

He adds, 'I tore my hamstring against Australia the week before. It was a tough week for me, trying to prove my fitness. I was happy with my performance, but that miss is a big regret. It could have put us two scores clear with six minutes to go. There were reasons behind that miss that I might go into in the future, but I'll leave that to a later date.' When pressed, Sexton confirms that his hamstring had flared up earlier in the game. He divulges no more on the 'other reasons'.

'If I got another chance [against New Zealand] I would have backed myself to get it,' he says. He believes being able to shut out the misses and refocus on his game stood to him in the 2014 Six Nations. 'I missed a couple of kicks against France, but knew I'd learn through it. I've kicked a lot of big kicks, so it's not the occasion that got to me. I had just missed a kick like every kicker does.' He took that attitude into the second half against the French, and scored his second try of the game before adding a vital penalty in the fifty-second minute.

The All Blacks miss festered, he admits, and hung like a fog for months. Being over in Paris did not get him away from his own thoughts. 'I will have to live with it,' he says, 'but that's the fickle nature of being a professional sportsman and a kicker.'

He continues, 'If we held on, made better decisions when we had the ball, didn't make defensive errors, a missed tackle in the corner, then no one would remember the kick. Still, I have to live with the fact that if the kick went over we would've had a better chance to win the game.

'Being the kicker is a thankless job at times. Neil Jenkins has a phrase: "No one thanks the postman for delivering the letters." People expect kicks to go over. The misses make you stronger. They make you want to practise more. It has made me a better kicker.'

# 16

## 'COMPLETELY ALIEN': THE NEXT GENERATION OF IRISH RUGBY STARS

Mick O'Driscoll went straight into the IRFU academy from college in 1998. The union was still overseeing the next generation from a central hub and would do so for six more years. 'In my second year out of school I played my first game for Munster,' he says. 'It took off from there and I got my first contract later that year. We weren't as professional then as we would have been from 2000, but we were still professionals in an amateur era. We were still probably drinking a little too much and all that, but you learn from that.'

Asked how much times have changed over the past fifteen years, O'Driscoll sits back, raises his eyes to heaven and ponders the question. 'The younger lads are completely alien to what we were,' he declares. 'There's no comparison. There is actually no comparison. None ... A lot of that, too, is that the world is different. When I was coming through, I remember that I was lucky as my parents would drop me everywhere, but, when they couldn't, I was always getting buses or trains. I remember getting trains with Donncha O'Callaghan up to Dublin, and walking from the train to the bus station. Not that it's far, but God forbid if a fella would have to do that now.

'They have everything given to them now, whereas when we were coming through you worked for everything. That was the difference. They rock up now for their first day of training, get handed a bag of gear and get their shakes, protein and whatever else it is. That certainly wasn't the way it was with us. We were begging, borrowing and stealing everything we could. On the rugby side of things, because the game is that much more professional now than when we were coming through, these guys have access to that from schools and clubs.'

***

'We have moved from the amateur era to the professional era, and are now entering the commercial era,' says Gary Longwell. The former Ulster lock is now performance-skills coach at the Sports Institute of Northern Ireland. Before he took up the role, in 2012, Longwell was head of Ulster Rugby's academy. 'There used to be a tradition of looking after players off the pitch and when they retired,' he says. 'Now it is much more ruthless. Players are earning a lot of money now, but there is no ethos of looking after people.'

There is a long-running practice, Longwell notes, of top rugby schools actively recruiting some of the best talents from non-traditional rugby schools and clubs. 'Schools like Methody [Methodist College] and Blackrock in Dublin, for example, have five professional coaches and a strength-and-conditioning coach. Young lads are experiencing professional set-ups way before they ever get to the academies. When your local team is professional, it is a much more reachable target. Look at someone like Craig Gilroy. He's a Bangor lad who went to Methody because he wanted to be a professional rugby player. As a ten- or eleven-year-old he would have headed off on the bus each morning and went past two or three schools, just so he could play at Methody and pursue that dream.'

Longwell believes that the school set-ups and structures are now so good that talented players outside that system will struggle to break through. 'Young lads may have greater natural talent and skills, but they lose out because the schools already have their guys in that professional mould. The schools' players will be bigger, stronger, faster, more durable. They will be squatting 120 kgs.'

Longwell left Ulster Rugby in 2012, and his place at the academy was taken by a coach who led the province to the Heineken Cup that May, Brian McLaughlin. Two players from the last set that Longwell worked with stand out as prospective mainstays of the next generation in Irish rugby. 'Iain Henderson will be a British & Irish Lions lock if he can stay fit over the next couple of seasons. We are only starting to see Stuart Olding's potential realised now, but he could well be on that next Lions tour too. He is supremely talented.'

***

The first steps on the road to becoming a professional rugby player, with Leinster, come in the Shane Horgan Cup. Five teams are selected to represent different regions within the province. Players who catch the eye during 'The Shaggy' go into an Under-17s programme and an Under-18 Leinster clubs side. The best players from that team will be merged with the finest schools players and placed in the province's sole Under-19 squad. Leinster have one Under-20s team, and the elite players from that group will then be signed on an academy contract.

I am greeted by Girvan Dempsey at Leinster's purpose-built head-quarters and training facilities on the grounds of University College Dublin. After getting a run-through of Leinster's structures and pathways, I asked the former fullback (and occasional winger) about the predominance of schools rugby in the province. 'We are still at probably eighty to eighty-five per cent coming through our schools system, which is very high,' Dempsey concedes. 'That is, traditionally, how it was set up, but you are definitely seeing that change over the last number of years.'

Dempsey adds, 'It can be quite tough for those "year one" guys to adjust, but the senior players are incredible, and the new set up in UCD has facilitated that. Daily interaction is key. One thing that Joe Schmidt introduced here was the culture of greeting. Everybody greeting each other in the mornings has been massive and infectious. Even when Brian

O'Driscoll was here. For someone like Brian to go around and meet and greet every year-one academy player every morning just means they feel part of it.'

Leinster's academy is similar to that of Munster and Connacht in that twenty-two to twenty-four players are included. Ulster generally run an eighteen-man academy. As Dempsey explains, there is a lot more that goes into running an academy than choosing the twenty-three best players from across the province: 'Our selection is determined by player characteristics and also on succession plans to the senior team. We are currently looking at the age profile of our centres, and also looking at front-row players. I meet with the senior management and coaching staff to see where the gaps (are) and where guys are contracted to. That would impact on our decision as academy staff on who we intake into the academy. We don't want to have a backlog of players in certain positions. It's just making sure that link is there for the senior team.

'If you look at the way Noel Reid has progressed and, even this year, Stevie Crosbie has moved. He is capable of playing at out-half and also in the centre, and he has been shifted more towards twelve. He's had a good few involvements with the senior team and now is playing twelve for the A team. You are looking at all players and who can replace the senior players. I don't think there is ever going to be anyone who can replace Brian O'Driscoll. He's a once-in-a-lifetime player, but you never know.'

Garry Ringrose is one of Leinster's current academy crop. He was born in January 1995, seven months before the game turned professional. His favoured school [Blackrock], position [outside centre] and goal-kicking exploits have led to early comparisons with O'Driscoll. The fact that he was called in to train with the Irish senior team in November 2014 only adds the linked narrative of the Blackrock alumni. He mixes his studies – Law and Business at UCD – with gym sessions, training with academy colleagues and running occasional drills with Leinster's first team.

He says, 'I'm going to be perfectly honest and say the thrill still hasn't worn off, of shaking Rob Kearney's or Ian Madigan's hand. In my eyes, they are the players I would have looked up to all the way up during school. To get to train with them or if you are in the gym beside them, you are still almost like, "Jeez, I can't fail on this lift now." I like maintaining that attitude, that I'm lucky to be in the position I am, because I know, certainly going out of school, there are a lot of my friends who would give an arm and a leg to be in the position I am.'

Ringrose has, to date, progressed with little hindrance through a competitive set-up he describes as intense and cut-throat. For every disappointment or setback, such as injury or non-selection, he has been buoyed by training alongside men he has looked up to and benefited from coaches such as Matt O'Connor and Joe Schmidt. 'The worst thing I could ever do is become complacent and think I am the complete player,' he says. 'All the time, all the time, you're trying to improve. I'm twenty [in January], so to think you are the finished product at twenty is stupid.'

***

Connacht academy manager Nigel Carolan takes up on Mick O'Driscoll's extraterrestrial theme. 'The nineteen-year-old that came into the office and sat in front of us in 2004 and the nineteen-year-old that sits in front of you today, they're like aliens. They are two different people.'

Carolan revisits the troubles that can arise from going from 'the big fish in a small pond' to the academy and professional grind: 'A lot of the guys, you find, have never sat on a bench before. They get up to the interprovincial games, for example, and they have never had that view before. They're like "What's this?" These things come as a shock, but it is part of the programme and part of a rugby player's existence. In some ways they need to be able to deal with these things maybe before, or as, they arise. They have to put that in perspective too. Some of a rugby player's problems are really small in comparison to other people's lives.'

Carolan, who was appointed Ireland Under-20 coach a month after our chat, says mental health is now considered just as vital in a player's development as their physical conditioning or skill-set. 'Mental health wasn't even invented, if you want, in 2004. Now, personal development has become a huge part of our programme. Not only trying to develop the player, but the person that supports and underpins the player. We've had to take a look at personal values and how a player shows up on a day and behaves. It's not only coaching them how to play, but how to become a professional rugby player as well.

'There will be ups and downs along the way, so it is about trying to resource them to be able to deal with all those adversities. There is a lot more going on in their life – social media, pressure with college, money issues. They seem to be under a lot more pressure. There has to be an understanding that there is a life outside rugby; keeping a social and academic balance. There are no guarantees in this game, but while they are in it, they will be given the tools to succeed and no stone will be left unturned for them.'

The resources Carolan refers to are personal development, psychology, psychotherapy, nutrition, technical and physical development. By the time a player advances to the professional world, all the structures are in place and individuals will be expected to handle being dropped. The next generation, says Carolan, are comfortable with admitting when they are having problems. He adds that Connacht cannot afford 'to let any X-factor player go just because he has an issue off the field or some issue with his character. A door has to be open, too, for a late developer, and that could be physically or in his maturity. It is widely accepted in the psychological world that a guy hasn't fully developed until he is twenty-one. We have eighteen-year-olds coming into our programme, and if we think they are all going to be well rounded we're mistaken. It is our job to smooth the edges and take a holistic approach in building their characters.'

A late developer, in provincial rugby terms, is Robbie Henshaw. The Athlone native played schools rugby with Marist College, who would be far removed from the traditional Connacht powerhouses. Henshaw starred for Marist as they captured the Connacht Schools Senior Cup and, within six months, was making his senior debut. 'Robbie is not someone who would have shone in the Under-17s or Under-18s,' says Carolan. 'However, you're dealing with a guy who is very coachable, self-motivated, ambitious, willing to work hard and who is honest with himself. That makes it easy.'

A constant conundrum for Carolan, his academy team and community-development officers is the shallow player pool in Connacht. The province has just under eight per cent of the national population, and the GAA pursuits of football and hurling dominate the sporting landscape. One way of tackling the issue is recruiting players from the other provinces and abroad. Connacht have given playing opportunities to the likes of Kieran Marmion, Niyi Adeolokun and Eoghan Masterson in recent years, and continue to cast the net far and wide.

Tapping into the GAA seems an obvious route, but Carolan is keen to stress that good working relationships are vital on both sides of the aisle. 'We're not going to compete with the GAA. It is inherent with every community in the west of Ireland. In some ways we work with it. We don't stop any player from playing GAA, nor would we. On the contrary, we work with the clubs and their coaches. What we then see is that the players coming out are multi-skilled because they have been exposed to a wide variety of sports, especially those that require hand–eye coordination, spatial awareness, peripheral vision. It can only add to the repertoire of skills they can bring into rugby.

'We may lose one or two players when they are younger, but the door is always open. We work, and have a reasonable relationship, with a lot of the Minor managers across the province. By seventeen or eighteen, however, that decision does need to be made – I don't see a player coexisting between GAA and rugby well into his twenties.'

***

Munster assistant coach Ian Costello takes a philosophical point of view when considering the promotion of a young player from academy or A rugby. 'You say, "Have we got the best structures, resources and systems in place to make sure these players are ready?" First, you look at your systems at academy and development level, and if they are where they need to be. Then you look at how you integrate them into a squad and how often they get to train with the first team. How often do you look at them? We had twenty academy lads in for pre-season, and kept eight or nine in for a few weeks longer. So we're building up all that information. Then we use our experience or instinct to see when we think they're ready.'

Costello, a former academy chief at the province, believes the step up from A to senior rugby is not the punt it may have been in the past. He explains, 'Look at what happened with James Cronin. We had Killer [David Kilcoyne] the year before, who was involved in that A semi-final against Leinster at the RDS. Himself and Paddy Butler were the stand-out players. Suddenly David breaks through, and we're thinking, "Jesus, we'll miss him on the A team." Then James comes in. So, because he was successful with the As, he gets a crack, and now James is an Ireland international less than twelve months later. David's breakthrough cleared a path for him. So, if we keep doing our jobs right, there should be another prop on the lot, ready to go.'

Two other players who crossed Costello's path in their formative years are now Munster and Ireland regulars. 'I remember first coming across Peter O'Mahony at Under-19s when I was coaching the side. He stood out like a beacon. His skill level was incredible, his physicality was exceptional. That was almost an easy one. He stood out straight away as the captain of that group. Within a week of training, we knew who our captain was going to be.

'Conor Murray was a little more understated with the presence he had back then. When you looked at Conor, he just had exceptional fundamentals. It's hard to think that people were questioning anything about Conor's pass, as it is the fastest pass and one of the best worldwide. The power he gets off his wrist ... you see him doing things in training with one hand that a lot of guys can't do with two. His kicking is world-class as well. They were in place from an early age. His fundamentals were so good, so you knew he could accelerate [his advancement]. Sometimes, they just need the opportunity.'

Players such as Munster and Ireland flanker Tommy O'Donnell, Costello explains, are examples of slow-burners: 'Tommy had exploded onto the scene before going back and going a little bit quiet, before exploding again. You're looking for that presence, too, and that ability to stand up and make a decision. Will you do something in training – the right thing at the right time – rather than worrying about what others will think? You look at players who are comfortable at getting on the ball. No one wants to see a player who makes a mistake retreating into the background. We love to see the player that makes a mistake and can't wait to get back and atone for it. That's what you look out for, and you see that in the top players. Top-class players don't worry about making mistakes, and they push themselves into the forefront of every training session and every game as they excel. It requires that belief, that bit of mental strength and mental discipline on top of that ability. They're the lads that make it to the top.'

Unfortunately, Costello concedes, desire and commitment do not always add up to careers as professional rugby players. For every Murray, O'Mahony and O'Donnell, there are young men who are forced to face an unwelcome reality, rather than the dream of representing their province. 'A rugby and league selection might not be the Heineken Cup final, but, for a certain player, this is his time, his dream. If you're not going to pick him, you need to make sure you have made the decision for the right reasons. The only way I know how to do that is you work as hard as you can to make sure you have as much information as you can. Then you make a decision based on your experience and instinct on top of it. If you're letting a guy go or feel he is not going to make it as a professional player, the way

I rationalise it (and it never gets easy … Jesus, it is never easy to leave a guy out of a team, never mind telling him he is not going to be a professional rugby player) is just make sure that you have done everything you can to get that information to make the decision.

'Then you try to let it go afterwards, which is easier said than done, as you get very attached to players and you want to see them succeed. You can't help but feel responsible for their progress, and feel, to a certain degree, that you've let them down – that you haven't done enough to bring them through.'

For the players who do impress, however, there is no instant crock of cash. Former Ireland winger Niall Woods now runs Navy Blue sports agency. As Woods explains, a player can be signed up at any age, with some joining agencies around the same time as targeting Senior Schools Cup success (sixteen to eighteen years old). Woods steers clear of schools players and will only sign academy players if approached. 'I would generally meet the parents first,' he says. 'There is real need initially. If they sign a contract in the academy it is a three-year deal.'

Woods continues, 'The IRFU changed the academy contracts without speaking to me, around the time when I was leaving my [chief executive's] role with IRUPA. They all used to be one year. It ties the players in, obviously, for three years. It is ludicrous, and the parents think it is great because they are going to Leinster and they just sign them up. Leinster are clever. They signed seven guys into the academy from the Ireland Under-20s during the summer. They have seven of them on €4,000 a year for the next three years.

'Jordi Murphy is a client. In the second year of his academy contract, he was in eight match-day squads and played six times. There was an argument to bump him up, which they didn't. At the start of the third year, he played ten of the first twelve games, so they eventually did. Before that, Jordi was on €4,000 a year, playing with Brian O'Driscoll and Jamie Heaslip, who were on between €400,000 and €500,000 a year.'

'If a player progresses,' says Dempsey, 'they are jumped up. It's academy contract, development contract, senior professional contract – that is the way it works. But if a player in the academy progresses at such a level that they are just bumped up, they are not held back in any way. It has happened over the last number of years. Jack Conan would be a case in point, where he would be in the third year of the academy now, but he is no longer there. He has moved up to the senior contract.'

'There is an argument,' Woods suggests, 'about having an agent before they go into the academy, if they are outrageously good in school, because they are going to get €4,000 a year for three years. There are numerous clubs in England that are over here looking at school players – that have relationships with schools. If you are strictly interested in money, you would probably get €15,000 or €20,000 if you signed a one-year deal.'

# 17

## ROAD TO RECOVERY: INJURIES AND THE SPECTRE OF RETIREMENT

'In terms of injuries,' says former Connacht hooker Adrian Flavin, 'I will start from the top and work down.' He lists:

- Fractured eye socket
- Scratched cornea, which then got infected
- Both cheekbones broken
- Multiple breaks of the nose ('It must be close to ten,' he says, 'but the worst I got was by running into Bob Casey's elbow. It spread my nose across the side of my face and made Mike Tindall look like Brad Pitt.')
- Broken neck (two operations needed; one involving trimming discs down)
- Subluxed SC joints
- Subluxed AC joints
- Three right shoulder operations (two for cartilage repair, one reconstruction)
- Two left shoulder operations
- Right bicep torn off
- Both thumbs dislocated and broken
- Multiple fractures of fingers, dislocations and breaks
- Hernia operations on groin (both sides)
- Hip operation (resurfaced – bone pared down)
- Torn hamstring

- Strained knee ligaments (left and right)
- Snapped ankle ligaments
- Plantar fasciitis (tendon reattached to big toe).

'In 2003/04 I broke my neck,' Flavin continues. 'I was twenty-three years old and starting for London Irish. I was out for seven months, and got the all-clear one weekend and turned up, eager to go, on the following Monday. In that first training session back I snapped my ankle ligaments. Other than that, I have been pretty lucky with injuries in my career. I've probably had two or three bad injuries in a sixteen-year career, so can't complain. You list it out and it sounds bad, but in my seven years at Connacht I only missed out on a handful of games through injury.

'You play on through pain a lot, but you quickly get acquainted with that feeling. You were never forced to play, and we had a brilliant physio during my time at Connacht in Keith Fox, who would have kept a close eye on all of us and made sure we were not pushing ourselves through too much. But you just got on with it, either through stupidity or toughness or a mix of both. It is probably why I needed so many operations [four] when I finished up. I may need a full hip replacement in a few years, but the resurfacing has done the job for now. I'd say I will be in bits when I'm older, but hopefully not for a long time. I'll be a big follower of medical science in my latter years, believing some miracle procedure can get me back together again. As I've always said, I couldn't sing or dance, so I had to do something.'

\*\*\*

A 2009 study carried out at the University of Leicester found that a dump tackle (lifting a player off their feet, and their legs above the horizontal, before spearing them downward into the pitch) by a sixteen-stone player 'exerts a force akin to what a driver would feel in a 50-kilometres-per-hour car crash into a solid wall'. The study also found that for two players running head-on into a tackle, the force felt is akin to a crash at sixty kilometres per hour. According to a February 2015 report, carried out for *The Irish Times*, rugby players' mean body size has altered significantly in the past twenty years. The average height (188 centimetres) has increased by 4.7 centimetres, while average weight (105 kilograms) has increased by 9.4 kilograms. There is five per cent less body fat, but more muscle mass to produce greater speed and explosive power.

Every match-day jersey of Ireland's provincial clubs carries a global positioning system (GPS) unit. As well as monitoring distance covered, rest time, sprints and other useful data, the unit can register the G-force impact of tackles and collisions. Eight to ten G is regarded as heavy impact – an F-16 fighter-jet roll is equivalent to nine G of force. In November 2009, in the final minute of Ireland's win over South Africa, Brian O'Driscoll connected with a huge defensive tackle on Zane Kirchner that registered fourteen G.

Four years on, against Wales in the 2013 Six Nations, a hit on the Irishman almost doubled that recording. O'Driscoll received a pass from Johnny Sexton, but was shattered by Welsh centre Scott Williams before he could move the ball on. It was the biggest hit the Irishman received in his career – registering twenty-seven G on his GPS unit. In his book *The Test*, O'Driscoll states, 'As I hit the floor every last ounce of breath is gone from my body … I'm barely aware of any pain, but it feels like the closest thing to dying – unable to breathe, panicking.'

Jonny Davis, head of strength and conditioning at Ulster Rugby, has experienced the steady drift of rugby injuries in the past five years. Soft tissue injuries, such as hamstring pulls and calf strains, have been reduced in number and recovery time frame, but there has been an increase in bone breakages and fractures. Elbow breaks would have been extremely rare over the past decade, but in the space of one game, against Toulon, in January 2015, Ulster suffered two – Paddy Jackson and Stuart Olding. Connacht's head of fitness, Paul Bunce, says, 'Everyone else is getting big and strong, so we need to too.' The problem is, players are growing in size so much, and increasing lean muscle, that they are literally breaking each other's bones in contact.

***

At any time, Ulster's medical staff expect twenty to thirty per cent of their squad to be unavailable for selection due to injury. Indeed, during a 2011/12 season that included a visit to the Heineken Cup final, Ulster had forty-three per cent of their playing staff injured, with another twenty per cent away on international duty. Dr Michael Webb, medical director at Ulster since 2010, notes that over the four seasons from 2011/12 to 2014/15, the province has averaged fifteen per cent unavailability on the first day of pre-season. 'This illustrates the hangover from the season before and means we always seem to be playing catch-up,' he says.

In the 2013/14 season, Ulster had 151 'time loss' injuries. With a senior playing staff of forty-four, that works out at three-and-a-half injuries per player each season. That, Webb explains, is when a player is not available to train or play for a period exceeding twenty-four hours. 'Clearly,' he says, 'many players will receive medical attention but miss no time, and also some players may miss training early in the week but be fit for selection for the next game.'

Webb continues, 'We're moving away from those quick fixes in rugby – patching a guy up and getting him back out there. We look at it more in the long term. If a guy needs an extra few days or weeks, we'll take those. The coaches are great about that, and it minimises your risk of re-injury.'

Ulster secure a 24–9 victory over Llanelli Scarlets on 6 December 2014. The result keeps their slim Champions Cup hopes alive, but there has been a heavy price to pay. The province has installed a state-of-the-art medical centre at Kingspan Stadium (as Ravenhill Stadium will be known until 2024) as part of a €5.4 million redevelopment. Planning ahead, with worst-case scenarios in mind, Ulster's medics requested four beds for the centre. At one stage of the game there are five bad injuries. All four beds are occupied, and Stuart McCloskey, who has damaged elbow ligaments, alternates between lying on a changing bench and pacing the floor.

For Webb, it is one of those nights. 'Five significant injuries,' he remembers. 'Stuart's elbow, then hamstrings for Nick Williams and Wiehahn Herbst … We had two concussions, and both were diagnosed before they came off the pitch. No matter what they did in their [Head Injury Assessment] tests, they weren't coming back on. One guy [Franco van der Merwe] had a suspected loss of consciousness and the other [Stuart Olding] didn't feel well … They both performed well in their tests, but the bottom line is, if there is any doubt, you get them off the pitch.'

He adds, 'You think everything is going well, in the season or on a night. Then, all of a sudden, you lose two inside centres in one game. You just don't know what's around the corner.'

*****

Brian O'Driscoll fielded questions, in October 2012, at the offices of *Ultimate Rugby*, a website he has a stake in. He was three games into his fourteenth season with Leinster and Ireland, but already the questions were about a possible retirement the following summer.

In a recently released autobiography, *The Open Side*, New Zealand captain Richie McCaw admitted he had hidden a suspected broken foot from his teammates and coaches so he could lead the All Blacks to World Cup final glory. Given his injury profile and willingness to put his body on the line, I asked O'Driscoll if he had ever done something similar to McCaw. 'Some players react differently to injuries,' he began. 'Some guys like to play when they are near a hundred-per-cent fit, and won't play if they're not. A lot of guys never play a hundred-per-cent fit. Yeah, you can tell, it tends to be the very mentally tough guys that are able to. I can see it in the guys in the squads that I've been involved in. Guys that are capable of playing through serious discomfort.

'Sometimes it is about striking the balance,' he added. 'If you're eighty-per-cent fit but you feel as though you're doing a better job than someone else who is a hundred-per-cent fit, then you have to make that call for the team's sake, not just your own selfish point of view – wanting to be involved in a game. I think you have to be capable of making that balance.'

A little over two years down the road, I posed the same question to Ireland prop Mike Ross ahead of his team's November international with Australia. Ross confessed he had never gone into a match at a hundred per cent. He said, 'Apart from pre-season, most guys will go into a game with some sort of a niggle. That's the same in the majority of cases. I don't think you're ever going to feel a hundred per cent, but if you're ninety-five per cent that is generally good enough.'

Ross laughed when told about O'Driscoll's eighty-per-cent level, and thanked me for the comparison. 'You just have to go by how you feel,' he explained. 'If you're offering value to the group at whatever level you're at, then you go ahead. If you feel like you're going to be a hindrance, then it is upon you to be honest, to put your hand up and say, "I'm not right," and leave a guy who is to come in.'

***

July 2014, and a new season awaits. Leinster hoosh Sean O'Brien out for as many interviews and launches as possible. His previous season looked to be over before the New Year, as he was helped off the pitch with a dislocated left shoulder. The Tullow Tank had missed Ireland's 2014 Six Nations campaign and his province's Heineken Cup exit to Toulon, but returned in time to win a second Pro12 league title. Joe Schmidt had spared his newly healed shoulder a summer tour to Argentina. Taking a seat for a round-table yarn, following the launch of a competition to redesign an expanded RDS, O'Brien is keen for action to commence.

A month has passed since the retirement of Irish teammate, and friend, Stephen Ferris. 'His retirement did hit home,' O'Brien admits. 'He's only a year and a half older than me, so, yeah, you would be getting your skates on to plan for the afterlife – or "after rugby", I mean – and trying to be as best organised as possible if that happens. It's obviously a thing now, where the game has gone so physical now and it's a pressure environment. Injuries happen though, and you just have to go with it.'

He continues, 'We were a big, physical back row. Ferris used to go around smashing people. It would leave me to carry a bit more ball, while Jamie [Heaslip] had a bit of everything. To the opposition we would have been a big, physical back row that had a couple of strings to their bow.

'Injuries are something you deal with, and it is something you have to manage, as well. Everyone, no matter who they are, is tipping away and doing some form of rehab every week. That's just a part of rugby, and we put our bodies through that; but we wouldn't want it any other way. I've been more unlucky than some lads in the past while, but hopefully I'll have a good run of it this year now.'

Asked about life after rugby, O'Brien remarks, 'I know I'm going to be broken up.' From a farming background in Carlow, the loose forward would like to maintain an interest in that field, but cannot envisage a full-time return to bovine pursuits. 'It is something you'll have to think of when it comes along,' he says, 'but there's no point in me worrying about if I'm going to be broke up. I've to make the most of what I'm doing at the minute and go along with it. Everyone says that to me, "Why do you do what you do?" or "Why can't you mind yourself a little bit more?" You can't mind yourself in this game. It's the type of position I play and the way I play. That's the way it is and that's the way it will stay.'

O'Brien captained Leinster in their opening game of the season – a 22–20 loss to Glasgow – and completed the full eighty minutes. That match, on 6 September, would be his final game of 2014. In early October Leinster coach Matt O'Connor confirms the bleak news of shoulder reconstruction: 'The [shoulder] graft didn't take, and as a result he needs that tightened up. Because of the softening of the tissue with the infection, the screws that were put in weren't as successful as we would have liked.'

O'Connor adds, 'You never want to see world-class players on the sideline. That is the reality of it. But the nature of the game is blokes get injured. Hopefully not as often as Sean. He is pretty positive. He's looking at the upsides as you have to do in these situations, and hopefully he will come through the other side of that when he is right in February or March to play a significant part in the back end of the season.'

Leinster went into their first ever Champions Cup (a rejigged Heineken Cup) without O'Brien, Cian Healy, Fergus McFadden, Luke Fitzgerald, Dave Kearney and Marty Moore. Team captain Jamie Heaslip declared, 'We're not playing table tennis here. Lads get hurt. It's part and parcel of the game.'

***

I caught up with former Connacht and Munster player Paul Warwick in June 2014, three days after he announced his retirement from rugby, at the age of thirty-three. The Australian had moved to France for two seasons after Munster had been informed by the IRFU that they could not offer him any more than a one-year deal. He transferred to Worcester Warriors for 2013/14 before injuries caught up in a flood. Having overcome a thumb injury to make his Worcester debut in October 2013, Warwick played a handful of games before knocks became life-threatening encounters.

'Against Sale, in February 2014,' he says, 'I made a tackle and got up to go for the ball. One of my own teammates – one of the second rowers – came through and collected me with a knee. I was completely concussed and my whole body had that funny-bone feeling. It was weird; as we were playing Sale, Sam Tuitupou was the first guy I saw. I remember him looking at me and saying, "Are you okay?" I was like, "No." I was numb all over. It was a bit scary. I was stretchered off and went away for all the checks. Everything was okay, so I was free to go home.'

Warwick played again, three weeks after the concussion. He was listed to start on the Worcester bench in their penultimate game of the season, against Saracens, but injured his neck for the second time in three months. 'I got hit from behind while I was holding a [tackling] pad,' he explains. 'I was completely not expecting to be hit. Again, there were pins and needles down my arms, and they both went dead. That's when they scanned me.

'The doctor, before that assessment, mentioned retirement as unlikely, but a possibility. After the scans, the doc then said it was probably best to give up. He had been pretty conservative in his estimates [in the past], so I thought it would be silly to risk anything for the future. It's disappointing, but my family and my health come first. I don't want to be in a wheelchair after a few years of rugby.'

Warwick has taken up a coaching job with Worcester and feels fortunate to be earning a living in the sport he loves. His most cherished memories are playing for the Barbarians, pushing the All Blacks to the brink with Munster, and his Heineken Cup 2008 winners' medal. 'As you mature and grow up, you appreciate that part of your life, because you'll never get it back again,' he reflects. 'I'm proud of that part of my life. A lot of things fell into place for me. Rua Tipoki got an injury and I got a chance to play, against Sale, at fullback in my first Heineken Cup game. I scored a try and kicked a field goal, and it turned out to be a really good day. I guess the rest is history.'

*** 

Keith Earls splays his arms across a bay window in the University of Limerick's restaurant and bar, and watches the action below. Munster are going full tilt ahead of their Champions Cup opener with Sale Sharks. Simon Zebo goes hell for leather after a Felix Jones up-and-under, but the ball rebounds off his shoulder. Head coach Anthony Foley resets the play, while Paul O'Connell goes through a solo training session in the far corner of the pitch. Several students from UL stop to watch the plays unfold, before ambling on to their next class.

Earls has yet to feature in the 2014/15 season, and surgery on his knee in early October means he will miss the entire group stages of the Champions Cup. The latest injury setback occurred during Ireland's two-day camp in August. Earls stepped hard off his right foot and felt something pulling. Taking a chair by a table reserved for the squad's lunch break, Earls says no return dates have been set. 'The knee had been niggling me for a while, even last year,' he explains. 'I was supposed to play against Glasgow last year and I tweaked it, but it was nothing major. It was over the summer, and tendons like to be worked – kept active. I had the month off, and thought the rest was going to be doing it good. I got back into pre-season and it was a bit sore, but I got rid of it.'

Earls underwent rehab after the jarring in Irish camp, but the tendon swelled again as he neared a playing return. He travelled from Limerick to London, where he was met by Ireland team physio James Allen ahead of a date with Swedish surgeon Håkan Alfredson. 'Surgery was the next step, and when the surgeon opened me the tendon was in fairly bad condition. He kind of scraped away the top bit and, please God, that's it now.'

Earls continues, 'James left on Monday night. I had my surgery on the Tuesday, and my partner flew over that night. We returned on the Wednesday as I didn't want to leave my daughter without her parents for a couple of nights. I was going to be in the hospital but didn't want to drag them both over, so my partner flew over to bring me home on crutches.'

Earls insists he is looking upon his latest spell on the sidelines as a positive: 'I can look at a different part of my game, or put on a bit of size in this time. With the World Cup coming up, I want to try and get my body as right as it can to give me a chance to be selected.' At the time of our conversation it had been nineteen months since Earls' last game for Ireland. Earls had left midway through the first half of the 22–15 reverse to Italy in March 2013. Schmidt was named Ireland coach two months later, but, training aside, Earls was unable to stake a claim on the wing or in his preferred role of outside centre. 'I've been in camp a few times with

Joe,' he says, 'and he's a fella that strikes me as someone who really knows his stuff, and one I want to work with. Unfortunately, he seems to be a bit of bad luck for me – I seem to get injured every time I go to Irish camp.' Medial ligament and shoulder injuries have accounted for some of his time away from the international scene, but illness prevented him touring Argentina in the summer of 2014. 'I got sick a couple of days before that trip and was told to stay away from the lads,' he explains. 'I had it a couple of years ago as well. It's some stomach problem I can't get to the end of. It comes every so often and knocks me out for a week or so.'

Earls' father, Ger, was a Young Munster flanker of ferocious regard in the 1990s, and featured in Munster's famous win over Australia in 1992. Keith played for local club side, Thomond, in his formative years, before playing a season with Garryowen. He was called in for his first training session with Munster on his nineteenth birthday. 'A couple of weeks later Deccie [Declan Kidney] offered me a developmental contract,' he recalls. 'That was grand, because I was on a building site, as an electrician, for about four months beforehand.

'I stayed with Thomond captain Eddie Fraher; he gave me a job. I learned a lot from that, about life outside rugby and how fellas lives were. Even when you come into rugby, the young fella gets a hard time. It's to see what character you are. It was the same on the site: a lot of donkey work, but I appreciated it. I had a job. I was chasing walls for wires, drilling holes in the timber for wires to go through, and I was pulling them through the roof. I was second fixing. In fairness to Eddie, he taught us straight away, and put us into the deep end.'

Earls made his Munster debut, aged nineteen, against Ospreys in April 2007, and was an Ireland regular within eighteen months. He made the British & Irish Lions squad in 2009 and was Ireland's leading try-scorer at the 2011 World Cup.

Injury to Brian O'Driscoll afforded Earls an extended run at outside centre in the 2012 Six Nations. That summer he was named No. 12, but played most of the first Test against New Zealand at Eden Park at No. 13, as Kidney experimented with a new role for O'Driscoll. The backline talisman was partnered by Gordon D'Arcy for the following Six Nations, with Earls reverting to the left wing. With O'Driscoll now retired to the world of book launches and punditry, I ask Earls if his injury ahead of the November internationals is even more frustrating to bear. 'I have to concentrate on getting fit first,' he replies. 'If I get the game time here [Munster] at thirteen, it increases my chances of Irish selection there. Over the years I've got caught up in it, but now I've brushed it by me.'

Self-doubt will always be a part of his psyche, Earls concedes, but each season sees him grow more comfortable in the skin of a top professional rugby player. 'I'm twenty-seven now, and if I don't cop on now I never will. A lot of guys in the country, as rugby players, can be too humble at times. We need to have, not a cockiness as such, but a confident mentality. As Irish people, we're often obsessed with other people, other players – thinking, "Jesus, they're from New Zealand. They have to be better individuals than us and blah, blah, blah" – instead of saying, "You're just as good as him, and you're going to go out and show him."'

Switching off away from Munster has become more of a necessity since the arrival of daughter Ella-Maye in 2012. 'I get completely away from rugby, completely away,' he says. 'When you go back to her, she only knows you as her daddy and she loves you. She doesn't rate how you played or anything like that. She's great craic. It's great to get away from it. You can't be moping around about rugby for her sake, and for her mother's sake. It's another folder in your life. You have your rugby, your family and your friends. You can't be bringing one problem into another.'

Earls was one of twelve senior internationals to have contracts extended by the IRFU during 2013/14. 'It can be a tough time, during negotiations,' he says. 'This time next year I'll be negotiating again. It just comes around so fast. It can be distracting at times … Injuries didn't help me last year with my hopes of negotiating in France or wherever. Definitely, at some stage of my career, I think I'd fancy it – heading away with my family and doing something different. Whether it is two years' time, four years' time or later, I have to keep my options open.'

'Strange' is the word Earls uses to describe the feeling of watching his teammates rip into each other four days before the return of European rugby. 'You have to concentrate on getting back, but hopefully the lads will do a job [in the pool stages],' he says. 'I have to get my body conditioned, and right, so when I do get back I'm not leaving the lads down. It is going to be tough, watching them on the telly. It was hard the last couple of weeks, knowing I should be playing. It's the same for any rugby player, but you have to try and find the positives ... No matter what game you're watching, you're trying to break it down and study the moves. Because I know the moves here, I know what's coming a lot of the time.

'I called over to Mike Sherry's house to watch the Munster–Leinster game. The two of us are banjaxed at the moment. We said we'd go through the hell together. It's tough watching the lads. We were roaring and shouting at the telly when lads were making a break.'

Earls walks me out of the bar, and we swap parenting tales before he leaves me with a handshake. How is the rest of his day fixed? 'I get the stitches out today,' he says, 'and I'll be able to sweat them as the wound is closed. I'll start my rehab tomorrow and take it by every day, every week. I'm looking forward to sweating and hurting again. If I'm not doing that, I don't feel like I'm working.'

# 18

## FRENCH FLIRTATIONS AND THE RISE OF RUGBY WAGES

Irish rugby has advanced significantly with regard to paying players over the past twenty years. The first payments of any sort were made to Leinster players who had competed in the 1995/96 Heineken Cup. Each player was given the princely sum of £180. For handing over the money, the Leinster branch, in turn, was carpeted by the IRFU, as it had yet to finalise contract offers and payment procedures. The first full-time contracts, for £25,000, arrived the following year. In 1997, Peter Clohessy signed a £50,000-a-year contract, as he had been called up for the British & Irish Lions tour to South Africa. Injury meant Clohessy never played on the tour, but he was named in the squad. A stipulation was a stipulation. Contracts edged into six-figure sums when Irish Lions such as Keith Wood, Paul Wallace and Eric Miller were tempted home for league and Heineken Cup tilts.

Ireland's highest-paid players can now command anywhere between €450,000 and €550,000, depending on their age and injury profile, and position. Additional money can be secured by the union or province acting as a conduit for sponsorship deals with companies such as Topaz, 3 Mobile or Canterbury. As reported by *The Irish Times*, Johnny Sexton's salary – through wages and sponsorship deals – will top €650,000 when he returns to Leinster for 2015/16. Sexton, quite rightly, says he could earn a much greater amount by staying in France with Racing Métro, but he is satisfied with his new deal and the feeling of being valued by the IRFU.

Jamie Heaslip had previously been Ireland's top earner, before the Sexton deal. I ask rugby agent Niall Woods if Heaslip should have inserted a clause – as Roy Keane used to do when he was at Manchester United – whereby his salary would jump to match that of any player signed to a better contract. 'If I was advising him, I would say forget about that,' says Woods. 'You want to get paid whatever your market value is, and it is up to the agent to dictate what the market value is and find out what it is. The IRFU might not like what the market value is, or contest it, but they have to put their best offer forward.

'Then there are ways of structuring it to make it more appealing for him to stay. Tax incentives and sportsman's tax relief are huge, because it gives them an extra sixteen to seventeen per cent per year. But when it comes to France, the after-tax money in France, you can't really compete. You could have a player's gross salary in Ireland that is less than his net in France. Particularly if you are married and have a number of kids, you are down into single digits. That is just the tax system in France. If you are married you pay less tax. If you have one kid you pay less, two, three, four, five. It just gets less and less. That is why, for the older guys, it is more appealing, because generally you are married and might have one or two kids.'

The IRFU appear to have learned the lessons from Sexton's shock Top 14 departure in the summer of 2013. In one of his first press conferences as Ireland coach, Joe Schmidt bemoaned the amount of game-time his starting out-half was playing for Racing. Sexton had played twelve matches in thirteen weeks, and was summoned back during the November Test window to sit on the bench for the Parisian club. It was a muscle flex that irked many involved in Irish rugby. The previous tactic of stalling negotiations until the final months of the season was scrapped. By February 2014, the union had tied up star names such as Heaslip, Sean O'Brien, Conor Murray, Rory Best and Keith Earls to new deals. By November 2014, three-year deals had been announced for Rob Kearney and Tommy Bowe.

'The threat of France will always be there,' Woods says, 'but it is harder to use it as a negotiating tactic. Clubs in France don't believe the players will go … They just believe they are looking to get a higher offer here, which probably, ninety per cent of the time, they are. So it's harder, for the one or two guys that want to go and play in France, to be taken seriously. Again that is up to the agent. You have to convince the clubs that they are serious. It doesn't help when other players make the trip over and you know quite well that they are not going to leave. Again it's just the market. Johnny Sexton going probably helped the market believe they would go, whereas him coming home and the other two boys [Heaslip and O'Brien] staying last year has worked in reverse. It could be one big name who goes this year. The biggest thing that is keeping them here is playing for Ireland. Unless you are out-and-out number one, if you go to France you probably won't play for Ireland.'

Leinster chief executive Mick Dawson comments, 'Ever since the game went professional and the players left in 1995 and went to the UK, the IRFU made a big decision to get them back, around 1998/99. Nothing has changed in the union's outlook or our outlook. We want the best Irish players to be based in Dublin or Ireland. Well, Dublin particularly. That is still our view.

'French clubs have an unbridled tap,' he adds. 'If you've got an owner who's a billionaire, and he decides he wants to spend a lot of his money on rugby players, it is very difficult to compete. Our model is very different. That's why a new stadium [an increased capacity RDS] with extra revenue, the new Champions Cup with its extra revenue, all of those are vitally important to us.

'France is a worry for us, but so far we've managed to do remarkably well. You're not going to win them all, but if we create a winning culture and this [Dublin] is our hometown, then we will definitely be able to hold onto most of our players. But it is a worry. You can't compete with someone who's got a billion quid.'

Ronan O'Gara, who has coached Sexton at Racing since August 2013, agrees that the IRFU has weathered the storm, for now. 'It will happen again,' he says. 'It is going to turn into a monster over here. There are teams in the Pro D2 who are going to get millions if they get into the Top 14. The Irish players are paid very well at home – and deservedly so because they are big names – while over here, average players are paid well. That's the difference, as average players are not paid well in Ireland. If a [Top 14] president is interested in you, he'll offer you big, big money, and that is how it will kick off again.

'You'll easily get that €1 million a year player, within three years or even in eighteen months, after the World Cup. If Kieran Read came on the market, he would get over a million a year. Look at what happened to rugby in fifteen years. If it continues, going from £7,500 a year for my first contract to €750,000 for Matt Giteau, it is not long before you will get a fella signing a five-year deal for €5 million.'

In December 2014, three months after O'Gara's prediction, his club Racing Métro announced the signing of New Zealand out-half Dan Carter on a lucrative three-year deal. The New Zealander, as reported by *Midi Olympique*, would receive a basic wage of €500,000 a year from the club, while standing to earn at least the same amount from his image rights and sponsorship agreements, through Arena 92. The business is tied in with Racing and will run the club's new stadium upon its 2016 opening. However, by separating Carter's contracts into playing and commercial, it allows Racing to stay within the salary cap imposed by the French rugby federation.

'I wouldn't rule the €1 million-a-year deal out in Ireland either,' says Woods. 'Not for everyone, obviously, but, say Brian O'Driscoll appeared now the way he was in 2000/01 and then in 2003/04, he would be getting a million in three or four years. It might not all be in salary. It might be split into image rights, but you would have to, to keep him, because he would get offered €1.5 million or €2 million in France at that stage. Some of the French clubs can just be looking for that position, and you are at the top of your game. You are the best in the home unions or the world. You get a crazy owner who will just want to outbid the other clubs.

'Then it is up to the player, if he thinks it is right. The public have a thing about money, but it is a short career. Sean O'Brien is injured now [October 2014]. He might not play again. He could have gone to Toulon last year. He could have got €200,000 more this year and next year, and he could be retiring now. The argument is: he should have gone, from a financial point of view. If he is going to get injured, he might not have got injured over there. Everyone says, "You are going to damage your body over there," but you are going to damage your body here as well. It depends on the player, depends on the club and what the squad is like for cover in that position. Sexton struggled last year because of the injuries. That is because he was played so much, but if you are a prop and you go to France, you go to the right club, you are probably behind international props. They only play you for fifty minutes in France. You could be playing fifty minutes or thirty minutes, and getting well paid for it.'

IRFU chief executive Philip Browne addressed the French threat in July 2014. Browne was speaking at the publication of the union's annual report, which showed revenues more than trebling over the past decade to €69.7 million in 2011, up from €21.6 million in 2001. As reported in *The Irish Times*, Browne said, 'The sort of money that is available in France, of course we've got to be concerned. We've done pretty well with limited financial resources and limited playing resources over the years. We have to look at our business model, number one, and maybe have to look at bringing in private money. Some of the provinces have been successful at bringing in private money.'

With rugby entering the era of €1 million-a-year players, I use Colombian striker Radamel Falcao (£260,000 per week at Manchester United) as an example, and ask Jamie Roberts if the game will ever mirror football for exorbitant wages, and if fans have a right to feel envious of players. 'I think [that attitude] is quite naive of football fans, to be honest,' Roberts responds, 'because if there is that much money in the game, the people that deserve to be earning the money are the players.

'Football is such a bigger machine. If there was that much money in rugby, the people who deserve it are the people that produce the product – the players. From a personal point of view, for the fans to say, "Look at the money he's on. That's ridiculous" – for me, that's not true. People pay a lot of money to see those people play, so they deserve the money. Rugby is nowhere near the same machine as football. Worldwide, you can see it's growing, it's getting there. In the UK it is growing, and with the Guinness Pro12 [formerly the Celtic League], Sky Sports coming in is huge. I think over the next few years it will grow and grow. It's interesting. Whether or not it will get to the point football is at, I'm not sure. We'll see.'

***

Woods has handled most sides of the rugby cube, having played as both an amateur and a professional, worked with players' unions in England and Ireland, and branched out into becoming an agent. One of his clients is former Munster forward James Coughlan, who secured a lucrative move to Pro D2 side Pau in the summer of 2014. 'I started Munster contract talks on James' behalf in November 2013,' says Woods, 'and the deal was done at the end of the month. I remember James was astonished. He said, "You're telling me I don't have to worry about this over Christmas?"

'That for him was a worry in previous years. Negotiating goes from now, early October, to March and April for some players; the lower down the pecking order, the later you get left to negotiate. You are worrying about it.' The fear of injury, Woods comments, never goes away, but it is shunted to the back of players' minds.

Leinster head coach Matt O'Connor speaks about his players' ability to compartmentalise and push injury worries aside. 'It's their desire,' he says. 'That's what they want to do. Since they were six, seven, eight, nine, ten, they've wanted to play rugby at the highest level. That's an incredibly powerful driver, and, from that end, you wouldn't question it. It's not my business to question it, but to fuel it.'

An IRUPA survey of its members, in 2013, revealed that the average length of a professional rugby player's career – from the first full-time contract until retirement from the game – was seven years. Woods moved on from the players' union in 2011, but fought many battles during his eight years as chief executive. Using live examples (players who had major injuries or had retired), he explains, was often the only way he could grab the attention of players. 'As soon as they're out the door,' he says, 'they are going training and going out smashing each other, they are going to forget about it. That was the hardest part – it's not the sexiest thing talking about insurance, post-career options or talking about networking. They don't really care. When you talk about match fees and win bonuses, they are all over you.'

In 2002, Irish finance minister Charlie McCreevy introduced a deal whereby sportspeople, upon their retirement, would be able to claim back forty per cent of the income tax they paid over their most lucrative ten years. For a rugby player making, for example, gross earnings of €600,000 over ten years, that would mean a retirement pot of €93,780.

Woods comments, 'When sportsman's tax relief nearly got shelved by the government a couple of years back, we [IRUPA and players' agents] would have lobbied for six or seven months to get it kept. In typical Irish fashion, it was kept at the last moment.'

As of January 2015, there were 194 Irish professional rugby players at Irish provinces and clubs abroad. Approximately sixty had high-earning contracts, funded by the IRFU. After all its behind-the-scenes negotiations and lobbying, the players' union received just one 'thank you' letter from a player in the national team – it was sent by Rob Kearney.

New Zealand's Jonah Lomu rides roughshod over Ireland at the 1995 Rugby World Cup.
© INPHO/Billy Stickland

Peter Clohessy and Denis Hickie, two of Ireland's first full-time professionals, dejected after an away defeat to France during the 1998 Five Nations. © INPHO/Billy Stickland

Malcolm O'Kelly, Keith Wood and Brian O'Driscoll have a laugh on the Irish team bus on the way to training. © INPHO/Billy Stickland

Francois Pienaar of Saracens gets to grips with Munster's Peter Stringer during a 1999 Heineken Cup clash. © INPHO/Andrew Paton

Gary Longwell, David Humphreys and Andy Ward celebrate Ulster's Heineken Cup success in January 1999. © INPHO/Andrew Paton

Ronan O'Gara leads An Taoiseach Bertie Ahern into the middle of Irish celebrations after they defeated England in the 2001 Six Nations. © INPHO/Billy Stickland

Ireland coach Warren Gatland stands back as his players engage in a half-time team-talk at Lansdowne Road. © INPHO/Billy Stickland

Brian O'Driscoll and Paul O'Connell take a breather midway through Ireland's 36–15 win over Wales in 2004's Six Nations. © INPHO/Billy Stickland

The Irish players celebrate winning the Grand Slam at the Millennium Stadium in March 2009. © INPHO/Morgan Treacy

Shane Horgan celebrates with friends and family after Leinster clinched their first ever Heineken Cup title, in May 2009. © INPHO/Morgan Treacy

Andrew Trimble of Ulster and Ireland, pictured after he was awarded the IRUPA Players'
Player of the Year. © Brendan Moran/SPORTSFILE

The final whistle at Wellington Regional Stadium spells victory for Wales and World Cup
2011 devastation for Ireland. © INPHO/Dan Sheridan

Johnny Sexton reacts after he misses a crucial penalty near the end of Ireland's 22–20 loss to New Zealand in 2013. © INPHO/Ryan Byrne

Munster captain Peter O'Mahony rejoices after his team defeats Leinster at the Aviva Stadium in November 2014. © INPHO/Dan Sheridan

Rob Kearney takes a moment to reflect during Ireland's national anthem, ahead of their 2014 Six Nations clash with Wales. © INPHO/Billy Stickland

Ireland captain Paul O'Connell shows off the Six Nations trophy to a phalanx of photographers as night falls at Murrayfield, March 2015. © INPHO/Billy Stickland

# 19

## A TRIP TO FRANCE: GRENOBLE VERSUS RACING

There were fifty Irish players operating on professional contracts in the top two tiers of English and French rugby in January 2015. One glance at the Top 14 fixtures for 2014/15, and my trip was confirmed. Expenses be damned; I would travel to Paris and onward to Grenoble to watch seven Irishmen and an honorary Wolfhound (former Ireland A player Andrew Farley) doing their thing in the south of France.

A lazy narrative was already forming in my head as I booked my flights on Friday 30 August. I would speak with the Irish coaching trio of Ronan O'Gara (Racing Métro), Bernard Jackman and Mike Prendergast (Grenoble) ahead of their sides' weekend clash. The focus, however, would be on the kicking battle between Racing's Johnny Sexton and James Hart of Grenoble. Twenty-four hours later, Sexton had his jaw fractured by a Toulon hooker. He would miss six weeks of action, while Hart was slowly on the mend from a wrist injury and had fallen down the pecking order behind South Africa's Charl McLeod. It was a costly lesson not to pour plans in concrete while relying on a rugby player to stay fit.

### Tuesday 23 September

'Spot the Irishman,' jokes Ronan O'Gara as he walks past me to take a seat in the corner of Racing Métro's hosting area. We are in the reception of the club's headquarters, but a flat-screen TV, cosy seating and a steadily engaged coffee machine blend for a relaxed interviewing space. The former Munster out-half is kitted out in a Racing tracksuit, and greets a couple of local journalists before ushering me to a corner for a babble. O'Gara is right about one thing: compared to the daintily dressed French rugby correspondents, I do stand out as a Behanesque Irishman.

We talk Munster, Ireland and the pressure of place-kicking, before the conversation turns to retirement. After 128 matches for Ireland, O'Gara's international send-off involved applauding the victorious Scotland team off the Murrayfield pitch and receiving an ominous knock on his hotel-room door. Declan Kidney cut a seventeen-year cord, but lost his own job six weeks later. I ask O'Gara if he felt a tinge of jealousy for the bombastic farewell afforded to Ireland teammate Brian O'Driscoll the following season: there was hardly a dry eye at the Aviva Stadium as the soon-to-retire centre turned on the style to beat Italy, and waved goodbye in the shadow of floating 'Thank you Brian' banners. 'No. I wouldn't have been able to handle a year like that,' O'Gara concedes. 'When you're in a decision-making position, you just can't do that. There is too much scrutiny on you.

'It was probably a little drawn out for everybody, but it's hard to know that before you do it. I don't know what his thoughts are on it, but I was at the game and, to be fair, the IRFU did a great job for him. He's an O2 ambassador too, so everything [with the banners] added to it. It was a marketing dream.

'If I'm honest, a send-off like that probably would have been nice for my family. But for me? No, because I never operated like that. For me, when I was in the dressing room and was able to look my own players in the eyes and thank them, that was it. Once I finished, after Clermont, Munster were doing their damnedest to organise a farewell for me, but I didn't want a show. It's very final – very brutal. I didn't want it, because what about all the other hundred fellas I played with over the years? The fellas in the dressing room were very important, but there were another eighty that were equally as important to me. I was very grateful for how it ended [with Munster], and I wouldn't change it.

'Coaching is completely different,' O'Gara muses as the conversation brooks on. 'Being a good player doesn't mean anything, but it takes a bit of time for that to hit home. Essentially, with a lot of coaching you have to be a teacher. As a player, you're not really aware of that, because it's you who can do the actions. You now have to teach the actions or try to get them across the best way you can.

'Tony McGahan always made a good point, and it sticks with me. He said, "Never fucking assume." You know, you never, ever assume what people know. You have to start at the start and teach them … I don't know if it is any easier this season, but I'm further down the road in terms of what I am trying to teach them.'

O'Gara had a passably high level of French upon his arrival at Racing, but, he argues, speaking and living the language are different sides of the coin: 'It's like a French person joining us here. No matter how good he is, (a) if he doesn't get the slang and (b) if he doesn't get the accent, he's on the hind foot. That's what happens. It's not easy in that regard. If they want to lose you, then they can speak quicker and your argument is lost.'

Recruited to the tightly knit coaching staff of experienced duo Laurent Labit and Laurent Travers, O'Gara endeavoured to make an instant impact. Six weeks into his first season he noted the ongoing lack of a defence coach and put himself forward for the job. 'It kicked on from there,' he says, 'and I think the two lads enjoy someone who is proactive rather than reactive. I've got to know my place, but I'm driving it on as hard as I can.'

*** 

Mike Phillips finishes dissecting his Twitter spat with One Direction singer Niall Horan for a French journalist before taking his leave of the Racing reception. His Welsh teammate, Jamie Roberts, emerges from a gym session and orders a coffee. Taking a seat beside me, he places the coffee beside two Activia yoghurts, and asks about the book. He praises O'Gara's transition to coaching: 'I know that Welsh and Irish competition is always there, but he is a true rugby man and commands respect. When he speaks, people listen … His French is very good, so it's easy for him when he's presenting to the team, but a bit of English slips in every now and then, certainly on the microphone after games or after a few beers on the team bus.'

Roberts is one of four Welsh players at Racing. Phillips joined as a free agent the previous season, Dan Lydiate arrived after the British & Irish Lions tour, and Luke Charteris was recruited over the summer. Roberts is a rare breed in modern, professional rugby, in that he chose to complete a medical degree even as his star was on the rise. The language barriers in France have stilted his doctoring ambitions, but he is not ready to allow an eight-year investment of time, effort and tests go to waste. 'Being a doctor is something I don't want to give up on,' he says. 'I want to pick it back up. I miss learning, I miss developing as a person, basically. I mean, Wednesdays can only consist of so many coffees, eating out or riding the sofa watching TV. You need your downtime, but when you're in your twenties and straight out of school you have to keep learning, keep evolving and furthering your mind.

'I always found that university was a great escape from rugby for me. I could completely switch off from rugby and have a different bunch of mates. I'd come off the training field or I'd be training, and would look forward to going to uni, hospital and doing different things. And by the end of the hospital day, I'd love to go back training.

'There was a huge temptation to quit as rugby got bigger,' he concedes, 'especially in my third and fourth years. I was very close to going with full-time rugby, but you're a long time retired from rugby, and if I could do them both then, why not? I've always felt at my most productive when I was very busy. My days off [from Cardiff Blues] were always hospital days, on my half-days I was at the hospital. I studied on Sundays. It was my most productive as I put pressure on myself to make sure I ticked all the boxes in rugby.

'Life after rugby goes one of two ways. You either follow your pathway and what you want to do – like I would in becoming a doctor – or a lot of rugby players get in touch with a sponsor in their final few years of playing and end up working for them. We'll see … A lot of my mates really enjoy their lives as doctors. It's a good life and certainly a rewarding one.'

Becoming a doctor would have seemed the best financial route for Roberts to take when, aged nineteen, he was offered a Cardiff Blues academy contract of £500 a year. 'That grew steadily, but I got my chance with the Blues because of an injury to Chris Czekaj, the winger. He was on tour with Wales in Australia in 2006, and he had a spiral fracture of his femur – a really nasty injury. I was a fullback in those days, but had my chance on the wing and it went well. I was capped that season, and had my first cap with Wales in 2008, when Warren Gatland took over after the World Cup.'

Just over a month shy of his twenty-eighth birthday during our chat, Roberts is already reflective about his career to date. 'In the bell curve of a rugby career I'm over the top of it in regard to age, in a weird way, and I need to appreciate it. I need to look after my body, more than anything, because I like to think it's my body that will give up before my mind.

'A lot of players now are trying to hang on as long as they can. We earn really good money as rugby players, compared to the normal world. Players may be earning six figures a year as a rugby player, and when they come out of that environment, there aren't that many jobs around where you can earn fifty or sixty grand a year nowadays. A lot of guys play at an advanced age because of that. A lot of players still feel they can contribute, but much of it depends on what you've got set up after.'

While central contracts arrived a couple of seasons too late to stop Roberts from fishing out his passport, by August 2014 the Welsh Rugby Union (WRU) had moved to mirror the successful Irish system. Player welfare and managing game-time were totems of a deal that took over a decade to implement. The likes of Alun Wyn Jones and Sam Warburton would be contracted to the WRU and loaned out to the regions under the proviso of playing no more than sixteen games a season. 'It's something that could have happened a while back,' Roberts concedes. 'I like the Irish system. The way the players are managed and how they peak for international periods. It's spot on. The clubs and union appear in complete harmony. We're getting there with Wales. From a players' perspective it is great, and they will feel well looked after.'

As Roberts speaks about player welfare, I glance down at a fifteen-centimetre scar that tattoos his left ankle. Injuries are a common factor in his line of work. 'I've had reconstructions to my ankle, knee, shoulder and wrist,' he says. '[The ankle scar] was a tendon dislocation. I had the wrist reconstruction after the Lions second Test in 2009. The shoulder when I was eighteen, and the ACL [anterior cruciate ligament] after the Six Nations in 2012. I missed the summer tour to Australia that year, and did my ankle in my second game here. They are the four main ones – the ankle was only three months, but the others were six-month injuries … They're tough, very tough, but every rugby player has them.' He adds, 'You would never play to your full potential if you think about injuries. It is a contest where you have to launch yourself into it a hundred per cent, and the minute you don't you get found wanting.'

Racing had beaten Montpellier away and Toulon at home during the opening weekends, but two away defeats had seen them lose ground to Clermont, the early pace-setters. Reversing that trend against Grenoble would propel them to third in the standings. 'I can't get my head around it,' Roberts confesses, 'how little teams win away from home. I'm still trying to put my finger on it. Whether it is a mind-set … playing at home is a massive thing. I think the refs have a huge part to play. Any fifty–fiftys go the way of the home team. It's a very French condition. You play away from home and after thirty minutes or halfway into a game and you're down, you can forget winning as [the players] know they've lost the game. In the UK we go for the full eighty. It might not always be reflected on the scoreboard, but it's flat out. Over here, you have to go in at half-time knowing you can win the game, otherwise ... it's interesting in that respect. Hard to understand.' With his French lesson utterly missed, and a brilliant excuse for it, Roberts takes his leave. Before he goes, he asks about 'the Irish scrum half down there' at Grenoble. I inform him Hart may be on the bench, but former Ulster centre Chris Farrell should start. 'Oh, okay, I must keep an eye out for him so,' he replies.

**Thursday 25 September**

The first thing that stands out about Stade Lesdiguières (home to Grenoble) is the stadium's easy access. Two of the main gates are open yet, loyal to my profession, I take the media entrance. There is no obvious reception, so I follow the yap of voices up the main stairs and walk in on two props enjoying their breakfast muesli. I give them a knowing, 'I'm supposed to be here' nod before backing out through the door. Access to the main stand at the 12,000-capacity stadium is gained through the president's box, but the pitch below is empty. The early-morning sun is generating some heat and snow has yet to settle on the imposing Alpine mountains to the east and west. Slowly, from what appears to be a banqueting tent, the Grenoble players emerge.

I receive a nod or '*bonjour*' from each of the passing players before I spot, and flag, James Hart. He asks about my trip to Paris and Ronan O'Gara's start to coaching, and speculates on Sexton's new deal with Leinster. Backs coach and former Munster scrum half Mike Prendergast joins us, and asks if I will be sticking around for the Racing Métro game. 'Big match,' he says, 'but I think we've a real chance.' Prendergast has been in touch with Anthony Foley and Paul O'Connell, and believes a home win over Ospreys is vital to kick-start their season. He believes the loss of Donnacha Ryan will prove more debilitating to the team than that of Keith Earls. Both are key Munster players, but Ryan offers the Munster pack much-needed bulk and a scrapping presence.

We agree to catch up later as Bernard Jackman, Grenoble's head coach, approaches with an extended hand. The banqueting tent, he chides, is the team gym, while the sturdy Portakabin beside it houses his office. Taking in an entire training session, he informs me, is no problem. Each Grenoble training session is open to the public, with an average attendance of forty (a mix of supporters and press). Irish provinces allow the media vision-access windows of ten minutes before cameras are shut off. Top 14 clubs release their training schedule for the week and open the doors. 'It's a social thing for many people,' Jackman explains. 'The age of retirement is lower in France [sixty-two], and the welfare payments are better. A lot of guys will come along to watch the sessions, then go for a coffee.' Easy access means greater media speculation on team selections, although Jackman does like to run the odd diversionary play to keep writers and bloggers honest.

I attempt to nail down my starting fifteen as I take a seat in the shaded stands near the gym. There are two female reporters and a young mother pushes her child back and forth in a pram along the sideline barriers, but the watching crowd are predominantly male. Yellow bibs are swapped around backline players so often that I begin to lose track of my suspected starters. Hart and Chris Farrell rarely feature in the same plays, so I discern that one will start while the other may have to settle for a replacement's role. Farrell and experienced New Zealander Nigel Hunt are paired in midfield for most of the plays. Hunt, a former Sevens player with soft hands, runs hard lines and pops passes for his partner to take on the charge. McLeod, the South African scrum half signed from Sharks, is the most vocal. He often pauses between Prendergast's moves to seek clarification or make a suggestion on angles of attack.

An invite to join the team for lunch is accepted, but I grab a word with Prendergast before sampling Bruno Delatte's fare. Praised by O'Gara for 'taking the hard road' in coaching – Young Munster and his Grenoble apprenticeship – Prendergast believes introducing Irish players to the club has given others an idea of the graft needed to make it as a professional.

'At home, we really appreciate it when you get into a system, academy or professional side, as there are only four teams,' he says. 'In France you have the Top 14 and Pro D2, so that's thirty teams. They know if they are let go from one they can get into another. In Ireland, we work very, very hard to stay within those systems.

'It's good to have guys coming from different backgrounds. Here, we have the French lads, your South Africans, your Australians, New Zealanders. When you bring it all together, it can be a good mix, but it has to be channelled and come from the top. That's what Bernard has brought this year. He is trying to bring in a culture to a club, which can be hard in France as there is a lot of movement in players – twenty-one left after last season and we have fourteen coming in – but we're well on the road to doing that.'

Having split spells at Munster with a season with Bourgoin and Gloucester, Prendergast retired at thirty-two. He became director of rugby at Young Munster, and had a part-time role with Munster A before Jackman placed a good word in Fabrice Landreau's ear. He came on board in 2013 as skills coach and, when Landreau was promoted upstairs, took on the backs brief in the shake-up. His daughter, Emma, was two during his playing stint in France. Now aged nine, she goes to the same school as Jackman's children, and is making a better fist of French, Prendergast jokes, than her father. To help reacquaint himself with French rugby, Prendergast signed up for Fédérale 1 (French third division) side Chambéry. 'The league is semi-professional with a lot of full pros in it, too,' he says. 'It would be like the All-Ireland League, going back about ten or twelve years. They had a few injuries at halfback, so asked Fabrice. He told me it would be good experience – very much a French club, so it was good in picking up the language. I did it for three or four months, but it was great. Met a couple of hard nuts down there, I can tell ya.'

Chef Bruno serves up wondrous spaghetti bolognese, and Prendergast talks about the team's pre-season tour to Argentina. The lunch room is filled with French, spoken in Australian, South African and Fijian accents. I skip dessert to grab a few words with Ireland Under-20 prop Denis Coulson, who is two months into a developmental contract and training with the senior team. 'Bernard said it to me [about signing for Grenoble] because I knew I wasn't going to get a spot in the Leinster Academy,' says Coulson. 'There is a hell of a line of loose-heads there. That was last September, but we were in touch all year … It eventually came about as he was watching me in a couple of games in the Junior World Cup and offered me a spot.'

A member of the all-conquering St Michael's College Leinster Schools Senior Cup team, Coulson travelled to the Junior World Championship in New Zealand with his future undecided. He helped Mike Ruddock's Irish side get to the semi-final – their best finish since Brian O'Driscoll's Under-19 generation – before Jackman intervened and steered him to the south of France. He had coached the prop at St Michael's before his Top 14 ascension. Coulson says, 'The final number of us that graduated into professional teams, from that St Michael's squad of twenty-three, is eight: Ross Moloney, Nick McCarthy, Ross Byrne, Cian Kelleher, Dan Leavy, Rory O'Loughlin and Rory Kavanagh, who played Pro D2 with Auch last season. That was a special group.'

Playing primarily with the *Espoirs* (academy side), Coulson hopes to break into the senior team in the coming months. Opportunity is likely to arise in the Amlin Challenge Cup, a competition Prendergast says Grenoble see as secondary in terms of importance and a proving ground for younger members of the squad. He will cheer the seniors on at Stade des Alpes on Saturday, but will be early to bed that night. 'The next day we have six hours on the bus to Perpignan for an *Espoirs* game,' he says. 'Play that and get back on the bus for another six hours.' It is certainly one way to see the country.

Chris Farrell spirits away from his scheduled French class to sit down for a talk about his first few months in the Isère region. He sits for our twenty-minute back and forth with an ice-pack held against his chest. It is hard to believe the Fivemiletown native is still only twenty-one years old. His name has been in the ether for the past three years – a towering, talented centre destined for international honours. He played in the same Ireland Under-20 team as J. J. Hanrahan and Ulster teammates Paddy Jackson and Iain Henderson before injuries ram-raided his progress. In the past two seasons he missed nine- and four-month blocks due to an anterior cruciate ligament tear and a metatarsal break. His departure from Ravenhill had taken many by surprise in the off-season. 'I'm definitely not happy with what I achieved in Ireland, especially considering where I was at eighteen and nineteen,' he concedes. He feels Stuart Olding 'leapfrogged' him into the Ulster midfield during his time on the sidelines.

'I said to my agent, "I feel like a change of environment,"' he adds. 'I was in with Ulster but was a bit miserable, as I was in with the rehab squad for a year and a half. It gets a bit monotonous, and I wasn't sure where I'd be in the pecking order coming back in. Humph [David Humphreys] tried to convince me to stay and not to make a move to France, but I went with it.' Munster, Connacht and several English Premiership clubs made enquiries, but Farrell was sold on Grenoble after chatting to Jackman.

Grenoble are playing all of their league games at the 20,500-seater Stade des Alpes this season, and Farrell recalls his first outing at the stadium. It was as a nineteen-year-old against the French Under-20s in February 2012. Ireland won 13–12, thanks to a late Hanrahan penalty, but England clinched that season's Six Nations. Farrell has known since Tuesday that he will be starting against Racing. The Parisians will find that out the next day, at midday. 'If you'd have had told me a couple of years ago I'd be playing in France, in the Top 14, at the age of twenty-one, I'd have dismissed it,' says Farrell. 'It is a different direction from where I believed my career would have gone, but I'm looking at it as a positive. My focus is all about this season, and hoping it goes well. I have no idea at this stage whether I want to go back to Ireland, stay in France or go elsewhere …

There is interest already from a couple of places, but I'm trying to keep my head down and play rugby. All I need is that injury-free run. I haven't had that the past two years, so it is all I'm looking for.'

Farrell drops me off at the offices of Andrew Farley, former Grenoble captain and now team manager. The affable Australian played six seasons with Connacht before finishing out his playing career in the south of France. Officially a day older than me, his career trajectory is headier. Deadpan, Farley lists out the highlights of his time in Galway: 'The races, the art festival, living with Bernard.' Aged thirty-four, Farley's coordinating role – providing a bridge between Grenoble's business and sporting departments – keeps his mind off thoughts of a dramatic return to rugby action. 'I haven't found that I want to get playing again, but it is probably because I'm at the desk here from 7 a.m. until 7 p.m. each day.'

Having arrived at Swansea in 2002 with the intention of giving rugby in Europe a proper go, Farley has been the Aussie abroad ever since. He helped Connacht crawl off the canvas in 2003 – soon after it had been put there by the IRFU – and says Grenoble has delivered everything he was promised back in 2009: 'It was a very ambitious project. I had some dinner with [president] Marc Chérèque and Fabrice, and they said, "Okay, we're going to stay in Pro D2 for two or three years and build a team, not just to win that league, but to stay up in the Top 14." And, what happens? First year we come fifth, then we come second and miss out [on promotion] by a point, then we won in the third year. We stayed up and then stayed up again, and have built the new training facilities. They were the best years of my career. Everything has come to fruition.'

My final interview of the day is with Jackman, in a sparse meeting room. Farley and Prendergast have been pragmatic about the club's collapse last season from fourth to eleventh. Injuries, a stretched squad and a tough fixture list are cited as reasons the club went from challenging for European Cup places to staving off relegation on the last day of the season. Jackman cuts to the core of the matter and gives a refreshing take on openness within a ruthless profession: 'We had a group of guys that got us out of Pro D2 and kept us up in the first year, which is the goal of every team that goes up, but our squad is ageing. The club would be ambitious about becoming a top-six side. So we had to make a choice – stick with that group and always be a club that were hovering up or down, or change the group and staff. That decision was made, that in order to be a top-six club we basically had to start a new cycle.

'The guys we let go – sixteen players – were really good servants for us and good guys. We felt it was better ... you can drag people along, but it's not fair. We could have dragged them along until April and said, "Listen we're not sure, blah, blah, blah, we're looking at our options," and then tell them to find a new club. By January we had the majority of our points and we all thought we were safe. We then felt it would be better to tell those guys early and let them find a club. We did that, but from there on we had half a squad that would only be there the next season. We then got injuries, lost games and it was hard to regain momentum.

'We were winning games just off passion. A little bit of organisation, but mainly desire and the old-school thing of dragging teams down to our level. When you have that and don't have good systems in place, if you are not unbelievably motivated you are not going to have a chance ... It's very hard to play twenty-six games of the year with just madness.

'Once you get rid of sixteen guys out of your group,' he adds, 'and they're thinking about their next project, it's very hard for them to go out and die for the jersey.'

Jackman has been coaching since he first took a training session at Tullow RFC as a twenty-three-year-old. The former Connacht and Leinster hooker kept his coaching eye in throughout his playing career, with roles at Newbridge and Coolmine. Upon retiring, he oversaw the Clontarf Under-20s and St Michael's College, leading them to Schools Cup success in 2012. Finding opportunities limited in Ireland, he looked abroad. 'Grenoble had just lost a Pro D2 [promotion] semi-final against

Bordeaux-Bègles,' he says. 'It was second plays fifth, so a massive shock. The club had been thinking they were going up, but they now had to work with a smaller revenue – TV money, crowds, merchandise. There wasn't an awful lot of money around, but Fabrice thought we needed to change things up and improve. Their attack had been good, but defence had been poor. I said to Farls [Andrew Farley], "Get me in front of him." He convinced him and over a couple of Skype interviews I convinced him I was worth a punt.'

Jackman worked with Grenoble during the 2011/12 pre-season, and provided video clips and analysis from Ireland. The modest pay arrangement, added to money earned coaching schools, Under-20 and college rugby (Dublin City University), made for a good living. By the beginning of 2012, he knew Grenoble would be going up. They won the league at a canter, and Jackman upped sticks to become their full-time defence coach. He served two years under Landreau before being appointed head coach. The road has rarely been straight for the Carlow man, let alone easy. He toured with Ireland to South Africa in 1998, yet won his first cap, against Japan, in 2005. He was twice approached to play for Leinster – his home province – but IRFU rulings and Eddie O'Sullivan's wishes intervened. When he eventually got there, he helped Leinster win a league title and European Cup.

'I've always had to prove myself,' he says. 'It means I can empathise with players going through a bad patch. I appreciate that I always wanted to be a coach. Now, I get to do that as a professional and with a club in the most competitive league in the world, with some of its best players and a chance to advance my role here each year.

'I'm massively proud of being the only Irish head coach in the Top 14. Yeah ... I think it's cool. I'm goal focused. I like to tick off boxes. I like to be sought after, achieving things that others aren't achieving. I'm competitive ... Being here in itself is an achievement, but now I want to be a successful Irish coach.'

## Friday 26 September

'Imagine you worked for a newspaper, and in January you were told, "In the summer you're gone." Your boss then tells you to write your best ever articles over the next six months. What would you think?'

James Hart sums up the predicament of being honest with a squad of players when it comes to renewing contracts. The Captain's Run at Stade des Alpes is over and Hart is out of the changing rooms. He has put in an extra hour of kicking and passing drills with skills coach Philippe Doussy. As I watched him I asked Bernard Jackman if he would be starting. Charl McLeod was in at scrum half but Hart 'would get his chance'. The head coach clutched a Dunnes Stores carrier bag as he spoke with me. A Connacht rugby supporter had made one of his regular trips over to cheer Jackman on at his new club. He had arrived at the ground – for another open session – bearing gifts: Butler's chocolates and handcrafted bog oak, the latter courtesy of Connacht prop Ronan Loughney.

Denis Coulson had sought me out and provided good company as the session drew to a close. We had looked on as local journalist Yves Feltrin interviewed Chris Farrell with the aid of a translator. The Ulster man had made an impression in his opening games in the northern hemisphere's toughest league. A sizeable media contingent had coalesced in the away dugout during the Captain's Run, cherry-picking the in-form players and those possessing the greatest sound-bites. An hour on, Hart spoke, in the same dugout, about an uncertain future: 'You can see how much things change. You go from being the guy who is starting the whole time and everyone wanting to talk to you, to suddenly being back to – I wouldn't say square one – but times are tougher and you're not the guy … You know who your real friends are. Your family is always there, and that's important. It just goes to show you that once you finish your playing days you're no longer the main man. It's like that now with Charl. He's playing well and there's no complaints. I can't complain about anyone if he is playing well and doing the business on the pitch.'

## Saturday 27 September

Six hours before kick-off in Grenoble, Johnny Sexton returns my call. He is out for a Saturday afternoon drive with wife Laura and newborn son Luca for company. A fractured jaw – picked up after a late hit from Toulon hooker Craig Burden – wiped out his September involvement at Racing. The injury did not prevent a three-night stay in Maynooth for Ireland's autumn camp. The out-half's return target is the Parisian derby with Stade Français.

'[The injury] was not ideal timing. I might play six games for Racing, but I'll be a hell of a lot fresher than last year. Then, I had played fourteen matches going into the November internationals,' he says. 'The jaw is still sore. I went a few weeks of no food – no chewing. I was on liquid food while it healed up. There was no operation required, so I was lucky. I had the operation done before, and it was not too comfy, to be honest. I broke the jaw in the quarter-final of the Heineken Cup in 2010. I got a shoulder charge from [a diving] Morgan Parra while I was lying on the ground. I didn't know it was broken at the time. It was different this time. I knew the feeling and thought I had broken a few teeth.

'I rested for two weeks, had another couple of weeks light training, and I'm going hard at it from Monday for another two weeks. I'm fifty–fifty for the Stade game, but, hopefully, I'll make that. It is one of the biggest fixtures of the season for Racing, and I don't want to be rusty going into the Champions Cup.'

The Irish media had zeroed in on a greater comeback story. Eighteen months after his shock move from Leinster to Racing Métro was announced, Sexton had signed a four-season deal to represent his home province from 2015/16 onward. In an email sent around by the IRFU, in September 2014, canned comments from player and union spoke of soldered harmony. Rapid bridge-building had taken place since May 2013, when Sexton had told me he felt significantly undervalued by the IRFU. 'They, obviously, have a different plan to Leinster and myself,' he had said. 'They didn't rate me as highly as I rated myself, maybe.'

Two months into his second, and final, season in France, Sexton is pleased to have his playing future mapped out until November 2019. 'Players want security,' he says. 'I have been given that now with a long-term contract. I have a big nine months left here [at Racing], and I want to make the most of it.'

Although Ireland teammates Sean O'Brien and Jamie Heaslip, took their contract negotiations down to the wire, both had recommitted to Leinster, and the Top 14 exodus had yet to materialise. 'A lot of guys would've asked what France was like,' says Sexton. 'I let them know, but the experience is different for every single person that does it. It's hard as I can't give them a full picture. I'm only here fourteen months. It could be totally different for the next guy. It is a step into the unknown. Saying that, I'm sure more Irish guys will make the move in the future.'

There is no getting around the fact that Racing's contribution to the final Heineken Cup tournament was squibbish. They started the 2013/14 season winning ugly and were plain ugly during winter, but ended the regular season in winning form as Sexton's growing influence in plays began to tell. Reams of reports in Ireland told a different story – of a man ill at ease with Parisian life and desperate to secure a one-way ticket home. 'I found the reports strange,' he admits. 'I try to judge my performances on what the coaches and players here think. The coaches must have been happy if they offered me a four-year contract. I don't pay too much attention to the media, but it was frustrating at the time. I would give an interview that was generally positive, but if I was honest about settling in, the reports were that I was not happy. There was always a negative spin. People have different agendas, but I didn't really have a big problem with those stories.

'We were ninth or tenth at one stage. There were a few games where, if we lost, we could have been drawn into a relegation battle. The Top 14 is that tight. As it turned out, we finished top five, but I think we should have got a home quarter-final. We went down to Toulouse and won there, but obviously that took a lot out of us. You're playing against the crowd, who have a massive influence over here. Away teams don't get the rub of the green from the ref. We played our best match of the season in that quarter-final, but came up against the best side in France [Toulon] in the semis. We deserved to get that far, but we were too inconsistent to be considered champions material. We're on a better track already this season, getting better results and scoring more tries.'

Racing were on their upward tilt, in March 2014, when the first reports came of a Sexton boomerang to Leinster. Peter O'Reilly stated, in *The Sunday Times*, that the province wanted the out-half back in time for the following season. As it played out, Sexton remained true to his two-year deal, but talks of a 2015 return began soon after he landed in Ireland following the summer tour to Argentina. The four-year contract Sexton eventually inked will pay him approximately €500,000 a year, while – as an established senior player – he has secured additional sponsorship and ambassadorial agreements that should augment his yearly salary by a further €150,000.

I put those figures to Sexton as he drives his family away from the congested innards of the French capital. 'I'm not doing any press. I've done nothing. Everything I say seems to get into the press, so I'm trying to keep the head down. There has been a lot of speculation that is wide of the mark. People are thinking that I was playing a game. I have made my decision though, but there has been nothing said, from my point of view, on the deal.'

A large focus of the speculation centred on whether Denis O'Brien had supplemented Sexton's wages in return for a close working relationship between the player and the media mogul's Communicorp operation. This was fuelled, no doubt, by an interview Sexton gave to O'Brien's Newstalk radio station after the IRFU contract was confirmed. 'I don't know anything about that, to be honest,' declares Sexton. 'I have given away a lot to come home. The deal was structured to make it attractive to me. I don't know where the speculation on extra deals has come from. Leinster has helped me to secure sponsorships, that's my business. The playing contract is with the IRFU and is not funded, as far as I know, by private people.' Ronan O'Gara has worked closely with Sexton ever since, in 2011, they put their Munster–Leinster differences to one side. Sitting in the Racing reception area in Paris, O'Gara had appeared crestfallen when contemplating the Dubliner's move back to Leinster. 'When you consider in the first season where we came from, he did well. Some people wanted him to fail … but it is very easy to give an opinion on something when you don't have a clue and when you're on the other side of Europe. It's the same as anything, knowledge is power and to have a valuable opinion you need to spend time somewhere.

'He's a good player, like, and there aren't many tens around in the world. That's the reality of it. The standard of tens, I think, is not very strong at the minute. If you're looking to [recruit], Matt Giteau is under contract, you have Owen Farrell for England, Dan Biggar or Rhys Priestland for Wales, Scotland, I don't know. Three really good New Zealanders, but two of them [Aaron Cruden and Beauden Barrett] are young, and Dan Carter would cost an arm and a leg. When you think about it, that's why we would've wanted him. Johnny would only have got better here, the more time he spent here. The more he got to speak French, it would get easier and easier for him. But I have to agree with him – if you get a good offer to play for Munster or Leinster and Ireland, it is an opportunity you shouldn't pass up.'

Sexton reflects, 'If you told me a few years ago that I'd move to Paris and that we'd have our first child there, I'd have laughed. It's nice, just me, Laura and Luca. In other ways, it is challenging. It's nice to have close family around and, in fairness, they are good for coming over. There are arguments about who is coming over on what weekend as we only have the one spare bedroom. It's tough, too. I was away in [pre-season] camp when he was born. Laura has been great with him. She does about ninety per cent of the work and I cover the rest. All we seemed to do for the first three months was change nappies, but he has grown up so quickly. He's starting to give a little back now.'

### *Le match*, 27 September 2014

Ronan O'Gara is perpetual motion. The man never stands still for a moment. Sitting is out of the question. He occasionally rests his weight on one knee before sprinting off to chase down an errant kick or offer up some advice. Armed with a complimentary *jambon-beurre* and water, I take a seat in the media tribune well in advance of kick-off. I'm joined for the match by a friend from home, Ken Darley. All the work has been done midweek, so coaches Bernard Jackman and Mike Prendergast save their breath until it is needed. O'Gara, at the far end of the pitch, is a blur. He primarily works with Jonathan Goosen, who has the kicking duties for the evening, but Benjamin Dambielle and Marc Andreu are nodding beneficiaries.

Grenoble start the match poorly and fall 3–0 behind, before a sketchy Racing line-out, flung to no one in particular at the tail, provides the opening they need. A rapid, jerked pass from Charl McLeod, and Henry Vanderglas is barrelling towards the line. He is held up, but Grenoble climb into the resulting scrum, occupying the entire pack long enough for McLeod to make a snipe for the line. By the time the light-blue-and white jerseys reach him it is too late. Jonathan Wisniewski converts the try to make it 7–3, before missing a penalty to stretch the advantage forward. Down on the sidelines, moments after he is scolded by the fourth official for barracking his players, O'Gara checks an alert on his phone before resuming with his bellowed instructions.

Stoked up, Grenoble's backline land big hits on Dambielle and Jamie Roberts before showing their worth with ball in hand. McLeod feeds his halfback partner after a solid home scrum. Wisniewski, in turn, finds James Hunt, who takes two giant strides towards the Racing twenty-two before popping up a pass for Chris Farrell. Roberts has been drawn forward, eager for the defensive hit, and not trusting his midfield partner Henry Chavancy to make it without him. The outside centre arrives at pace, angling his run in, towards Roberts, before stepping off a strong right foot and making for the corner. He evades a despairing swat from Mike Phillips and tosses the ball into the night sky after dotting down.

A mental lapse by Andreu – kicking the ball away to prevent a quick line-out – costs Racing another three points. The visitors hit back with a spell of sustained pressure, but leave the Grenoble twenty-two with nothing after Dan Lydiate is pulverised for his ball-carrying temerity. The cavalry go off their feet and Wisniewski punts clear. Grenoble's Fijian winger Alipate Ratini is denied a try as the half winds down. Roberts fails to make it forty minutes as he limps off, to be replaced by Benjamin Lapeyre. His exit goes unnoticed and unremarked upon by the majority of the 15,500 crowd. Goosen knocks over a penalty on the stroke of half-time, but Racing trail 17–6.

Wisniewski drops one over from thirty metres out to increase Grenoble's lead and Goosen is sent to the sin-bin, but Dambielle lands two penalties of his own to make it 20–12. On another evening, Ratini would have four tries and a king's chair off the pitch. On 27 September 2014, he has yet another close call shot down as his left boot is in touch. With twenty-five minutes to go, Goosen is back in play and popping over a penalty to make it 20–15. Minutes fifty-eight and fifty-nine contain pure, chaotic, joyful broken-play rugby as both sides take wild swings at each other. O'Gara and Laurent Travers (one of Racing's two head coaches) are beside themselves with gesticulations and admonishments. Julien Caminati and Wisniewski's line breaks sweep Grenoble to within yards of the Racing line. The forwards take up the running, and we have another video-referee decision. It goes in Racing's favour.

O'Gara goes from studying Racing's successful defensive scrum to jogging back to his sideline spot. He arrives in time to dry the ball for his hooker, Jérémie Maurouard, ahead of a line-out. Racing win the throw, but are soon reeling as they lose possession. Grenoble's replacement hooker Anthony Hegarty busts the defensive line, Wisniewski's cut-out pass finds Rory Grice on the run up the right wing, and he dishes to Ratini. He outpaces lock Juandre Kruger and bounces his way over. Inevitably – it is Ratini after all – there are countless video replays, but the score is given. Wisniewski embellishes a fine personal contribution with a sweetly struck touchline conversion for 27–15.

The starting Grenoble front row are on the bench for the closing stages and unable to prevent Racing from munching through scrum penalties. Goosen makes it 27–18 after sixty-eight minutes, rather than kick for the corner and chase a try. It becomes clear that the visitors are targeting a losing bonus point rather than a comeback win. A winning bonus point is achieved in Top 14 rugby by scoring three or more tries more than your opponent. By preventing this, losing teams can leave with a point to their name.

Rather than press for the try that will kill the game, Grenoble drift back and invite trouble. It is not helping that their scrum is getting shaken back and forth like a canine chew toy. Racing thunder forward, phase after phase, but their bonus point hopes look dashed as Adrien Planté spills a pass with the tryline gaping.

Grenoble are faced with a defensive scrum with two minutes to play. It's not the match-winning introduction Hart was hoping for, but he replaces McLeod with defensive work to do. He can only urge his pack on as they cave to Racing's late heaves. Scrum half Xavier Chauveau, on for Phillips, gets the put-in, and the Grenoble pack can no longer hold the tide. Hart flings himself at Antonie Claassens' ankles as the South African picks and dives. Racing get their point, and the final whistle is consumed by a chorus of boos. Grenoble flanker Fabien Alexandre storms off towards the dressing room. '[Alexandre] was gutted,' Jackman reveals post game, 'but that's a really good sign for me. Last year the place would have been hysterical and a fanfare atmosphere.'

Whether he gives interviews in French or English, Jackman is restless despite his team's climbing to fourth. 'I'm not happy because we're better than that,' he says. 'It's great to win. Racing are a very good side and people in Ireland may think it's a surprise, but we're very ambitious. We prepared well, had a good game plan and I felt we were the only ones who really were attacking. Once we got the third try we switched off and started to play conservatively ... We let them back into the game. The players are there, the game plan is there. The next thing is creating that culture and being ruthless.' It is the first time this season that Grenoble had allowed a team a bonus point (either attacking or defensive) and the head coach was rueful: 'If we want to think top six, they're a team that are going to be up there. We missed an opportunity to get five points while they got one. I am annoyed ... Listen, I knew with ten minutes to go that we were going to win the match. I'd much prefer if we were looking for the fifth try, sixth try, seventh – showing our fans how we want to play – rather than hanging on until the end.'

Farrell ambles into the press room and leans back against a heavily sponsored wall. I wait for the local journalists to get his take on the match – and his second try of the season – before descending on him like an old friend. Is that what all those Nigel Hunt pop passes in training were all about? 'We recognised that their defence was soft; they were drifting,' he explains, 'ten, twelve and thirteen were very tight together and drifting out,' he says. 'It was just up to me to find the gap. It was Nigel's pass that created enough space, and then I was carrying enough momentum to get to the tryline.'

'A great try,' Jackman enthuses. 'We analysed Jamie Roberts during the week. We created a move to try and interest him to jump out of the line. Everything worked perfectly.'

Where it fell to Hart in 2013/14, the Ireland call-up mantle had been passed to Farrell. Yes, he answered, Joe Schmidt had been in touch to say he was being monitored, and Grenoble had been emailed to say an invite to Ireland training camps may be on the horizon. Farrell hovers a pro-tective arm over a chest that needed mesotherapy and anti-inflammatory injections before kick-off. He says, 'It may be nothing, but it's good that Joe was in touch. I haven't thought anything about it. It was just a catch up and, for me, that's way out of my sights at the minute. I just want to keep playing well here. There's no point changing things if you're doing that.'

## Sunday 28 September

Waiting for a train to take me to Lyon Airport, I pick up a couple of newspapers to read their take on the match. *Le Dauphiné Libéré* has a section of titbits and interesting facts from game night in Grenoble. One headline catches my eye – *Deux journalistes Irlandais au Stade des Alpes* (Two Irish journalists at Stade des Alpes). It is reported that my colleague and I were in France to cast our journalistic eyes over Chris Farrell.

Not far off.

# 20

## THE SPECIALISTS: IRELAND'S FOREIGN LEGION

While hosts of Irish players head abroad to pursue their rugby careers, the provinces continue to augment their squads with foreign talents. Munster were the first to reap rewards through the shrewd recruitment of John Langford, Jim Williams and Trevor Halstead. Though they played a combined eleven months in Ireland, Rocky Elsom and Brad Thorn seared their way into Leinster legend. Felipe Contepomi's four seasons at the RDS are lauded by the Leinster faithful. Ulster has been a revolving door for South African talent since B. J. Botha's arrival in 2008. Springbok scrum half Ruan Pienaar and New Zealander Jared Payne have been vital in Ulster's ascent in European rugby. Connacht benefited greatly from Dan Parks' two seasons at The Sportsground, and, in the summer of 2014, made transfer coups by attracting Super Rugby talent Bundee Aki and All Blacks Test centurion Mils Muliaina.

The IRFU moved to stem the flow of Non-Irish-Qualified (NIQ) players in December 2011, when they introduced new guidelines. Holding court in a West Stand suite at the Aviva Stadium, Philip Browne and Eddie Wigglesworth presented a document entitled 'National Player Succession Strategy'. From the beginning of the 2013/14 season, the three provinces of Munster, Leinster and Ulster could field only one NIQ player in each of the fifteen field positions. Connacht, still looked upon as a special project, were exempt. The IRFU duo also announced that the expired contracts of NIQs would not be renewed.

Writing in the *Irish Independent*, Ruaidhri O'Connor explained the strategy would have ramifications around Ravenhill, Thomond Park and the RDS in the coming years. He added, 'You won't have felt anything, but the foundations beneath Irish rugby shifted yesterday.' The union held firm in their contract stance, with notable casualties including Wian du Preez, Isa Nacewa and Doug Howlett – the latter two opting for retirement when their provinces were denied the chance to offer extensions. Ulster found the IRFU in a good mood in October 2013, however, as they were given permission to sign Pienaar to a three-year extension.

The exception to the foreign-import rule was the 'special project player'. The IRFU officially introduced the system in 2012, and Richardt Strauss – signed by Leinster in 2009 – was the first to take advantage. The system allowed provinces to sign players who had not received a Test cap for their country and could represent Ireland after three years in residence. The early signings – Steven Sykes, Peter Borlase, Clint Newland – did not work out, but shrewd moves have led to international breakthroughs. Strauss became the first special-project player to earn an Ireland cap in November 2012, and, fittingly, the opposition were his native South Africa. 'When I left there I made a commitment to play, and that I'm an Irish rugby player,' he commented. 'If the public want to go on about me being a South African, back in South Africa, that's up to them. I don't see myself as a South African rugby player at all. There's no ill feelings there, it's just that I see myself as an Irish rugby player.'

Connacht's Rodney Ah You and Nathan White have both trained with Ireland, while Strauss' fellow South Africans Rob Herring and Robbie Diack earned Test debuts in June 2014. Diack commented, 'I always wanted to represent Ireland, as soon as I came to Ulster in 2008. To get that cap was a huge honour for me and I really enjoyed the opportunity. It has given me the hunger and motivation to get more caps, and to be involved in that set-up with Joe [Schmidt] and his coaching staff. It's incredible and the squad is fantastic … My goal and motivation is to get back there.'

Centre is a position that Ireland have targeted for replacements –

be they Irish or project players – since before the 2011 World Cup. In November 2012 Connacht's Danie Poolman gave an insight into Ireland's progression planning. He said, 'I have my sights set at playing for Ireland in three years when I qualify [in August 2015]. I was looking into getting a move overseas to gain more experience. I talked to a few people about it, and I heard Ireland were looking for a centre. I am financially secure now for three years while I chase my goal, but it was a difficult decision to leave South Africa.'

Payne's first season at Ulster was virtually wiped out by an Achilles injury, but he returned, in September 2013, to excel at fullback. He became eligible to play for Ireland a further year down the road, and provided line breaks, deft passing and an innate ability to locate space when moved to outside centre. Speaking to the *Irish Examiner* ahead of his November 2014 debut against South Africa, Payne said, 'People are entitled to their opinion. They can say what they want. I've been over here for three years now. I'm pretty passionate about it, seeing the environment Ireland have created over the last three years.'

Payne, Diack and Strauss offer the national side primed, battle-hardened qualities, but provincial acquisitions in 2013 and 2014 hinted at a new direction in the IRFU's special project. Munster signed up twenty-four-year-old back Tyler Bleyendaal from the Crusaders. Connacht followed up the capture of Kiwi flanker Jake Heenan (twenty-one upon arrival in Galway, in 2013) with the marquee signing of Chiefs' twenty-four-year-old centre Bundee Aki.

\*\*\*

I am greeted by Heenan in the reception of the Connacht Hotel in Galway. Summer 2014 has stretched into September, and it is tee-shirt weather in the west of Ireland. The open-side flanker had featured in a weekend win over Newport Gwent Dragons, but left early due to a shoulder-injury flare. We had met for the first time at the announcement of Connacht's renewed partnership with sponsors Mazda. Interviews completed, writers, players and sponsors had been ferried over to Moran's Oyster Cottage for lunchtime seafood. Heenan had ordered the 'biggest, ugliest' lobster, and told me about his upbringing in Pataua North, situated in the bottleneck of New Zealand's North Island. I had just finished Donald McRae's *Winter Colours* and wanted to talk Josh Kronfeld and Michael Jones. 'I was probably still in the front row when they were playing – a bit early for all that,' Heenan remarked.

One week on, the flanker remembers the lobster fondly. I am keen to find out, however, about Heenan, the teenage prop. 'I grew up playing rugby,' he says. 'Started as a prop, moved to lock around twelve, thirteen and did a bit of back row. I finished in school early; I was a bit young for my year. I was at a bit of a crossroads and didn't really know what I wanted to do, so thought I would give rugby a crack. I went back to school again to play schoolboy rugby … I probably could have topped up on a bit of education as well. I went to one of the Blues secondary schools, which was quite different for a fella like myself. That is where I met Pat Lam. That's where I became a No. 7. They asked me to play there, and it was fortunate in a way as it fit like a glove.'

Schools from across the Blues region – which includes Auckland, North Harbour and Northland – nominate players to take part in trials for an Under-18 representative team. Once on the team, players take part in a national competition over a week-long period. Heenan recalls his opening half of the first trial game as terrible, but he improved after the break and his side won. He was selected for the New Zealand Schools side, and had a 'huge game against the Aussies'. Soon after, he was contracted by Auckland.

The year 2011 was Heenan's first with the academy in Auckland, and, fortunately enough, he was at the epicentre of New Zealand's World Cup ballyhoo. 'They had a house for the academy guys – the boys from out of town – which was literally across the road from Eden Park,' he explains. 'I've hit three golf balls onto Eden Park from my back yard, with a pitching wedge as well. That's how close we were. The World Cup was unreal. We would have been given close to $2,000-worth of tickets just because we lived there. People show up with too many tickets. Give them a beer when they come in your gate, and there you go: a spare ticket. Picked up a ticket to New Zealand versus France, the first one [group stage], for fifty bucks. Was given a ticket for the semi-final. Outstanding.

'We converted our basement into a bar, so we ran a line through the wall and trickled some beers out for folks coming in off the street. It was actually neat. We had a few, what we'd call famous New Zealanders – they're not really famous at all – would come in; we'd have a beer with them. [Comedian] Leigh Hart was one of the guys.'

He adds, 'That semi against Australia, that was the game where Australia played well, but the All Blacks were, well, another class. It was almost like that last Bledisloe we saw [late August 2014], Australia weren't that bad, but the All Blacks were on. The thing that stands out about that game is that they don't play flashy rugby. They do the basics extremely well. The only thing that sets the All Blacks apart from the rest of the world when they're like that, when they're hot, is they do the basics extremely well. It is very similar to what Joe Schmidt is doing with Ireland.'

Heenan played under former Auckland out-half Ant Strachan at the academy, and had two seasons with the club's Under-20s. Teammates included current All Blacks Malakai Fekitoa, Charles Piutau and Steven Luatua. Patrick Tuipulotu was the year below him. 'In my third season I played with the New Zealand Under-20s and thought I was fairly unlucky not to get a run with the ITM Cup side. That was possibly, probably part of the reason for me coming here. It wasn't looking in my favour … I didn't feel like the guys ahead were better than me. To me, at Auckland, the coaches would hum and haw for over a year. That year, when I came back from the [national] 20s, there was a guy who I had played against a few times and had been quite comfortably better than. He ended up playing [for the seniors], so that was a bit disheartening.

'With my home province, Northland, their coach said he wanted to offer me a contract, but I never heard from him again. Coaches saying, "Yeah, perhaps," and offering club rugby, which is a bit of a gamble.'

Ultimately, a phone call from Lam convinced him to take a cross-continental gamble. Heenan had played with Lam's son at Auckland, and had often profited from Lam's technical and personal interest. 'Coming here wasn't a business decision for me; it's hugely personal,' he says. 'It's my whole life coming here, not just my rugby. That was big, that he made it personal, said he wanted me, and he was a coach that was willing to back me. That was very important for me at that point in my career.

'That was a great sensation. A coach wanted me to play full-time rugby, and to make some real money for the first time in my life. It was exciting. The next sensation was the one of leaving my family and thinking, "Shit, this is actually happening." Then, I got here, and it was about adjusting. It was back to the small picture and, "Right, what am I going to do tomorrow to achieve my goal?" – that goal is, first, being the best No. 7 in Connacht and, then, the best No. 7 in the world. You get thrown into day-to-day life, and I haven't really missed home at all yet.'

Heenan got his chance early on in Connacht's season as open-side Willie Faloon succumbed to a foot injury. He played eighteen games for Lam's side and was immense in league tussles against Ulster and Leinster, while playing a pivotal role in the province's shock away win over Toulouse in the Heineken Cup. Within three months of his debut, Heenan was being quizzed on representing Ireland in 2016, if and when he became eligible.

'I didn't come here to sit on the bench,' he says. 'I've never played a game of rugby to make up the numbers or to play a solid game. I always try to play an excellent game, try to influence the game. Again, I was lucky enough that Pat gave me the opportunity and feel that I put in enough work during the week to go out and influence games like that. So I was hugely thrilled to have an impact and do what I can for the team. My leadership within the team and trying to guide the team towards victories would be my most important thing this year.'

He continues, 'Last year I didn't feel I was in a huge leadership position. I was very much head down and worrying about my own game. Because of that, the performances didn't really worry me as long as I was on top of my stuff. The thing that hit home to me is just that word "professionalism". For some games last year, I wasn't really mentally excited and pumped up. That's the nature of rugby, though. You can do that for a few weeks; then it gets on top and you can get quite tired. You can't help it. But, for me, even if I wasn't fizzing – like last weekend [against Dragons] – I can still show up, do my job, do it effectively and play a good game of rugby.

'That's what is important in a competition that is as long as this one. You need fifteen players to play a good game of rugby, and you need three or four of them to play outstanding. Obviously, you won't have every guy playing outstanding each week, but you need guys that will play solid rugby and who'll step it up now and then. You can't have guys just fall off the radar. That has probably cost us. Some guys will show up or they won't show up for a game of rugby. It's hard work when you have thirteen-and-a-half players on the field.'

I tell the New Zealander a Malcolm O'Kelly tale about heading west to play Connacht. O'Kelly had said, 'I found myself in the toilets in Athlone. I remember we stopped off in a hotel, being in a toilet and literally having my head in hands, trying to find focus. Getting myself up and there was literally the pane of glass of the hotel being pulled off the wall by the wind and the rain. I understand the dread before those kind of games. It evaporates very quickly once you get out there. Once you get into the game you love it for the reasons why you started playing in the first place – the test, thrill and combat of it all. Sometimes those local games can be the best ones.'

Heenan nods in agreement as I relate O'Kelly's words. 'Something my dad told me, and I keep quite close to me,' he says, 'is that it doesn't matter what happened during the week or the morning of a game – from the time you step on that field, you have to show up. A hundred per cent. We all have those days. It's just about how you react and how you perform, even if you're not right up. There's stuff like finding the game early, that bit of contact, getting your hands on the ball. Find something in that first five minutes of the game to get yourself into it.'

Heenan's stated goal is one day to emulate the career of New Zealand captain Richie McCaw. The Cantabrian has been the standard bearer for loose forwards the world over since making his Test debut against Ireland in 2001. As soon as a fifteen-year-old Heenan settled on open-side as his position, he pored over footage of McCaw. 'The first thing that stood out about McCaw, for me,' he says, 'was watching a game where he secured two, maybe three, turnovers against Australia. A good day at the office. "How does he do that?" I thought, so I watched the game back. He would have flown into about thirty rucks. Looking at that I saw it was a low percentage play, but he was having a crack. It was something I wasn't doing at the time.

'The second thing was the lines he would run defensively. They'd be going wide, and he'd almost track backwards, see what was up and then come back in. You could say it was unnecessary work, but the way he would see it is if they did break through he'd be there. He's running lines that people don't see, and that is just in case. I read his book, which is actually very good and in depth for a No. 7. He talks about what he does and the four things he worries about on the field – carrying, tackling, pressure at the breakdown and support lines. That stuck with me. You get all these things thrown at you, but the more you simplify it, the easier it is.'

The Irish player that has made the greatest impression on Heenan since his arrival is the current Munster captain. The New Zealander says, 'I thought Pete O'Mahony was excellent last year: very strong over the ball, and a guy who is capable of producing good rugby week on week. My watching rugby is as far as, "How am I going to beat these guys?" as opposed to "How I'm going to be them?"' Heenan adds, 'Robbie Henshaw is absolutely beautiful to watch playing the game of rugby. Ultimate gentleman off the pitch, very angry man on it.'

Cutting out mistakes or, at the very least, not repeating old ones is key to Heenan's quest for improvement. He is striving to add attacking and defensive elements to his game, and to become an on-field leader, but believes consistency is a vital component in the make-up of world-class players. 'To be a leader, you have to be able to walk the walk,' he says. 'That is something I have always lived by. You have to be prepared to have a go, and not be afraid to fail. It can be quite nerve-racking, too, to get up in front of a bunch of guys and say something that may be wrong. That's one thing I have to work on – not being afraid to have a go. If I get things wrong, I won't the next time.'

Heenan knows international rugby will be the true proving ground if he is to achieve world-class status. By the summer of 2016 he may have to choose between declaring for his homeland, Ireland or, thanks to his mother, England. 'I knew coming here would give me a big opportunity … the move gives me the option to focus on my rugby,' he explains. 'The way I see it, when I'm twenty-four years old I will be eligible to play for three countries and have three years of fully professional rugby under my belt. What a great position to be in.

'My five-year goal is to play Test rugby. I've said it before, but I do want to be the best No. 7 in the world. To do that, I have to be on the international scene, quite frankly. All I have really done is kept my options open. The three years, to me, are more about developing as a young man and a rugby player. I could swear my allegiance to Ireland tomorrow, but it is not going to make any difference as I can't play for them for another two years.'

There are no limits to Heenan's ambitions, but he knows he is responsible for building on a promising, if injury-hit, start to life in Ireland. 'To be honest,' he says, 'if I never play anything higher than Connacht Rugby, I won't be at all disappointed. If I only play as high as Connacht and I don't try to go further, I will finish with a lot of regrets. That's all it is to me. If I don't have a go at being the very best in the world, I'm always going to regret it. Whether I get there or not, who knows? Between now and, what will we say, 2024, I am going to give it a hundred per cent to achieve it. And I do believe I can achieve it.'

He leans forward: 'I have achieved the first step in convincing myself I can do it. That's the easy part.'

Heenan's appointment with the doctor happens two days later, and the news is bad. Further surgery is required on his right shoulder and the comeback forecast is five months. I send on a message wishing him well with recovery. He responds, 'It's all good mate. Looking forward to finally getting the bastard right.'

***

Mick Noone is a member of the Ireland Under-20 class of 2010. His teammates included Peter O'Mahony, Jack McGrath, Dave Kearney, Matt Healy, Rhys Ruddock and Ian Madigan. His inclusion in that grouping was little surprise to those who watched him play Leinster Schools Cup, with Presentation College Bray and then CBC Monkstown.

Ireland Under-20 coach Mike Ruddock was impressed with the back-row forward during a 2009 Six Nations campaign that promised much, but tapered off after defeat to Scotland. Many of the team were earmarked for a rapid rise through the senior ranks. Rhys Ruddock and Dominic Ryan had made their Leinster debuts in September of that year. Noone was with the Blues' academy and picking up Leinster A caps under Colin McEntee. When he finally struck a first stumbling block, it left him floored.

Noone was training with the senior squad at UCD, ahead of their Heineken Cup quarter-final against Harlequins, when he broke his leg. He rehabbed with the province over the next two months, but learned, at season's end, that he would not be graduating to the next academy level. It was Noone's first glimpse of rugby's harsh reality.

Training is done with for the day, on 14 October 2014 and Noone, now a second row with Jersey RFC, is heading home. Originally from Greystones, in Wicklow, the twenty-four-year-old is happy to train in the fresh, sea air.

After battling back from his leg injury, Noone moved from Seapoint to Blackrock, to gain AIL experience, before English Championship side Doncaster came calling. He says, 'It was a move I found I had to make if I wanted to stay professional … I knew I had to get playing at a high level. It was something I was not willing to throw away, just yet.' After a season with Doncaster, he was set to move to Rotherham before, in 2012, he got into a pre-season 'scuffle' with player-coach Lee Blackett.

Fortunately, Leicester Tigers coach Richard Cockerill drafted him into the Premiership squad. He remained for two seasons before stalling behind Geoff Parling, Louis Deacon and Graham Kitchener. Noone was offered a new contract, but felt his progress flat-lining. 'I had a decision – do I stay, play a bit and hold the bag for a couple more years,' he explains, 'or do I go somewhere else and play week-in, week-out rugby, and try to make that step up again?'

Moves to other Premiership outfits fell through before Championship side Jersey RFC stepped in. 'The money is quite good, certainly at this stage in my life and career,' he says. 'You get paid significantly better here than at other Championship sides, excluding Worcester and Bristol. They are paying £220,000 to £230,000 a year to internationals. It's not a dreadful salary. It is not what you would earn with the top Premiership sides or in France, but it is, in and around, what you would be paid at Leinster as a second- or third-choice senior player.'

Jersey are ambitiously investing in talent and facilities as they target a promotion play-off. Asked if he would like to see out that journey or clock up game time before moving on, he responds, 'The latter.' The Premiership and Pro12 remain his playing targets. He says, 'Sean McCarthy made the move from Jersey [to Leinster], Sean Dougall to Munster and Robin Copeland went from Rotherham to the Pro12 [Cardiff Blues] and back to Munster. It's happening all over the place. It's just about timing.'

Noone is four seasons out of Ireland, but glad a professional career did not slip away as he hobbled out of Leinster's exit door. 'Don't get me wrong,' he says. 'The provinces and academies are great for your development, but most of the Leinster guys are playing AIL week in, week out. It is a pity that the Irish second tier is not strong enough. It's not really doing anything for them as rugby players, even if they're playing there and living that lifestyle. It is a credit to the provinces and the IRFU that they are producing so many great players, but a shame that there are not enough clubs for them once they reach a certain age. It takes a bit of courage to step out and leave your country to keep the dream alive.'

# 21

## DIVERGING PATHS: JAMIE, LUKE AND FEZ

Ireland's final Test match at Lansdowne Road, in November 2006, coincided with debuts for two Leinster players and a back-row sensation from Maghaberry in Ulster. Led by Fijian lock Simon Raiwalui, the Pacific Islanders were to play the earnest fall guys as Irish rugby packed up and contemplated a cross-town move to the GAA headquarters, Croke Park. Eddie O'Sullivan's charges had finished second to France in the Six Nations and claimed a second Triple Crown in three years. Over the previous two weekends, Ireland had vanquished South Africa and Australia. There was less than a year to go to World Cup 2007 and O'Sullivan was eager to augment his battle-hardened team with youthful vigour.

The head coach made ten changes to the team that had defeated the Wallabies 21–6 the week before. Shane Horgan was switched to inside centre, alongside captain Brian O'Driscoll. His place on the right wing went to nineteen-year-old Luke Fitzgerald. The Wicklow teenager's father, Des, had played internationally as a prop, so his sheer pace and caterwauling, broken-field play must have derived from his mother's side of the family. A Schools Cup background with Blackrock College and early signs of raw talent had already led to O'Driscoll comparisons. Eight Leinster caps was his total when he was awarded an international debut.

Stephen Ferris, like Horgan, had arrived in the provincial set-up through club rugby, rather than the well-trodden schools route. He had featured at the 2004 Under-19 World Cup in South Africa and returned with a singular conviction to make his mark at Ulster. That determination saw him leave his £170-a-week job paving driveways to join the Ulster academy. Within a year he was making his provincial debut against Border Reivers. European rugby proved none too tasking a step as he flung himself headlong into the giants of Toulouse. He was twenty-one when O'Sullivan named him as blindside flanker.

At twenty-three, Jamie Heaslip was by far the oldest of the players to earn their first cap. Sean O'Brien, who was making strides as an eighteen-year-old with Tullow RFC at the time, recalls Heaslip making an early impact for Leinster: 'I went to a lot of Leinster's games at Donnybrook, and remember standing behind the goal, in the terraces, watching Jamie warm up. I think it was his first cap [against Ospreys]. The size of him! He was twice as big as he is now – had a little bit of weight on him.' By the time Ireland came calling, a little over eighteen months later, Heaslip had played thirty-eight games for Leinster, had scored six tries and was holding down a regular spot at No. 8. He was a leaner version than the one O'Brien had watched warm up at Donnybrook. A devastating turn of pace and ability to side-step opponents meant he was an attacking evolution of the man he replaced in Donnybrook that day – Victor Costello.

Eight years on from that win, I catch up with Heaslip, now the Leinster captain, at a provincial show-and-tell in Clondalkin. Heaslip has been a leader in blue for the best part of a decade, but head coach Matt O'Connor made it official by handing the forward the captaincy once Leo Cullen jumped from the playing to the coaching staff. The photography and interview duties are almost at an end, and Heaslip has promised some of Clondalkin RFC's young players one more kick-about before he sets off to check on business ventures that include a restaurant, technology innovations and a new bar he is opening with O'Brien and the Kearney brothers, Rob and Dave.

Heaslip remarks, 'You are running around like a chicken who has just got his head cut off. The whole day is a bit of a blur. I remember the three of us ran out at the same time, one in front of the other, in the old Lansdowne and up the steps. I have always missed those steps, even though it was a death trap for players in boots. I've missed that in the new stadium.

'I just remember running around like absolute lunatics, literally. Paddy Wallace got man of the match, and I remember trying to follow Paddy the whole day because he was making breaks for fun. I was trying to run off him and get the ball off him the whole time. You are trying to showcase yourself and also trying not to mess up, especially under Eddie's tutelage. I haven't thought about it in a long time. It was a very special day.'

Despite starring as an out-half in the Ireland Under-19 team that won the Junior World Cup in 1998, Paddy Wallace was making only his second cap for the senior team that day. The twenty-six-year-old had recovered from a serious leg-break and a spell back with his club side, Ballymena, to force his way back into the Ulster team. With David Humphreys retiring in April 2006, Wallace was next in line to deputise for Ronan O'Gara. His first cap arrived as a late replacement against Australia, and – given the starting nod against the Pacific Islands – he excelled the following week. Ireland hit the front as early as the third minute, but tries from Seru Rabeni and Lome Fa'atau made the score 16–12 some thirty minutes later. It took a lovely Wallace step inside, just before half-time, and a coughed-up score to Malcolm O'Kelly to pull the hosts clear. Thirty-one points were added after the break and Ireland signed off with a 61–17 victory.

'It was a great day,' Heaslip recalls. 'A special day for us all, gave it a good craic that night – obviously as new cappers and one of a few. Because it was the Pacific Islands, we all got up and sang a song with the Island boys. They sing songs the whole time at receptions too.'

For Ferris, the match would be a brisk, bruising education for a gruelling road ahead. 'I thought I was ready for Test rugby but, in reality, I was just a boy against men,' he said. 'I was coming up against guys like Alesana Tuilagi and Daniel Leo – these beasts, fast and strong. I knew, after that game, what needed to be done. No one would work harder, lift more weights or put in more work than me. By the time I played against a few of those guys again [in November 2009], I was a man. I was the strongest out there, and I knew it.'

Recognising a public craving for nostalgia, Leinster hosted Ulster at Lansdowne Road on New Year's Eve 2006 in the stadium's last game of any description. Neither Ferris nor Fitzgerald featured in 'The Last Stand', but Heaslip was there, right from the start. He played all eighty minutes and, with full-time drawing close, sealed Leinster's win with a try in the right-hand corner. It was only one game, but, in time, it would say much for the careers of the three men.

Season upon season, Heaslip defies rugby's roughhouse convention. He is an eighty-minute player, rarely leaving the field until his job is done or his team is spent. His lethal breaks off the back of scrums and rucks eased off once O'Brien made his rampaging senior breakthrough. Trophies have arrived in blue and green, and there has yet to be a significant breakdown. Conversely, Heaslip puts his longevity down to a devil-may-care attitude. 'If I'm going to get injured,' he says, 'I'm going to get injured. Ain't nothing I can do about it. Trauma injuries are trauma injuries, and they just happen. The best you can do is, any niggles you get, you address them, nip them in the bud early doors by doing a lot of pre-hab and strengthening. You have to work hard on it, in terms of preparing yourself, eating right, recovering right, finding what works for you. That is where the experience comes in.'

Heaslip is very much aware of the game's fickle nature, and reflected on 'the seven-, eight-year window' players get at the top after he led Leinster to their Pro12 league win over Glasgow in 2014. Before the game, Leinster had welcomed Eoin O'Malley into their dressing room. With Cullen (aged thirty-six) and O'Driscoll (aged thirty-five) lacing their boots for the final game of their storied careers, the twenty-five-year-old wished his former teammates well before taking his place in the stands. He had been forced to retire earlier in the season after a long-standing knee injury failed to clear up. 'It's quite a finite thing,' said Heaslip as the reclaimed league

trophy sat inches away. 'Your career could be over in the blink of an eye …
I'm already on borrowed time I suppose, but we all know guys who've had to
finish because of a sudden injury. To see someone speak emotionally about
what it meant for him to play for the club really gave a lot of guys focus.'

Two weeks on, Ferris was forced to call time on his career. The flanker
had damaged his left ankle in November 2012 against Edinburgh, and
fought back through dark days, bleak nights and countless setbacks for
seventeen months before returning in hard-hitting style, at Ravenhill, in
February 2014. The Ulster fans bellowed in Friday-night unison as Ferris
ran through Gareth Davies like a half-stuffed tackle bag. The cheers echoed
long after the final whistle as the No. 20 took the acclaim of the Ulster
faithful. A home Heineken Cup semi-final against Saracens awaited, and
it looked as if the twenty-eight-year-old and his team could go a step
further than their 2012 efforts and win Europe's top bauble. That dream
would wither four weeks later as a controversial red card for Jared Payne
left Ulster with fourteen men and fighting a losing cause against Sarries.
Ferris came off the bench to take part in a pulsating second half. His
thirty-minute outing would be his last in professional rugby.

I gave Ferris a fortnight's peace after he announced his retirement and
signed his name to Ulster's wall of legends at Ravenhill. When I reached
him on the phone, I found a player relieved that the fight was over, with
past battles still fresh in his mind. 'The idea was to give it forty minutes
in each game and see how it reacted,' he said, 'but the ankle kept digging
in and snowballed a bit. I worked so hard to get back and play in that
Saracens game and did fine for that thirty minutes, but the ankle was sore
again. I was missing training and it was swelling up. The Ulster lads said,
"You can't keep doing this to yourself, Stevie." I went along to a surgeon
and he said the ankle was not going to get better. Professional rugby would
only make it worse.'

Ferris added, 'The ankle will never properly heal. It will definitely
hamper me down the line. Every day I can feel it when I climb stairs.

Walking up hills is a nightmare. Most people walk up hills flat-footed, but I have to do it on my toes as I can't close the front of the joint up. It's like that deceleration when I'm running; the ankle bites and that's where the inflammation comes.'

Back in Clondalkin, Heaslip recalled the day serious injury first caught up with Ferris: 'We were in South Africa [in 2009], and I'm pretty sure it was a three-minute drill – that or the one-minute drill. Three rucking set ups, two guys with tackle bags and three sets of cones. You have to go through a gate, so it was Gats [Warren Gatland] in charge. He either called one, two or three, and you have to run to that. There were two guys there in tackle suits, and you had to make your way through. Four guys had to ruck over. I remember him hurting his knee then, and he was flying on that tour, absolutely flying, and I remember feeling gutted for him. We were in Durban. He turned around to me and said, "I'm gone. I have to go home." I was convinced that he was a shoe-in for the first Test. He was a Test Lion. As young as he was, things were going to kick on for him, and he was just gutted that day.'

I met up with Ferris just outside Carlingford a few weeks later. The blindside, who had collected thirty-five Irish caps since that Pacific Islands debut, spoke about the strange sensation of missing pre-season training. 'I would have loved to head over to Newforge and chat to the girls on reception, shoot the breeze, before going in for a game of pool with the lads. I'll still meet up with them for coffees and get-togethers, but I know I need to get some space between me and Ulster. Saying it doesn't make it any easier to do, but I know it is the right thing to do,' he said.

Luke Fitzgerald had also travelled with the British & Irish Lions in 2009, and had featured in the second Test against the Springboks. It had taken him eight months to get his second cap, while he came off the bench twice in the underwhelming Six Nations in 2008 that scuttled Eddie O'Sullivan. He was trialled at inside centre, alongside O'Driscoll, for the November internationals under Declan Kidney, before the new coach started him on the left wing – his suited position – for the 2009 Six Nations. He laced in a vital double against Italy in Rome, and started each of the Grand Slam games, earning a Lions jersey in the process. To celebrate, he won his first Heineken Cup with Leinster, and Heaslip, a month later.

Fitzgerald, Ferris and Heaslip were all named in the Ireland team to face Australia at Croke Park in November 2009. The game will be remembered for three reasons – David Pocock's gargantuan performance at the breakdown; O'Driscoll's last-minute, converted try to snatch a draw; and the gruesome knee injury that ended Fitzgerald's season. As the winger attempted to tackle Quade Cooper, his left boot stuck in the turf and his knee was wrenched. The medical term was 'a rupturing of the lateral collateral ligament'. Over the next five years, Fitzgerald would dazzle with his recantations of medical procedures and terms as he fought back from a series of injuries and derailments. He returned for the beginning of the 2010/11 season, but his form suffered as Kidney trialled him at fullback. A persistent and debilitating neck injury required surgery in 2012 and led to Fitzgerald missing his province's third Heineken Cup triumph. He got back into Ireland's Six Nations squad in 2013, but lasted eleven minutes, after coming on as a replacement for the injured Keith Earls in the first half. The reason: a torn cruciate ligament in that same left knee.

Fitzgerald played sixteen times for Leinster in 2013/14, and once for Ireland, coming on for a concussed O'Driscoll in an excruciating 24–22 defeat by New Zealand. A hat-trick against Northampton Saints at Franklin's Gardens in the Heineken Cup, reminded supporters of his sublime talent and merited some Sky Sports champagne. His season ended in frustrating fashion as groin and abdomen issues curtailed on-field involvement from March onward.

Heaslip commented, 'Luke has been told twice – his knee and neck – that his career is over. But Lukey, in his determination or stubbornness – whichever way you look at it – keeps coming back. It's a shame Fez has had to retire, but Luke is going well. He is one of those lads who is a game-breaker – he's got class, pace, skills, aggressive tackler, his pace at changing angle. He is one of the last game-breakers, and I hope he gets back playing. I'm a massive fan. He showed some nights last year when he was coming back; hopefully he gets back to that form and gets back playing.'

My final meeting with one of Ireland's class of 2006 took place in July 2014, amid a pre-season press chat at the RDS. Leinster's home would be being expanded, with naming rights for the revamped stadium open for bidding. Fitzgerald took his seat at a round-table and answered every single question that time would allow about his injury woes. He talked amiably and optimistically for fifteen minutes, and you got the impression he could have easily continued for another fifteen. The pelvis was the latest area of concern, and – as far as Fitzgerald was concerned – it was proving to be a nightmare.

'Surgery was about three weeks ago,' he began. 'Three weeks ago to the day, actually. I'm still in rehab at this point. It's a three-month injury, so I'm looking to probably get back for the first week of September, if not slightly before that. That's slightly within the time frame that I've been given, but I think most people aren't as lucky to be in a set-up like I am. That is probably [a time frame] for your average Joe Soap who isn't playing professional rugby, doesn't have a rehab coach, a physio, a strength-and-conditioning guy all available to him every day, so he [surgeon Gerry McEntee] thinks there may be a chance that I could shorten the time-scale.'

Fitzgerald did not need convincing that the latest fix would finally allow his body to do what he was telling it. He leaned forward, bridged his hands and urged us to believe him. 'This will be right,' he declared. 'I've just got to take the time now, let everything heal up, do the rehab correctly. It is just a matter of being exact on the three months.'

I drove away from the RDS that July afternoon wishing the best for Fitzgerald, his implacable pelvis and unswerving belief.

# 22

## FINDING THAT ONE PER CENT: STRENGTH AND CONDITIONING, ANALYSIS, AND SHEER MOTIVATION

Former Leinster full-back Girvan Dempsey tells a tale from his playing days, of sitting with teammates in the ballroom of Old Belvedere Rugby Club, watching grainy VHS (video) footage of the previous weekend's match. 'Fast forward, rewind, and don't forget pause,' he says. 'The screen would be jumping up and down, and you're trying to identify specific things about the match. You'd be sitting in that meeting and nearly falling asleep, because it would go on for hours before you'd finally go out to train.'

Emmet Farrell raises an eyebrow and laughs at a recalled memory when VHS is mentioned. 'The big technology then was when we got a big video recorder thing that had a wheel on it. So, with your finger you could roll the video footage back or forward. That was state-of-the-art stuff. There was excitement beyond belief about that,' he jokes.

We sit in a meeting room overlooking the Leinster players' gym at the Newstead Building in UCD. Dave Kearney and Fergus McFadden linger for a chat with Jordi Murphy after finishing their weights session. All three are injured and will miss the weekend's match with Wasps. Ian Madigan is doing floor exercises straight out of Mr Miyagi's 'wax on, wax off' teachings in *The Karate Kid* films. My insight into Leinster's video-analysis world began around the corner in a whitewashed room full of 'Be the Difference' catchphrases, dizzying statistical charts and six Apple computers. Farrell, Leinster's video analyst since 2003, clicks through folders to show individual video packages designed for each player. This week's homework includes a review of the previous game (Zebre) and a study on Wasps. 'Players have access to an app and they can view the clips on their phones or iPads, but many still choose to come in here and use the computers. We get their latest game reviewed, coded, packaged and up for the next day. Stats are up within four, five hours,' he said.

Led through a main office that contained Leo Cullen (forwards coach), Guy Easterby (team manager) and Bryan Cullen (Dublin GAA footballer and Leinster Academy strength-and-conditioning coach), I was greeted by Richardt Strauss. The hooker is back to full fitness and on his way to study clips of the Wasps line-out for chinks, patterns or both. 'In the professional game now,' says Farrell, 'there's always a game next week. The quicker you can view the game you just played, learn the lessons and put it behind you … it's essential. Instead of one or two days reviewing, you have moved on by Monday afternoon to the next game and that performance.

'Even if you have a bad game, there's still the next one coming up. Until you get knocked out of a competition or the internationals come around, there is no real break.' At Leinster, the rugby week begins with unit (backs and forwards) video reviews before the entire squad is assembled for a team review. This is followed by an afternoon training session, but already the focus has shifted to the upcoming opponents. 'We might do some drills if our tackling [in the last game] or breakdown was poor, but the session is primarily about the next match,' says Farrell.

Farrell played as a professional in England for two seasons before he joined up with Mike Ruddock's Leinster in 1999. He played eight games for the province, including a 22-point haul in a 32–10 win over Leicester Tigers at Welford Road. His career was ended eight months later when he ripped his 'patella, cruciates and all sorts' in a pre-season tie with Saracens. His comeback, one year on, against Swansea, lasted ten minutes. Once he was back on his feet, Farrell took a job as a sports-store manager before finding work with a company that was doing marketing and promotions for Leinster. The province advertised for an analyst in 2003 and Farrell found a new way of helping his old team.

The next technological advance, for Farrell, was a laptop with an editing programme, while the head coach got one of his own to tinker with. The coaching staff were then awarded a second laptop before the players piped up and, as a squad, got two of their own to play with. 'They were able to come into a room at the back of the containers we used to have [for offices] out in Donnybrook,' says Farrell. 'It grew from there, and now you have eleven computers they can look at and an app they can use at home.

'Every game now is on TV, but, back then, we were videoing it ourselves. I remember the first job I had to do for Leinster was ahead of a Heineken Cup game against Biarritz. I was sent over there with a camcorder. Their game was on a Sunday, but they could get me in only on a Friday – in the hotel on Friday and Saturday, off to the game Sunday. I literally had to sit in the stands with everybody else and try to record the game on a camcorder. I got back on the Monday and, at least at that stage, I could stick the camcorder card in the laptop and upload it. It was the only way of doing it because guys [from opposing teams] wouldn't send you footage or, if they did, would send it in the post and it would often arrive after the game.'

Streaming and file-sharing programs and websites, such as Dropbox or WeTransfer, mean Farrell no longer has to pack up his camcorder and jet off around Europe. Leinster also have their own ways of tracking statistics during a match, and, Farrell remarks, it is not often the ball carries or turnovers won that coaches and analysts will focus on. 'We look at stats that we think are relevant to us,' he explains. 'That way we can control the parameters of what is important rather than an outside body telling you a player did this many carries or tackles. We'll decide on what's a carry or what's a line-break. That way, we know the stats we produce are relevant to us. We have profiling of our team to tell us what we're good at or what we need to achieve to get a result.

'For most teams, exiting is very important. Getting the ball away from your goal line. Good outcomes from your line-outs, scrums, things like that. Possession is always important, but we'll look at a few secret things to hopefully give us the edge ... Speed to feet, to some teams that is important. To French teams, who are a little bigger, that is not as important, but to Irish teams it is. It's probably down to the fact that we're not as physically big, so speed of feet, speed of mind is crucial. Getting up off the ground and beating the opposition to the next phase.'

Having played the game in the early years of professionalism and studied it closely for the past eleven seasons, Farrell believes lines are blurring between forwards and backs. 'That's the difference with the amateur game,' he comments. 'The players have time to work on their skills. The clubs have two or three nights' training a week, so you just focus on getting your line-out right, scrum or rucking. With that bit more time, players can do their extras, their core skills, handling, passing, decision-making, they've got skills coaches around. The forwards have taken on more attacking responsibility. With the backs, there is a bigger emphasis on being physical, hitting rucks, being effective at traditionally orientated tasks.'

Los Angeles Angels' Billy Beane gained worldwide fame for advocating the Moneyball model of player recruitment, which focused on a new cross-section of baseball statistics and analysis rather than what he felt were outdated tenets, such as runs batted in or strike-out percentages. Farrell admits that every analyst dreams of finding the one statistic that turns the world around. 'The one thing I wouldn't have done if I was the Moneyball guy was advertised and told everybody what we're doing,' he says. 'We would very much keep it to ourselves – keep that advantage.'

Watching hours and hours of rugby occasionally rewards Farrell, and assistant performance manager John Buckley, in more than financial terms. The run to Challenge Cup success, including wins over Biarritz and Stade Français, stand out as particularly satisfying. Farrell recalls, 'Those games are the best example of training ground to pitch. Against Biarritz, we threw a line-out over the top to Devin Toner, he popped it to Isa Nacewa and Jamie Heaslip scored … that was a case of them having a five-foot-six hooker who was at the back of the line. We put Dev around the back, knowing that there was no way that guy was going to win the ball. Isa Nacewa ran in behind Dev, and it worked out perfectly with a pass for Jamie to score.

'In the final against Stade, we had two perfect scores, because we kicked the ball into the corners and attacked that space. We identified that as an area of weakness, the moves were practised on the training ground, we did the right thing in the match and scored from it.' Farrell gets as much joy from spotting the tells or weaknesses in the opposition, be it kicking poorly off one foot or a hooker's tell before a line-out throw: 'You just hope that guy you've targeted doesn't have a moment where he runs off the length of the field, scores and you're thinking, "Jaysus."'

In those rare weeks off, Farrell and the Leinster phalanx of analysts and coaches will get together and get introspective. 'We'll look at what we're doing, showing, what trends we've slipped into,' he explains. 'Sometimes, without being very conscious of it, it becomes really obvious what you're going to do when the ball is in your twenty-two. We'll scout ourselves. Sometimes after a game you will look at elements. If they chipped the ball in behind us three or four times, they must have thought we were really weak there. We'll look at that and see how successful they were. Clermont, in one of our recent games, attacked us around the ruck with pick and goes. We looked at that after and said, "Look, they must have thought they can get at us there," so we worked on that.'

Farrell predicts the next stage in analytical evolution will be in combining the video clips with data available from each player's GPS tracker. 'We'll get rugby-specific stuff out of the GPS,' he says, 'as opposed to quantity of running, sprinting, body loads.'

Increased access to statistics and video footage has seen television, websites and newspapers embrace rugby's new direction. Plays can be broken down as matches are being played, with an array of graphics praising and admonishing players for roles in scores, turnovers and seminal moments. Having been behind the curtain as a player and analyst, Farrell feels certain players may not get a fair shake in a digital age of instant player ratings. 'Sometimes the analysis of an individual after a game can be harsh, because the people that write about it don't know what the coach asked the player to do that day,' he says. 'He could have been told, "We don't want you carrying, but want you to hit forty rucks." Then it's written that this guy had a quiet game and didn't carry a lot of ball. He's reading it thinking, "Jesus, I did the job I was supposed to do, and I'm getting nailed in the press." It can be unsettling for a guy.

'The professional game is moving beyond that. The players now understand that we are seeing that they have done what they were told to do, and we're judging them on that.'

Farrell's mention of the selfless workhorse brings Heaslip to mind. The Leinster captain's breakthrough was accompanied by dashing carries and line breaks, but he now relishes rucks and freeing up ball for teammates. 'Mr Consistency!' Farrell exclaims. 'He does get criticised for not carrying at international level for some reason, yet he's first on every single team-sheet and is available every week. The way he plays, I don't think he comes off the field and the coaches are criticising him. Ever. You could read the press a while back, and they'd say Sean O'Brien and Stephen Ferris are making so many carries, but Heaslip only made two. Well, how are they getting the ball? Jamie is excellent at not saying, "I want to carry." He is brilliant at doing the job he is required to do for the team to win. I don't think there is a coach in Europe who wouldn't have him in their team. Shane Jennings is another guy like that: someone who works and works and works, but it doesn't get seen by everybody.'

Another enigma of the game, Farrell believes, is the tight-head prop. 'They might get the odd profile article, but in the summing up of the game they never get their name mentioned,' he says. 'The only time they are mentioned is when they don't do their job, and everyone realises it's all gone because they didn't play well.'

Farrell had the pleasure of playing a season-and-a-half with an emerging Brian O'Driscoll. I ask him if a focus on minute analysis and statistics could sap the spontaneity from the next generation of rugby players. He says, 'It's very easy to get a domineering coaching staff, who script what you're doing all the time and if you veer off that script you are reprimanded or taken off. Unfortunately, the nature of the professional game is that it is result orientated. That guy who tries something different would be very much judged on the outcome of what he tried.

'If it works, it is hard to give out to him. If not, and it leads to an opposition break or score, it will be tough for a coach, who is judged on his team winning or losing. What's important for us is if a player does something off the cuff, that they have a reason for it – they thought a move was on or that there was a bit of space. Hopefully they go back to a scouting video where they knew there was a bit of space there. It wasn't the exact move we talked about, but he felt it was a good time to attack that space. That's okay. You can't take that part of a game away from a player. It's when they do it and don't have any reason for doing it or say, "I just felt like I needed to do something today."'

I mention someone who I feel is a trump-card player – All Blacks out-half Carlos Spencer – in the hope of shaming Farrell for his editing-room advocacy. He is not moved. 'Spencer got away with stuff a lot,' he says, 'but, the way the game has changed, would he get away with it now? Everybody would know him and the analysis would be so much better. He was an exceptional player, but the analysis of the game was still growing. I think it would be harder for him to do those things today.'

A danger greater than the next Spencer comes from overloading players with too much information. Leinster, Farrell says, are conscious of outweighing the good with sheer statistical weight. 'Some players can take a lot in. Others a little,' says Farrell. 'They have to know themselves how much they can take in. Coaches too. What you have to emphasise is that they focus on things that are only important to the performance. You're not just throwing a blanket of stuff at them with some sticking and the others not. You have to be focused on message – this is how we're going to beat these guys and this is how they'll try to beat us. There's no point letting a prop worry about what the winger is going to do. He's got to be worried with what he has to deal with for eighty minutes.'

Finally, and most importantly, who checks if the players have done their homework? 'They're all mature, professional athletes,' replies Farrell. 'They should know what they need to do to be ready. Our job is to make sure it is there for them. If he decides to never look at the clips and is man of the match every week, no one is going to say "boo" to him. But if he does start dropping in his performance, things will be looked at.'

***

Mental coaching and visualisation techniques have been around in Irish rugby since the late 1990s, but have only taken hold in the past six to seven years. When Heaslip now speaks of winning eighty one-minute battles and the Irish squad being goal orientated and process focused, he is (probably) not pulling your leg. Heaslip and his Irish teammates are firm believers in mental preparation, and it has served them well in recent years.

In October 2014, Brian O'Driscoll spoke with Enda McNulty, on Newstalk's *Off The Ball*, about the former Armagh GAA player's work as a sports psychologist. The pair have worked closely ever since 2008, and O'Driscoll credits McNulty for reviving his career after he had completed a below-par season for club and country. O'Driscoll remarked that he had found most sports psychologists he worked with before McNulty as 'more than useless'.

McNulty said, 'Part of the conversation with Brian [in 2008] was getting him to focus on the things he did really well. Asking him, "What are you world-class at? What are your biggest strengths?" and getting Brian to

identify them and go back to being one of the best players in the world …
He wasn't that far away, but he knew that by going back and focusing on
his biggest strengths, he was centring himself at where he was best.

'Also, going back to the basics: it is unbelievable the amount of people
that talk about getting the complicated, small details right. If you get the
basics right all the time, it is amazing how the extraordinary things appear.
If you look at Brian's career and the best people in sport, in general, they're
the ones that deliver the basics, day in and day out, in performance. If you're
going to do that in sport, or business, it means that in your preparation you
have to deliver the basics day in, day out. If you ask a hundred per cent of
athletes how many of them hydrate well all the time, you're going to get
small percentages. If you ask a hundred per cent of athletes how many of
you do post-practice work, like Brian would have over the last four or five
years, not that many would have.'

McNulty touched on the sports-psychology mantra of WIN (what's
important now?) and said O'Driscoll used that to focus on a 2013 Six
Nations game against Wales in which he excelled. O'Driscoll paid credit
to McNulty for Leinster's league and European successes since 2008 and
for his 'work in the background' with the national team. He added, 'The
days Johnny [Sexton] would be out kicking, Enda would be out on the
side of the pitch in the pissings of rain. It's just the small, little add-ons.
Everyone who has played high-end sport knows that it is the "half-per-
centers" that are the difference. Sometimes a quarter of a per cent can be
the difference between winning and losing, and that's what you need. You
need to keep working on those tiny margins. That, along with a little bit of
luck, can be the formula for success.'

***

'It's funny,' muses Fergus McFadden, 'back in the day, when there might
not have been as much emphasis on strength and conditioning, you would
have seen guys with scrum caps or massive shoulder pads, but these days

you don't really see guys wearing pads anymore, because players, over time – whether in academies or going up through set-ups – build up mass with muscle. You get used to taking those collisions. After really big games you are sore on Monday and Tuesday, but it's a process you go through, and you just get on with it for the following week. I think the collisions each year are getting heavier and worse, and all you can do is adapt and go with it.

'I'm certainly getting stronger. The margins for getting quicker are probably a bit tougher than strengthwise, but Dan Tobin, our head of strength and conditioning in Leinster, does a fair bit of work on that – the dynamics of sprinting and stuff – which helps. But the last few pre-seasons I have been getting stronger, and you have to – the game's evolving every year and you have to keep up with it.'

A grin briefly breaks across the Leinster and Ireland back's face as he thinks back to his slighter self in 2004, as he transitioned from Clongowes Wood College to the province's Under-19s. 'I think there's a balance … you can be a weightlifter and you can be an athlete,' he says. 'You're trying to get a fine balance between having strength and having speed as well. It's important for me to be fast and agile on the wing. You can be a big lump, but if you're slow and not good at moving laterally, not good on your feet, you'll get shown up in that area. So it's about having the balance, and I think we've got the right guys getting us stronger and faster. I know what you mean, there is a level. I've probably come to the level in my career where it's more about maintenance.

'I think when you're coming up through the academies, you are getting stronger and stronger each year. They're only tiny margins after that where you'll make gains and losses. Look at someone like Drico [Brian O'Driscoll]; he wouldn't have lifted really heavy weights over the last few years. The game has taken its toll on his body, and it's more about maintenance – he just kind of adapted to it in that way.'

\*\*\*

Aidan O'Connell was part of the University of Limerick's first ever sports science degree course, in 1993. More than two decades later, the Cork native cannot shake the place. Coming from a Gaelic football background, O'Connell completed a master's in Edinburgh before taking up an internship under Mike Stone – 'the godfather of strength and conditioning' – in Connecticut. He threw himself into the 7 a.m. to 7 p.m. lifestyle, and worked with basketball, American football, hockey, football and baseball teams. 'I got a call, then, from my mother, saying, "You haven't a job. What's going on, like?"' he says. 'She had spotted in a newspaper clipping that the IRFU were looking for fitness staff, which, in 2001, was very unusual.

'There were no real, professional fitness-coach jobs going around in Ireland at the time, so it was big news if one came up. I came back and did a job interview with Ulster for their academy coach [role]. I was thinking Ulster … I don't know, but I went and did the interview. I got a call a couple of days later and was told I was unsuccessful – Phillip Morrow got it – but there was a position in Leinster, working in Dublin, and did I want it? I jumped at it.'

The union had a request for O'Connell before he took up his new post – three weeks at UL with the Munster players who – by age, form or choice – had not travelled in an enlarged Ireland squad to Spala, Poland, for a three-week 'hell on earth' training camp. O'Connell's band of merry trainers included Mike Prendergast, Paul O'Connell, Colm McMahon, and the Clohessy brothers, Peter and Ger. Finally earning a wage for coaching, O'Connell's three weeks were a mix of great craic, hands-on experience and man management. 'You would have still had a lot of fellas who were quasi professionals,' he recalls. 'Peter Clohessy, for example, had Fridays off. He would go to Kilkee. [IRFU director of fitness] Liam Hennessy asked me to go to him in Kilkee. Claw had his family and obviously wanted to spend time with them over the weekend. I thought it was strange that I'd be asked to drive all the way to Kilkee, so I rang Claw and ran it by him. He said, "Eh … no," so that was that; I prescribed him a routine and left him to it. I wasn't going to argue that one.'

After the short stint at Munster, O'Connell did four months with the Leinster Academy before getting involved with the senior team. O'Driscoll, Dempsey and Gordon D'Arcy formed 'the younger crew', Denis Hickie was in the middle and players such as Reggie Corrigan, Shane Byrne and Victor Costello were the established pros. He spent two years with the province, working under head coach Matt Williams, before he felt the itch to return to Cork. He discovered the Munster set-up, at Cork Institute of Technology (CIT), was not far removed from their interprovincial rivals.

'The lads trained in a public gym at CIT,' says O'Connell, 'so, in other words, they're doing their weights and Mary, Sheila, Tom and Michael are waiting to do their weights or looking at them when they're on the treadmill. The groups were so small that you'd have to go in over five hours with six sets of players. It was really time inefficient.' O'Connell found an ally in returning coach Declan Kidney in 2004, but there was give and take involved in the move away from public gyms. He says, 'We moved into a classroom and were there for a year. It was better as you could fit more of us in, but the height of the room meant you couldn't fit a six-foot-six-inch player. You had guys like Paul O'Connell, Donncha O'Callaghan and Tom Bowman, who had won a World Cup with Australia, who couldn't do the overhead lifts.'

Having witnessed the first-class facilities in which American athletes trained, O'Connell had a vision of what Munster needed. Progress was slow – a multipurpose gym was secured in late 2004 – but it was progress, all the same. 'The desire, the work ethic, was always there,' he says. 'Elite sport is driven by guys who are perfectionists and who want to test themselves against the very best. The mentality hasn't changed, but players are much more disciplined in how they live now. That's nutrition, recovery time, how they treat their body away from the games and training.

'We talk a lot, here, about the other twenty-two hours. It's easy to train hard for two hours, but what are you doing in between? [Basketball] Coach John Wooden talks about your moral conditioning – are you eating right, going to bed at the right times? That process has evolved at Munster in the last ten, twelve years. When it comes to nutrition, now, we supply a lot of the food. Back then [when I started], players were left to their own devices.'

O'Connell believes the increased training-and-playing schedule has cut down on the time players spend away from the provinces. Munster's season would be considered successful in the late 1990s if it spilled over into January. 'I remember Anthony Horgan telling me a story, just when I arrived, about him pulling his hamstring,' says O'Connell. 'He was in University College Cork at the time. He was gone, out of the system for two months, and when he got back the hamstring had naturally got better. Now it is much more intense and accelerated. You can be back from a hamstring injury in three weeks. Back then it may have been six, ten, twelve weeks, and you were recovering under your own steam.'

O'Connell met little resistance at either province, and his methods were fed into a malleable training week. He admits, however, that clubs were guilty of applying heavy training loads on their players in the early years of professionalism. 'In the early noughties,' he says, 'we had less of an idea about training load and how much you should do in a week so you could peak at the weekend. Put weight training, speed work and a Captain's Run on top of that … we will now do two main training sessions and a really light session. Because people were professionals, we thought you could do more as you had more time to rest, but a human being is a human being. We don't have an infinite capacity to recover.'

Munster's methods are more scientific today. Players are monitored 'subjectively and objectively', with stress and fatigue levels coming into play. When a player comes in for training, be it in Cork or Limerick, they log the hours of sleep and quality of sleep on their phones or personal computer tablets. Energy levels, soreness and mood are also scored between one and five. 'When they train,' O'Connell adds, 'they give us scores between one and ten about how they felt the session went. They have GPS tracking as well.' Munster have gone from having two GPS sets – installed into a pouch at the back of the jersey – to providing one for each player at training and in matches.

'The GPS covers the distance they cover, the quality of those distances, the amount of sprints they do, accelerations, decelerations, the amount of contacts they've had in a session,' explains O'Connell. 'That gives us an objective idea of how they went in training, and then they'll give us a subjective figure – how they thought they went. All that feeds back in, so we can tailor training to suit their needs and prescribe more accurate training in the future.

'We are much better at managing the training loads, whereas we were a bit blind, back then. You would have used common sense, of course, and would know if someone was doing too much on a Thursday before a Saturday match. Back then it was a constant battle with the coaches. It still is, a little bit, but there is a lot more education around that area … monitoring helps us ask better questions, but you will never replace that subjective, human element.'

Aled Walters, head of fitness at Munster, calls pre-season his favourite time of the year, as he is given extended periods of time with the player. 'As for the actual pre-season,' O'Connell continues, 'many lads will feel that it mentally and physically sets them up for the year. The younger players are behind when it comes to strength and power, so a good pre-season can set them up that way. The more seasoned professionals can condense that conditioning period into four or five weeks. It's not ideal, but they could. It's your foundation for the whole year, and the wider the base, the stronger the pillars you can build upon, the better. If a player has a shortened pre-season, through injury or illness, they are chasing their tail but, then, that's our job: to find opportunities, within that week or month, to build them up.

'Lads like Donncha O'Callaghan and Paul O'Connell will talk about how a good pre-season does them wonders. Physically, it does, but, mentally, it is also great for them. They feel they have put the work in. It makes them hungry for rugby as well. They start off with an eighty–twenty split between conditioning and rugby, but, by the time the season nears, it has gradually changed seventy–thirty, in favour of rugby.'

O'Connell shares Walters' view about getting increased time with players over the summer, but notes that another pre-season, of sorts, is set in motion the moment a player is out, injured, for anything over three weeks. 'You have to change their mentality, straight away,' he says. 'For example, "You have an upper body injury, this is your chance to get your legs stronger, more powerful and faster than ever before." We frame injuries, as well, as golden opportunities to improve another part of their game.'

O'Connell insists return-to-play protocols and recovery timetables mean he is rarely pressured to get players back for big matches. 'There are three subjective stages to assessing injuries, and a player has to pass them before he is moved on,' he points out. 'We believe in the process, and follow the process. If a player buys into that, it often accelerates their recovery. In cases, let's say, where there is a hamstring injury three weeks before a big game … first of all, we have to work together as a conditioning staff. Not only does he have to be ready from a conditioning point of view, but he has to be able to perform at the highest level. We do as much as we can. If it is a shoulder injury, we are working on every aspect of his fitness and conditioning – not just the shoulder – so he is ready to return. In the early days, going back to the beginning, you would rehab the shoulder and do a little bit of off-field work to keep him ticking over. Then, the shoulder would be right, but it would be two or three weeks before he was match fit.'

O'Connell adds, 'There are injuries where players are rushed back, but that is happening way less. It's like, you get back, get re-injured and you're out forever. If it's a final, for example, I suppose you have to take a calculated risk. It's a risk–benefit trade-off, but I think there is huge honesty [among the players] now. There is better education, too. It's multidisciplinary, so, are you honest with the physio, the strength-and-conditioning team, your coach, your fellow players? If you're working together, then everybody can make the decision. Before, it was much more isolated; perhaps physio, coach, player. Now, there are more layers to it … I would say rushing back does happen, but less and less. If a player comes back and re-injures himself, questions have to be asked, as he played when he wasn't right. I would like to say we've evolved to a situation where [those instances] have been eradicated, but we're pretty close to it.'

O'Connell talks of merging rugby and conditioning so players train at the optimum level and do not burn themselves out. He does not believe, however, that the days of players flogging themselves so hard that they throw up will ever completely disappear from the game. 'It's an artful science,' he says, 'and we do have to make the training specific to rugby, so you don't want to see a player getting sick on the side of a rugby pitch in training. But there are periods, sporadically, where you do have to put players into a dark hole – a black place. It is for their mental conditioning as well – to see how they react to adversity.

'We're much smarter about it now. Whereas you might have seen it a lot more a few years ago, we would now plan it in. It might be on every second Friday or for three minutes, instead of twenty, in one session. It's highly taxing on the body. A lot of lactic [acid] build up. It's not really specific to rugby, but it is specific to their mentality. We have to be clever, but definitely there is still a place for it.'

During my morning at Munster's training facilities at UL, I had noticed Paul O'Connell working on his own training regime. As teammates ran drills ahead of a Champions Cup match, the Ireland captain ran shuttles and grimaced through countless squats in the far twenty-two. Aidan O'Connell says his namesake is not the only player taking part in modified training. 'You modify for the older professionals, the young guys, players coming back from injury,' he explains. 'With an injured lad, he might be training twenty-five per cent, fifty per cent, seventy-five per cent, then play. That could take two weeks. The older pros might not do any contact if, for example, they had an ongoing shoulder niggle. That's what we do every morning. We'll spend an hour, hour-and-a-half, looking at all of our monitoring data, GPS, talking to physios and coaches. That way we know, going into the session, who's doing what. Player one can do A and B, but he's not doing C, contact, so he's doing skills work with another coach, and then D. That's a huge part of our jobs, the player management.'

Teams are beginning to take a more hands-on approach when it comes to dealing with the mental side of the game and a player's psychological well-being. While Munster do not employ a full-time psychologist, they regularly engage such services. O'Connell explains that friends, family and fellow players are frequent outlets. 'Players are a lot more open now and the coaching style [here] is more humanistic so, if they have an issue, they'll talk,' he says. 'It depends on the coach. Some coaches don't want sports psychologists around, but, by and large, we've always had someone the players can talk to, even when I first started at Munster.

'We have to facilitate, though, if they want to talk to someone outside of here, on a sports-psychology basis. We have someone here [at UL] the players often use, Dr Tadhg MacIntyre. There's Dr Declan Aherne, too. Players have always had counsel outside the rugby setting.'

Protein and creatine supplements have long since filtered into rugby, but, O'Connell insists, guidelines laid out by Dr Liam Hennessy keep a tight lid on what a player can and cannot take. 'There was whey protein then [1999], there's whey protein now,' says O'Connell. 'There are a lot of supplement companies around now, but it is well policed. There was a big scare around creatine, early doors, and it was banned in France, but it is around a long time now. It's hardly controversial at this stage. It's something some lads will take. Others won't take it during intense periods of training, but use it to aid recovery. It gives partial gains. Some people think they can take heaps of creatine, not train and get massive. It will aid their recovery slightly, so they can get back to training. Its use is widespread around the world, now, but it is not as natural as whey protein.

'There's caffeine,' O'Connell adds. 'That wasn't used that much before, but it is around now. It improves your alertness, and – depending on the dosage – it could improve your aerobic capacity. All of this, though, is strictly tested, and there are limits to it, as well. You work within your confines. You had lads drinking a Red Bull [caffeine drink] early doors, but that could well lead to a spike followed by a dip.'

Each province now employs nutritionists to advise players on diets, food plans and general health. 'We've had a lot of good nutrition advice and consultants over the years, but it is definitely an area where guys go looking,' says O'Connell. 'There can be a lot of fads out there, whether they are high-fat diets, protein diets, low carb, high carb. It's an area that's growing,' says O'Connell. When players are required to consume, depending on their position, anything from 4,000–5,000 calories a day, creativity is often sought to stave off trough-feeding images.

O'Connell concedes there are occasional tremors – and calls for new techniques and approaches – if a rugby nation leaps ahead of the competition, but, in general, the IRFU and provinces have a cogent fitness strategy in place. 'I believe, pound-for-pound, we're the best rugby nation in the world for producing players from the resources we have,' he says. 'We're punching above our weight and there is virtually no waste. I have been involved here for twelve years, and could probably name you two players that have been in the academy system and that haven't got through because of certain issues – social animals, or they didn't want it,' he said. 'What we deliver with the resources we have, only New Zealand can match us.'

# 23

## 'ELBOW, APPLE, CARPET, SADDLE, BUBBLE': CONCUSSION TAKES CENTRE STAGE

We played Canterbury and won in the end [28–10], but I don't remember much of it as I was heavily concussed. I took an open-handed smack to the face, right under my nose. There was no half-time break back then, so I can just remember standing in the middle of the huddle in a daze. I didn't know who I was, I didn't know where I was and I didn't know what was going on. I looked up and saw the crowd and the scoreboard and then looked at my jersey. I was thinking, 'Oh my God, I'm in a Lions jersey.' I started looking around the huddle and thought, 'Wow, there's Rob Andrew, there's Jason Leonard, there's Jeremy Guscott.'

*Scott Gibbs (former Wales and British & Irish Lions player), 2013*

'Momentum equals mass by velocity squared,' Ireland's team doctor, Eanna Falvey, tells an Oireachtas committee on concussion in sport on 2 October 2014. 'If you are bigger you are going to tackle harder. Look at the statistics in professional rugby. Players are much bigger than they were ten years ago. So if you have got a bigger man moving into a collision a kilometre an hour faster, you have much more momentum and bigger impacts.'

A sign rugby was heading in the right direction arrived in November 2013, when Dr Falvey decided to remove a clearly shaken Brian O'Driscoll from play in the second half of a Test match against New Zealand. O'Driscoll was reluctant to leave the field of play, but later thanked the team's medical staff for taking the decision out of his hands. O'Driscoll had, in fact, passed the pitch-side concussion assessment, but Dr Falvey was not satisfied with the outside centre and took him off.

The decision came seven months after the same staff were criticised for allowing O'Driscoll to retake the field after he had been left sprawling and dazed by French prop Vincent Debaty. Reflecting on the incident in his book *The Test*, O'Driscoll reveals he answered three questions correctly and was allowed back for the final four minutes. He writes, 'Maybe the story would be different if there wasn't so much going on, if they didn't have Luke Marshall's situation [concussion] to worry about as well, but I make my way onto the field.'

In a September 2013 interview for *Newstalk*, Pat Kenny asked O'Driscoll if studies linking concussion suffered in sports such as rugby to early-onset dementia and Alzheimer's were a concern. 'It is,' O'Driscoll replied. 'And I guess, to a degree, in the professional era we're somewhat guinea pigs, because we haven't had the progression of people going through their careers and getting to old age. We don't know the downside to the escalating collisions.'

O'Driscoll was clearly dazed, on two occasions, in Ireland's November 2013 match against New Zealand. He hit the deck after fifty-three minutes and was slow getting to his feet. Dr Falvey was quickly on the scene. O'Driscoll passed an on-field concussion assessment test, but the doctor made a judgement call and removed him from play. The shaken O'Driscoll later revealed he had asked teammates for tomato ketchup in the minutes after his enforced removal, adding, 'I don't know why.'

Senator Jillian van Turnhout referred to O'Driscoll's 'guinea pig' comments during Dr Falvey's appearance at the Oireachtas committee. Dr Falvey responded, 'The current players are guinea pigs in the sense that they have seen a dramatic change in rugby in the course of their playing careers. The average forward is ten kilograms heavier, and the average back is eight kilograms heavier, than when they started to play rugby. That is why there is a big change.'

Go back six days, to 27 September 2014, and Dr Falvey is going through the new Head Injury Assessment (HIA) process, at the Aviva Stadium, for the Irish media. HIA replaced Pitch-Side Concussion Assessment (PSCA), and an additional video-monitoring aspect had been added to the process – for top sides – in November 2013. The new direction is coupled with a ten-minute window in which a player is taken to a stadium's medical room and assessed away from the din of players and crowds. 'Before the introduction of the assessment protocol,' says Dr Falvey, 'occurrences of missed concussions were fifty-six per cent. That figure is now at slightly over thirteen per cent.'

Dr Falvey is demonstrating, with the help of a pliant assistant, how he would assess a suspected concussion. He checks the subject's neck, asks if they can move arms and legs, and then asks five 'Maddox' questions based on the game. 'One of the points worth making about the assessments on the pitch,' says Dr Falvey, 'is that studies from World Cups show that, from a player going down to play starting again, the average time is about fifty-six seconds. As fit as I am, it takes me about fifteen seconds to get out to the injury, so you have a very limited time to get through that. There is a lot of noise. You are in this situation. You are trying to, over the noise, communicate with your colleagues and with the player. We have gone from having fifty-six seconds from them hitting the ground, to getting up, to make a decision. You now have ten minutes to help you out with that. While I wouldn't argue that this is the perfect solution, it is better than what we have had in the past. I think anyone who has been involved in the game is happier to have that time to do something than not.'

The doctor adds, 'The assessment has gone from five minutes to ten minutes. I am involved in the IRB [World Rugby] working group that has changed that. The reasoning behind that was we added more cognitive testing to it. I always felt that, with PSCA, the tests were a little easy or were asking you how you were feeling. So you are asking the player if he is feeling unwell, all the signs of concussion. But if the player is prepared to lie about those, then, that is it, basically. They can pass the test. What we now introduce is cognitive testing. They are challenges that show if a person is up to scratch, and how they are functioning, or not.'

In an IRUPA study of its players in 2013, sixty-seven per cent said they had been concussed between two and three times in their career. The same study also found that forty-five per cent of players responded 'yes' when asked if they had ever hidden or underplayed a concussion in order to return to the field of play. The players' union believes the results indicate a distinct lack of recognition of concussion's seriousness in many cases. Whilst this figure would appear to be high, the union argued, it should also be considered that it is based on players' entire careers and 'may not be reflective of shifting attitudes in more recent times'.

Once Dr Falvey gets the player back to the medical room, he carries out word and number memory tests. One example is getting a player to repeat back five words he says in any order. On this particular day the assistant answers back 'elbow, apple, carpet, saddle, bubble'. Rugby boots are taken off for a balance – walk the line – test before five questions about the game are asked and answered. The final hurdles to clear include a symptom checklist (headache, dizziness, blurred vision, etc.), clinical signs regarding mental well-being and a video review of the incident that led to the suspected concussion. The wonder is how this test was ever carried out in five minutes in the past.

It is interesting to note that Dr Falvey uses a clip of a concussed Rob Kearney, from Ireland's match with France at Croke Park in 2009, as an example of video reviews being vital in making concussion calls. After taking a concussive blow tackling Clément Poitrenaud in the sixth minute of the match, Kearney stumbled twice and lost his footing once as he tried to take up his position in the defensive line. Fifty-five seconds later, and with play stopped for Jerry Flannery to receive treatment, the treatment Kearney receives amounts to a bag of ice on the back of his neck. Play resumes, and less than three minutes later Kearney is bowled over when attempting to tackle Sébastien Chabal. The fullback gets to his feet and, forty seconds later, outjumps Yannick Jauzion to a high ball. He plays on until the seventy-fourth minute, yet, to this day, remembers little of the match.

\*\*\*

As well as being Ulster Rugby's medical director, Dr Michael Webb is one of Europe's leading specialists on concussion in sport. Heavily involved in the sport for the past decade, he has noted one upward trend in injuries – that of concussions. 'It's not that more concussion has happened, it's just that we're getting better at recognising and diagnosing it,' he notes.

In less than two years, upcoming Ulster stars Luke Marshall and Stuart Olding suffered seven concussions. Marshall had five, spread over matches and training-ground knocks, between February 2013 and January 2015. Olding's two came two months apart – in October and December 2014. 'The greatest predictor of future injuries,' Dr Webb says, 'is prior injury. That is true of all injuries. What we do know is that, if you have had a previous concussion, your risk of future concussion goes up by around fifty per cent. Unfortunately, if you have had eight [concussions], you are more at risk of a ninth than someone who has had three is of getting a fourth. The risk goes up each time.

'Having said that, most of the studies that have been carried out have [covered] the older approach to concussion. Now, we're probably diagnosing the more subtle injuries. For example, if a guy gets dinged, dazed or – to use the American term – has their bell rung, in the past it might have been that the player would never reveal that and we'd be none the wiser to it. Now players are educated very strongly about concussion. If you get an injury, there is a danger period where you can pick up a second injury that is more serious. So we are saying to our players, "Even if the symptoms seem mild, or relatively trivial to you, it is really important that you flag it up so if you need to have rest, to recover, you get that, because, if you don't, your brain is almost primed for a second injury."'

Dr Webb adds, 'Guys are better at putting their hands up [after taking heavy blows] or looking out for their teammates than, say, five, ten years ago.'

***

It is 22 November 2014 and Falvey and his medical team are run off their feet in the second half of Ireland's pulsating Test encounter with Australia. It is a routine afternoon of caring for international rugby players until four Irish players ship concussive blows in eighteen minutes. The first player down is Gordon D'Arcy, on 57:27, as he takes a flat pass and is moshed back by Matt Toomua and Sekope Kepu. Falvey is by D'Arcy's stricken side by 57:50 as play continues and Ireland attack. On 58:10, play breaks up the right flank and Rob Kearney is tackled out of play by Henry Speight. Falvey continues to speak with D'Arcy, but, by 58:30, the inside centre's match is over.

On 67:06, Johnny Sexton takes an accidental knock to the head from the trailing leg of Wallabies lock Sam Carter. The out-half is slow to rise, so Falvey makes his way onto the pitch. Play has continued and Conor Murray has taken a Quade Cooper knee to the head. With Sexton deemed fit to play on, Falvey jogs over to Murray. There is a considerable break in play – just over ninety seconds – before the scrum half is given the all-clear. Forty-eight seconds after play resumes, Murray tackles Australian captain Michael Hooper, but play continues. Australian prop James Slipper knocks on and, as a scrum is about to be reset for the third time, Murray is summoned to the sideline for further assessment. Eoin Reddan takes his place.

By 75:11, just over four minutes and thirty seconds after leaving the field of play, Murray has satisfied Falvey of his ability to play on. The IRFU later confirm he had passed HIA test number one in the stadium's medical centre. As he dives on a loose ball, Murray receives a kick in the back from Cooper less than twenty seconds after retaking the field. His contribution for the remainder of the game is a box-kick and two hearty tackles on Henry Speight and Ben McCalman.

On 76:06, three Irish players – Simon Zebo, Kearney and Sexton – combine to bring down Wallabies winger Adam Ashley Cooper. Will Genia recycles the ball for Australia, but only Zebo is back on his feet. Sexton is prostrate while Kearney struggles to get to his feet. With 76:25 elapsed, Australian prop Benn Robinson knocks on before Robbie Henshaw passes back for Ian Madigan to clear. The kick fails to find touch, and Ireland – down to thirteen fit players – are exposed on the left flank. Both Kearney and Sexton are back on their feet, but tottering. Ireland defend four more phases before Hooper, with 77:02 on the clock, knocks on and allows Henshaw to kick clear and get the ball out of play. Felix Jones replaces the rattled Kearney while Reddan replaces Sexton and Murray plays out-half for the final three minutes of a thrilling Irish win.

The following day, with Ireland coach Joe Schmidt in St Vincent's Hospital recovering from the post-match removal of his appendix, the IRFU release a statement confirming the suspected concussions of their four players. All four will not feature for their provinces, and Racing Métro in Sexton's case, until they satisfy return-to-play protocols.

On the Monday after the 26–23 victory, Sexton is carrying out media interviews as part of his sponsorship deal with Aer Lingus. 'I'm fine,' he says. 'I just got a bang on the head at the end of the game. Under the new rules it's best to come off and do the tests. There was only a minute left, or not even, so by the time the tests were over the game was over.'

He adds, 'I would have liked to have stayed on until the end. It's always nicer when you're on the pitch when the final whistle goes. You feel part of it, I suppose. Even at the end of the Six Nations, I came off against France [after being concussed tackling Mathieu Bastareaud]. It's a stranger feeling when you see the final whistle from watching the TV. It's not quite the same.

'Players always want to stay on. It's the doctors who make the decision.

They probably look after us more now than they did, previously, in terms of the knowledge of concussion [that they have now], if you get any knock to the head. We're more educated now, and when you do get a knock it's, "Get them off, get them tested and, if they're okay, get them back on." Conor [Murray] came back on, and I'm sure myself and Rob would have come back on if there had been more time.'

Sexton's concussion is his fourth in a calendar year, but he insists he is not worried. 'It's not like I'm getting knocked out or anything like that or having memory loss. I've had one bad concussion in my life, maybe six or seven years ago. Obviously the one against France looked bad, but sometimes you can just get caught on the chin. I probably felt okay the next day, that night, so it's not something I'm worried about. I think they are looking after players more and the public is becoming more aware as well, and it's being written about more. People are more aware of it and it leads to more interest on the subject. As players, we're concerned about the effects it might have if you have lots of bad ones, but I'm okay.'

The out-half recalls struggling for a couple of days with the one, heavy concussion he did receive in his career: 'The symptoms afterwards are, for example, if you have a bit of memory loss, nausea, headaches, then it is more severe. If you are perfect twenty-four hours later, then it is not as severe. They are the markers you have to go through. You have to tick the boxes … three or four days after a suspected concussion you have to make sure you're good to go. It's great that we are looking after players now, that they are not making the same mistakes that were made previously.'

The smaller knocks, he adds, are equally important to monitor: 'Before, the small ones were just brushed aside. Now they are looking after us better which is a great thing.' Sexton returns to his club side in Paris and is left out of their squad for the following weekend's game. Racing initially cite 'workload' as the reason for Sexton's absence, but face more questions as the weeks pass. Eventually, the club releases a statement confirming Sexton has, on medical advice, been stood down from playing for three months. He comments, 'It is most unfortunate and I feel bad for the club. But I'm still not feeling a hundred per cent and with injuries like this it's not worth taking any risks.'

The Murray situation is less clear-cut. Having passed his first HIA test during the match, the scrum half is monitored at the post-match function. Falvey and Munster team doctor Tadhg O'Sullivan, who was on duty at the game, carry out HIA test number two on the Sunday morning. He passes that and returns home to Limerick. Dr O'Sullivan carries out the third HIA test on the Monday, and Murray is diagnosed with a delayed concussion.

Murray pens a newspaper column on Friday morning – 21 November – stating that he is doing well after following 'return to play protocols'. That afternoon, in an announcement for the Munster reserves, confirmation of the delayed concussion appears. A Munster spokesperson says, 'We followed on the process initiated by the IRFU on Saturday and Sunday, and player welfare was our priority at every point. It is not a case of saying, "You're okay now, you don't have to worry any more," once a player passes the first test.'

An IRFU spokesperson attempts to clear up the issue: 'Conor wasn't concussed on Saturday. On Sunday, the medical staff looked at him again and he was fine. The confirmation [of delayed concussion] is per the Munster medical staff.' There are inherent dangers for a player suspected of concussion being allowed to play on. In January 2011 Northern Irish schoolboy player Ben Robinson died due to second impact syndrome (swelling of the brain before the effects of the first injury have healed). Robinson had been knocked out early in the second half of a game, only to return and make further heavy tackles. The fourteen-year-old collapsed before the end of the match and later died from his brain injuries in hospital.

The union's spokesperson stressed that Murray could have been diagnosed with delayed concussion after showing a symptom as minor as a mild headache: 'In fairness to Eanna [Falvey] and his medical team, they have made the correct decision. Even in the past when a player has passed a test, they have still been taken off. It was not a case where a completely concussed player was allowed back on to the pitch.'

The spokesperson added, 'Having a headache forty-eight hours later doesn't mean a player was concussed. It is now the case, though, where the medical staff will say, "Oh, you have a headache. You are going to go through the return to play protocols." It is an extra layer of protection.'

By all accounts, Kearney and D'Arcy hit all of their return-to-play markers. The veteran centre is the only player of the four to feature in the following weekend's action as he comes off the bench to help Leinster defeat Ospreys.

***

Jamie Roberts is well positioned to speak on the issue of concussion in rugby, given his eight seasons in professional rugby and his medical degree, picked up in 2013, from Cardiff University School of Medicine. 'I've been concussed a few times,' he says. 'I fractured my skull in 2008, which was a big one. It was against Australia – a big clash with Stirling Mortlock. It was quite scary.

'I stayed on for ten minutes, a quarter of an hour, then my medical training kicked in. I felt some water in the back of my throat and my nose was bleeding, yet I hadn't hit my nose. I just went, "Erm, this is a problem," and went to the guys to say, "Get me off." I had tasted salt-water, which was brain fluid. I knew it wasn't right. As I was walking off I could feel … my head was squeaking. I knew it wasn't right straight away. It was scary at the time, but I was back playing within six weeks.

'I got knocked out against Argentina in Autumn 2013. I took a hit straight to the jaw with the top of the other guy's head. Bang, I was straight out. I was out cold before I hit the floor. Straight off, and I woke up in the medical room … It's a hotly debated topic at the moment. We can't stop concussion, but we can improve the efficiency of detecting it and managing it.'

Bernard Jackman won widespread acclaim for his honesty when writing about his struggles with concussion in *Blue Blood*. He says pressure to play was a more personal, rather than coach-driven, factor in his lining out for Leinster when far from a hundred per cent. He tells me, 'I was very ruthless, very selfish and I hid a lot of concussions. I obviously didn't have to hide as many because the work wasn't there. Sometimes I felt it doesn't matter if they know I'm concussed, because you can still play. But when you get older … you are thinking about it all the time, because rugby is a short career. Your contract is so short. If you are working from a one-year or a two-year contract, you don't want to miss a block of games. If you want to play for Ireland, every match is important. If you want to play in the Heineken Cup. All these things, these selfish reasons come into your head.

'Most players would play with a lot of injuries and concussion. You can easily play on with concussion, which is terrible. For example, if you break your arm, you can't play. If you pull your hamstring, you can't play. Unfortunately, if you get concussed on Saturday, more than likely you can play the next week. You mightn't be 100 per cent, but no one would ever know that. That is the big fear about concussion.'

Asked how players can beat the test, Jackman says getting a purposely low baseline score, repetition (immediately taking it again) and asking a colleague to take your place were three successful tactics that no longer work. 'The best thing,' he adds, 'was to not do it. Just avoid it, avoid it and avoid it. Suddenly the team is picked on a Tuesday, announced at a press conference on Friday. You would want to be a brave doctor to say to a player, "Listen you can't play, you didn't do your cog test." That's the way it was. Obviously, I pushed that a little bit. But, again, it wasn't smart, what I did. I'm definitely proud, now, that there is better care of guys.'

In France, he explains, a second concussion during a season means a trip to the neurosurgeon and (as seen with Sexton) a third means three months off. Part of Jackman's coaching remit with Grenoble is the collision area, and he admits – despite all of his knocks – that he still loves contact. 'Winning collisions means physically dominating your opponent,' he says. 'I have no problem with that. That is what I love about the game. I was just trying to make people aware that it is a very serious injury.'

***

Declan Fitzpatrick took time out from handyman jobs on his new house in Lisburn to watch Ireland defeat Australia in November 2014. 'They were brilliant and they are going to be a real handful next year,' he says. 'They are so efficient now and have cut down on so many errors. They are playing with a real confidence. From speaking to some of the Ulster lads, the training sessions are even more intense than last year.'

Fitzpatrick has played twice for Joe Schmidt since he took over as Ireland coach. He earned his first cap, off the back of Ulster's run to the Heineken Cup final, on the 2012 summer tour to New Zealand. He started at Eden Park against the All Blacks and appeared off the bench in Hamilton the following week. His Test debut came a decade after he arrived at Ulster via England. 'My parents are both from the west of Ireland and had spent every summer over here,' he says. 'I was sick of England, so had a construction apprenticeship set up in Dublin and was all set to move, hoping to get involved in a club side when I was there.

'The Exiles were playing a match in London and I was invited along to play tight-head. I had played underage for England, but hadn't made the breakthrough. Allen Clarke was down in London for the game and was having a look at players. He asked what my plans were and told me they were setting up an academy in Ulster. It wasn't long after my eighteenth birthday when I joined. Rory Best came into the set-up around the same time. I joined the academy and they got me a job as groundsman for Belfast Harlequins for a season. I was more of an assistant to the main guy, so helped him out, drove the tractor, put up barbed wire.'

Fitzpatrick played a handful of games for the senior team as Ulster won the 2006 Celtic League. Simon Best was forced to retire with a heart condition the following year, so Fitzpatrick got a run of starts and established himself in the squad. B. J. Botha was recruited from South Africa the season after, and was followed, three years later, by John Afoa. Fitzpatrick found himself backing up world-class tight-heads no matter who was coaching Ulster. He admits it was hard to settle for the replacements role, but – once he was satisfied with his form and contributions when called upon – life fell into an enjoyable pattern. That pattern included a 2011 marriage to Gemma.

'My wife is a surgeon, and we are lucky to have the security of her job,' he says. 'I can fall back on her salary if things ever take a turn for the worse. It is incredibly stressful being a professional rugby player, as it is very hard to make financial commitments to anything. The most you usually get signed up to are one- and two-year deals. A lot of rugby executives and directors want to hand out one-year deals, but, luckily, Ulster is moving away from that. If you get injured around September or October, the club might bring someone else in and you'll be struggling to get that contract renewed. There is insurance if you ever have to retire due to injury, but it is never adequate. IRUPA has been great in setting us up with courses and work experience. I've got a Quantity Surveying degree and am on the board of a charity called The Welcome Organisation. I'm building up experience on my CV for when the inevitable comes.'

Around the time of Fitzpatrick's hitching, Ulster were becoming a force to be reckoned with under Brian McLaughlin, whose two seasons at the helm culminated in that Heineken Cup final defeat to Leinster. 'We were envious of the results Munster and Leinster were getting, but knew there was only one way of rectifying that,' says Fitzpatrick. 'Ulster has always felt a little out of the loop in terms of Irish rugby. We are getting a lot more recognition and respect now.

'There was a split in the group after we won the league [in 2006], and a lot of players left. Financially, we did not have enough clout. It has been a long road for Ulster to get back to where they are now. We have a good crop of home-grown talent like Paddy Jackson, Luke Marshall and Iain Henderson coming through, which helps, and [Chief Executive] Shane Logan is doing an incredible job. I remember we had to get changed in a bar out in Newforge near the start. We were told it would only be a few weeks, but we were there for three years. They finally moved us to a tin shed, and again said "a few weeks". We were in there for another three years. So, when I first heard about a new stadium and training facilities being planned, I was sceptical, but Shane has delivered on all of his promises. We have no excuse not to succeed, now.'

Fitzpatrick was included in Ireland's squad for the November 2012 internationals, but a concussion jinx struck and would shadow him for the next two years. 'I've had six concussions in my career to date,' he says. 'I've had no massive ones – ones where I would be totally floored. It's like being buzzed. If you get knocked out, everyone sees it. If no one sees it – either in a match or a training drill – you still feel the symptoms. It is easy to say, "I'm okay, I'm alright," as you just want to make the match at the weekend.

'I hadn't received a knock for a few years but, that October, I got hit in [Ulster] training. Tommy Bowe jumped for a high ball and his hip hit me in the head. I went down to train with the squad for the November internationals, but I just couldn't. That left me with post-concussion symptoms and with headaches. I was out for a couple of months.' The prop featured in Ireland's opening Six Nations games against Wales and England in 2013, but a calf injury in training cost him further appearances. He toured North America with Ireland that summer as Les Kiss coached and holiday-making Schmidt keenly observed. Further outings against Samoa and New Zealand told Fitzpatrick he was an integral part of the international set-up.

Another concussive knock, this time in a league game with Ulster, sent him spiralling. 'I should've rested for a week or two, but those pressures came into play again,' he says. 'My contract was up, and though the new deal was ready I hadn't signed it yet. I had finished the game, but when I tried to push on in training I broke down. You can't catch up once you haven't taken yourself out of the firing line. I paid the price for it, mentally. I was incredibly down about it. I ended up getting headaches; then the migraines started, because of my mood. I have suffered from migraines all my life, but the knocks exacerbated it. They went from sporadic to frequent, more intense. There were times when I said, "Jesus, am I doing myself serious damage here?"

'Gemma knew something was up by the way I was acting, my mood. My personality had changed a little bit. I was suffering from it – a lot quieter. She was very pragmatic once we figured out what was going on. Whatever the doctors say, she told me, trust them a hundred per cent.' Fitzpatrick began mindfulness exercises, meditating twice a day, and changed his migraine medication. Both steps, he feels, have been hugely beneficial.

Fitzpatrick adds, 'I had started my contract negotiations with the IRFU in October 2013. I then signed a contract in January 2014, but – due to the injury profile – the IRFU then said it was subject to a medical.' The union's U-turn was the last thing a fragile Fitzpatrick needed.

He travelled to Dublin for tests and scans, carried out by Professor Tim Lynch, but faced an anxious five months before he was eventually given the all-clear. Once the positive results came back, in July 2014, Fitzpatrick says everything moved along quickly: 'I had to wait until a week before pre-season started before the approved contract was ready to sign – it was incredibly stressful. I went on holiday that June without knowing if I would be an Ulster player when I got back. From October 2013 to the following July – imagine that pressure and worry sitting on you for that long. It certainly didn't help that there was not a lot of communication back and forth about the deal. You're thinking of what people are saying – "Ah here, he's injured again."

'It wasn't until I went down to Professor Lynch that I got all the tests and the reassurances that I wasn't doing any further damage to myself,' he says. 'I've been fortunate in that I've had excellent help from a group of people that were dedicated in getting me back playing.' Fitzpatrick must have been worried, then, when he received another blow against Scarlets in the season opener. On the contrary. 'After the game I told the doc [Dr Michael Webb] and took the concussion test,' he says. 'I was fine, but when they ran the test again on the Monday I had mild symptoms and they took me out of it for a week. This time I just said, "Yep, I need a week." The protocols that have come in are taking those calls out of players' hands. A player is always going to say he's okay, but you now take that out of players' hands with the new tests. If those protocols had've been in place two or three years ago, who knows where my career could have gone.'

Regular concussion screenings have made Fitzpatrick an aficionado of the process: 'They do an impact test on you, which includes memory tests, scoring certain things from one to five, reaction times, shape memory, number memory and memory combined with reactions. That will give you your baseline score. When that test first came out, that was the only tool, but they now use observation, video replays and SCAT tests, which look at memory, brain function and balance. They collate all this and assign you a graduated return to play. In some cases you could be back in a week. Others might take a few weeks, or longer. People say it is easy to cheat the memory tests and get a low baseline score, but the education of players is so good now that you'd have to be stupid to do it.

'You can see the impact all of the coverage has, and there has been a lot more education of staff as well as players in the last few years,' he continues. 'If concussions are managed properly, it should be no different to having any other type of injury. Obviously, the knock-outs and major concussions still need to be managed so carefully. You can't be too careful with these things. You've only got one brain. You're doing the better thing now by taking the player out of it rather than letting him batter on.'

Fitzpatrick and his wife are now proud parents to a daughter, Alex. The two women in the forward's life have been to see him in action for his province, and, when we speak, he has been three months without a knock that goes beyond the regular rough and tumble of rugby. 'There is no way I'd be playing now if I thought there was any danger of jeopardising my health,' he says. 'You have to have faith in the medical point of view and the statistics that say things have improved greatly. They don't know everything yet, but they know an awful lot and can give you reassurance. If, at any point, they said to me I was doing damage to myself, I would definitely retire.'

Fitzpatrick's personal goal for the season ahead does not stretch beyond getting a run in the Ulster No. 3 jersey and serving his team's goals: 'I know I'm capable of getting there if I can reach that level of consistency and keep myself fit. Mike Ross has done a great job for Ireland at tight-head for the past few years, and Marty Moore did a job when my injury opened the door for him. I'm confident that if I got back in with Ulster, my Irish ambitions would come back into focus.'

In January 2015 Fitzpatrick suffered another head injury against Toulon and in April, following medical advice, announced his retirement rather than risk another blow to the head.

# 24

# THE ABERRATIONS

'Turning thirty is not a big deal for me,' says Andrew Trimble, two days after the big day, in October 2014. 'I don't know what the average life expectancy for rugby players is, but if I get to thirty-five or thirty-six I'll be happy. Jeez, I'd be delighted to get to thirty-six.'

There is no argument that the game of rugby, in 2015, features more explosive athletes and greater hits, and is played at a higher tempo. While the body shape of players has changed over the past two decades (see chapter seventeen), the average age of those competing at an elite level has not altered too much. The average age of Ireland's 1995 World Cup squad was twenty-six years and eleven months. For the four Irish provinces, the average age of their squad (as of 1 January 2015) was twenty-six years and six months.

Professional rugby is an exacting and punishing pursuit, however, and the average age of retirements now stands at thirty-one. It was thirty-two a decade ago. While Trimble's wish to play on until he is thirty-six may seem ambitious, many of Ireland's first wave of professional players are still around to set benchmarks.

## May 2013

'I have a goal to play on until the World Cup in 2015,' Paul O'Connell tells me ahead of the British & Irish Lions tour to Australia. 'Whether injury or form intervenes before that, you never know, but that is definitely something that will drive me over the next couple of years.'

I recount the conversation to Stephen Ferris. He remarks, 'Paulie was being conservative there. I bet he's eyeing that Lions tour to New Zealand in 2017.'

## May 2014

The interview area at the IRUPA awards is general mayhem and grab-who-you-can fare. I speak with Jordi Murphy about his breakthrough international season, hear Tommy Bowe's plans to claim a spot on whichever Irish wing he can and learn Gavin Duffy is considering a post-retirement switch to Gaelic Games. Donncha O'Callaghan, who will later receive an award for his charitable endeavours, is left on his own for five seconds. I sidle up for a chat, and, after two minutes, ask him about a decrease in game-time with Munster and potential retirement. 'I've signed on with Munster for two more years,' he corrects as I sell him twelve months short. 'I feel good. It's as competitive as ever. I'm probably disappointed with how this year has panned out for me. Once you get the taste – when you're involved in great things like the Six Nations and Grand Slams, even with Munster in Europe – once you get that taste of success you want more. It's mad how addictive it is. You just want to be there.'

O'Callaghan turned thirty-five in March, and had fallen behind Dave Foley in the Munster pecking order. After ninety-four Ireland caps it looked as if he had played his final game in that arena, too. Joe Schmidt had opted for Ulster's Iain Henderson for the bulk of the latest Six Nations. Hope has not deserted the lock, yet. 'You never want guys missing out through injury,' he says. 'If you're in the team, you want to be in there on merit. As competitive as that place can be, it's better for everybody. If the other guy is going out and he's picked ahead of you, you know he's a quality fella who produces the goods every week. You have that competition in the second row and you look at a few spots that are a bit sparse and you're thinking, "Bloody hell, why don't they have the fire up their arse like we have?" You go through each other on the grass, but there is massive respect there and you wish them well when they're representing us.'

## June 2014

Michael Swift has lost count of the Connacht jerseys he has worn, but he is getting used to modelling the new ones. The London-born lock is an icon out west, and poses menacingly in the newest set of threads. The 2014/15 season will be his fifteenth in Galway and eighteenth as a pro. He has signed his third one-year extension, and will turn thirty-seven in time for the Challenge Cup kick-off in October. Swift refuses to set goals on how long he wants to play, but it is clear head coach Pat Lam sees him as a crucial squad member. One aspect of the game he will not miss, he jokes, is the pre-season physical: 'You stand there in your boxers while a nutritionist pokes and prods at you, and the other lads slag you over how easy you took it since the last game of the season.'

The honorary Galwegian is facing competition in the second row from Quinn Roux, Mick Kearney and Aly Muldowney. Lam's penchant for promoting colts means he must keep Danny Qualter and recent Ireland Under-20 captain Sean O'Brien in their place. 'As senior players, it will be our job not to make things easy for them,' Swift proclaims. 'We'll be eager to get those lads into tackling and full-contact sessions. The lads who've been around a bit will be looking to hand out some hard lessons.'

## July 2014

Paul O'Connell is counting down the days until his fourteenth season in professional rugby. Positivity abounds throughout his round-table interview. He is coming to the tail-end of his first full pre-season in three years and enjoying every minute. 'I'm still managing myself a little bit,' he says. 'I'm not doing everything the lads are doing, but I'm doing the two big main fitness sessions a week and doing a lot of skills, a bit of speed as well. Yeah, it's a great feeling to be able to work really hard Monday to Friday and not be rehabbing or looking after a niggly injury.'

He adds, 'When I look back on some of the better years that I played my best rugby – in 2005, 2006, 2008, the year of the World Cup – they are all down to big pre-seasons. Certainly for my position, anyway. Go into the backs or go into the front row there are different skill-sets, but certainly for a second row it's such a work-rate position. You are trying to accumulate tackles, ball carries, rucks, and you need to have that big workload done in the summer to be able to replicate that workload in the games.

'The big thing is the monitoring; there are certain kilometres or certain metres you are trying to hit each week, whereas that probably wasn't measured as much in years past. You just got out there and got beasted and worked really hard. There is probably a lot to be said for that as well; but at my age [thirty-four] it is nice to have what you are doing monitored, to be able to step things up each week. The GPS monitoring allows the strength-and-conditioning staff to see exactly what you are doing, and it's a little bit more controlled as well.

'When I would have come back, when I was very young, I would have been eager, in week one, to get into the thick of it as hard as I could straight away. Now, it has been a gradual progression over the first four fitness sessions for me. I'd say they have learned a lot from the past in terms of how players accumulated injuries and injuries were picked up. I suppose by managing that and knowing exactly what we are doing week to week, they are able to avoid injuries, and that is probably the big difference – the monitoring from a GPS point of view. We have an app on our phone and every morning you have to fill in where you are with your various numbers, weights, stretches, all of that. That just contributes to keeping more guys fit and healthy.'

O'Connell confesses he has become selfish about maintaining his fitness in recent years. He rarely throws himself into the two big team sessions per day during pre-season training. 'At this time of the year I'm able to do the heavier of the two sessions rather than doing both of them,' he says. 'There are some days I come in and I know I need to just be careful what I do. I had a little bit of that yesterday, where I stepped back a little and did a bit of work with the physio instead. That has been a bit of a learning curve for me, because I have injured myself trying to push myself in training in the past. For me, it's about getting the two big fitness sessions in each week, and just making sure I stay injury free. I think I played something like twenty-four or twenty-five games last year. If I can put a good pre-season on top of that, stay fit throughout this season as well, I think I will be in very good shape.'

The World Cup is fourteen months closer than our pre-Lions chat, but O'Connell is taking nothing for granted. 'It's month to month,' he says. 'Look, I'd love to go to the World Cup, but it's something you only want to do if you're in really good shape. I'd love to go there with two big pre-seasons – this pre-season and next summer's pre-season as well. If I could get there with those I'd know I'd go in really good shape. But the game is becoming tougher and tougher; it's going to be a really tough November internationals and really tough Six Nations, so, really, the World Cup is a long way away for me.'

O'Connell is more concerned with getting Munster off to a winning start now that they are singing off new coach Anthony Foley's hymn sheet. Europe looms as large as ever for Munster, and the trimmed fat of the Champions Cup – twenty teams as opposed to twenty-four – makes for tougher pools. Under Rob Penney, Munster had reached the semi-finals in 2012 and 2013. O'Connell believes the younger members of the squad are capable of going two steps further. 'One of the big things the Irish provinces have,' he says, 'is that – you hate saying the amateur ethos – but we'll have players playing for us who grew up in the province, in a club that they grew up wanting to play for. In rugby – a sport where that emotion still plays a big role – the Irish provinces have an advantage over the other teams in that regard. Hopefully, in Munster, Leinster, Ulster and Connacht, we can make that count.'

## August 2014

Gordon D'Arcy is a week further into his pre-season and is struggling to match Paul O'Connell's self-flagellating enthusiasm. 'It's pretty horrific as every pre-season is,' he says. 'You've just about recovered, and then you walk in and you can barely walk out. You go home and sit on your couch, just about recover and do it all over again. It is kind of like groundhog day for ten weeks.'

The new season will be the thirty-four-year-old's first without Brian O'Driscoll in the same playing squad. There is no point mulling on that loss, he insists: 'You just do what you do in sport. You get on with it, you move on. You are never going to replace Brian O'Driscoll. Leo Cullen has moved ten metres upstairs and it is like he has been there all his life. It is just part and parcel of sport. You play big games, big players aren't there and you win. People [believe] there is an opportunity to win without these guys. That is not to say you wouldn't like them there, but, when they are not there, the collective has to pick up the slack.'

D'Arcy will be four months off his thirty-sixth birthday if Ireland live an impossible dream and reach the World Cup final at Twickenham. Joe Schmidt has yet to find a viable, sustainable replacement for the Wexford native in the Irish midfield. His best performances in green have been defensively driven since 2011, but dalliances at outside centre for Leinster have stirred attacking embers.

'I can't really control more than six months in my destiny,' he says. 'When I broke my arm in 2008 there was a six-month period where I was going, "You are probably never going to play again." I had three operations and it was fifty–fifty on whether I was going to play. Six months later we win a Grand Slam. So I've learned six months is a very long time in rugby.'

D'Arcy continues, 'I can't worry about what might happen next September [at the World Cup]. I can worry about the first half of the season, recovering from my shoulder operation, starting the season, getting as fit as I can, getting four games under my belt before the Champions Cup. Getting a good start in the Champions Cup to put me in contention for an Irish position and the second half of the cup – that is my immediate target.

'If I hit all that and flip over to the next half of the year, if I hit all those things, if I'm involved in friendlies, I can just put myself in the shop window. If Matt O'Connor wants to pick me, if Joe wants to pick me, I will deliver on every stage. I plan on being at least at the top of the queue for every game.'

## October 2014

Peter Stringer came off the bench in three of Ireland's Six Nations matches in 2011. Aged thirty-three and tussling with Tomás O'Leary at Munster, the scrum half had accepted his bench role with Ireland. Twelve of his last nineteen caps had come as a replacement to either O'Leary or Eoin Reddan. In between the home wins against Scotland and England had been a controversial away loss to Wales. There had also been a backup role to play at Thomond Park on 6 March as Munster doused the Dragons 38–17. Twenty-one-year-old Garryowen scrum half Conor Murray started in the No. 9 jersey and set up Mick O'Driscoll for the hosts' third try. By the time Stringer returned from international duty, Murray had a granite grasp on that jersey. Leinster visited Thomond and were met by a half-back pairing of Murray and Ronan O'Gara. Cian Healy, Sean O'Brien and Kevin McLaughlin all took runs at the young scrum half, but he picked himself up each time. Munster won 24–23. By the time Leinster revisited Limerick for the Pro12 final, Stringer was on the outside, looking in. Murray started again and – for the first time in his professional career – completed eighty minutes in a 19–9 win.

O'Leary had returned from injury in May, while Leinster's Eoin Reddan and Isaac Boss had taken part in the remarkable Heineken Cup final comeback triumph against Northampton Saints later that month. Stringer took four weeks off in June, but there was no summer blowout. The World Cup kicked off in September, and Ireland's pre-season would commence in early July. The call arrived for the scrum half in late June, but it was not what he was expecting. 'Declan selected a big squad in 2011, during the pre-season, and obviously I would have been hoping to be included,' says Stringer. 'I had a word with the coach and he told me he wouldn't be selecting me. It was massively disappointing. You will have these crushing moments numerous times in your career.'

Three years and three clubs on from that disappointment, Stringer is enjoying a (twenty) second wind in England. Having fallen out of favour with Tony McGahan then Rob Penney at Munster, Stringer went on loan to Saracens and Newcastle before Bath opted to bring the veteran in on a permanent deal. He started his Bath career as a loanee, but two tries on debut against Exeter set an impressive tone and his switch became permanent. I catch up with him three months into his seventeenth season, and find him plotting for twenty and refusing to rule out adding to his ninety-eight Ireland caps.

'Bath is a lovely city, a rugby city, too. The ground is right in the middle of town. There is a good environment within the club and they have been very welcoming. I'm thoroughly enjoying it, and loving the new lease of life the move has afforded me,' he comments. 'There were opportunities elsewhere, away from Munster, and my goal was to play well for my club side and take it from there. You're always hopeful that those efforts will be recognised at international level.'

He adds, 'Munster is a place I loved, and still love. For me, I felt I still had a lot to offer. I was not in the Ireland squad for whatever reasons, but felt I had a huge part of my rugby life left. I didn't want to finish up my career not playing, being part of a squad and being content with that. I still have a huge hunger for the game. I left my homeland with the point of view of getting more game time. Moving to England gave me an opportunity to extend my career and still enjoy it. I have a massive passion for rugby, and as long as that lasts I will keep playing. The norm for players, once they reach a certain age, is to go on year-to-year contracts. There are not too many players my age still playing the game. As long as I'm still playing, learning and contributing – telling the coaches things and coming up with ideas – I'm content.'

Bath had released a video of pre-season training that included Stringer flinging balls through the shell of a vacuum cleaner. What stood out from the promotional piece, however, was Stringer's lean, muscular physique. 'The body feels good,' he says. 'Generally I would've looked after myself well. I'm even stricter, now, in terms of recovery and preparation for training sessions, than I was a decade ago. Even in the grand scheme you are in the game for the short term, so you have to look after yourself, your body, what you eat.

'I can only speak for myself and know that Donncha O'Callaghan looks after himself well, too. He doesn't drink or smoke either, and, like me, is meticulous with his preparation. We were both like that from day one and would have similar attitudes. All you can do is give your body and mind the best opportunity to go out and play, and finish on your terms.'

Fitness, diet and dedication are simple ways of keeping up with the next generation, but Stringer confesses to often losing the run of conversations between his younger colleagues. 'I'm reminded of the age difference every day at training. You're training with fellas born in the mid 1990s, when I was leaving school. Once we get to the training pitch, though, we're all just players. Teammates. I'm still near the top of all the fitness tests. There is still that perception of being the senior citizen. I use that in trying to set an example for the young guys while, at the same time, learning from them and improving my game any way I can.'

***

O'Callaghan testifies to Stringer's philosophy and backs it up on 4 October 2014 when he appears for Munster A at Donnybrook. They defeat their Leinster counterparts 18–8, and the veteran lock packs down with promising forwards such as Jack O'Donoghue and Shane Buckley. Reflecting on the match a week later, O'Callaghan states, 'The drive for me is no different. I played that A match and wanted to play like I was nineteen again. The hunger and the desire to get in the senior team is still through the roof with me. I love it. I love togging out; rugby means everything to me. I love Munster – it's part of my DNA at this stage. The values, the standards and the team; I'd like to think they're my life.

'I've played for Munster A and I've played for Ireland A, and – I've no problem saying it – I was disappointed with some of the senior lads I played with because they bitched and moaned at having to play. That's easily done, but I see it as an opportunity, playing with this quality of players, having a chance to try and earn their respect. That's a big thing, you tog out with a guy for the first time – you might have heard of things he has done in the past, but it isn't until he sees you in the real moment when you need to be more than a team player, you need to give it your all. If you can do that and try to earn these guys' respect … that was the big driver for me.'

### March 2015
O'Connell admits he may retire after the 2015 World Cup or in June 2016, adding 'there's no point codding myself too much here' about stretching his impressive career into 2017. David Wallace responds to the news by predicting his former Munster teammate may yet make it to New Zealand – in a British & Irish Lions jersey – in 2017.

### 15 June 2015
A little over a week after playing his final game for Munster – a Guinness Pro12 Final defeat to Glasgow Warriors – the IRFU confirm that O'Connell will be released from his provincial and national contract following the World Cup. The Ireland captain signs a one-year contract with Toulon, the reigning European champions. An option for a second year, which would take him up to June 2017, is included in the lucrative (reportedly €600,000 a season) deal.

# 25

## 'IT'S TIME LADS GREW UP': HEARTBREAK AGAINST NEW ZEALAND

Victory over South Africa, in November 2009, saw Ireland climb to second in the world rankings – their highest-ever position. By the time Declan Kidney, who had masterminded Gram Slam glory earlier that year, departed in April 2013, the country had slumped to ninth – their lowest.

Two matches, played within seven days of each other, would sum up the Irish team during the final years of Kidney's tenure. In Christchurch, on 16 June 2012, Kidney's men played the game of their lives, only to lose to New Zealand through a late Dan Carter drop goal. The following week, in Hamilton, the same players (bar the injured Jamie Heaslip and Gordon D'Arcy) were destroyed by the All Blacks. Nine tries were scored without reply. Ireland lost 60–0.

Captain Brian O'Driscoll was asked if he was sick of playing the All Blacks by this stage. 'You get sick of that scoreline pretty quickly,' he replied. 'That's a difficult one to take.' He added, 'It's hard to look back on other New Zealand performances [against Ireland] and think of a better one. The fact that they managed to 0 us is pretty impressive … They smashed us today, and, as a result, we weren't able to put together many phases. On top of that, the number of unforced errors we made really, really hurt us. A combination of things made them look good, but, on their own, they were doing a pretty good job on that front.'

Kidney batted away queries on his coaching future and remained in charge for a further ten months. His 2013 Six Nations squad was struck down with an entirely cruel injury jinx. He all but retired Ronan O'Gara after dropping him from a squad to play France, despite Johnny Sexton missing out with a tweaked hamstring. Kidney looked a beaten man when, on 16 March 2013, Italy broke a twelve-year habit by defeating Ireland. It was a grim, unfortunate way for a Grand Slam-winning coach to go.

*** 

After one win from his opening four games as Leinster coach, Joe Schmidt's credentials were openly questioned in print and across the national airwaves, albeit by a well-heeled minority. In the summer of 2010, the province had opted to appoint a man who had a solitary year of head-coaching experience at Bay of Plenty Steamers in his native New Zealand. Assistant roles followed at Auckland Blues and Clermont Auvergne, but it seemed a stretch to follow up the trophy-winning tenure of Michael Cheika with an unproven, yet eager, Kiwi.

Schmidt arrived with the ambition of making Leinster the best passing team in Europe. His side possessed players of undoubted flair with an ability to grind out matches when the need arose. He wanted to raise the skill ceiling and make his troops tactically and technically aware. 'That was something that wasn't supposed to leak into the public domain, but we had a few key targets … I thought there were some things they did really well and some things that, if they could do a little better, maybe we could grow our game,' he said. It would take time, but a six-game winning run, including European success against Saracens and Racing Métro, provided breathing room. By the season's end, May 2011, Leinster had claimed their second Heineken Cup title. By the time Schmidt left to become Ireland's number one, he had guided the province to another Heineken Cup, the league and the Challenge Cup.

Ewen McKenzie had been the early favourite to replace Kidney and interviewed for the job in a video conference call. 'Link' was openly angling for the Wallabies job, and secured it once the Australian Rugby Union dispensed with Robbie Deans after the Test series loss to the British &

Irish Lions. The other hat in the ring was that of Les Kiss, an Australian coach from a rugby-league background who had the backing of big hitters within the Ireland squad. Once it became clear that Schmidt was keen to take the job, the IRFU moved quickly. On 29 April, less than four weeks after Kidney's departure, Schmidt sat in the media briefing room at the Aviva Stadium and, looking like he had dressed in a taxi over from Leinster training at UCD, addressed a packed house.

O'Driscoll, who would be named in the Lions squad the following day, had yet to reveal whether he would continue playing. Schmidt remarked that he had planted fans chanting 'one more year' in O'Driscoll's direction at the RDS, and added that he would apply gentle pressure on his provincial talisman. Kiss would take charge of the summer tour to North America, and Schmidt revealed he had tried to recruit the Aussie when he first joined Leinster. 'This is a bit like when I came to Leinster,' he said. 'I didn't really want to be head coach, but I've enjoyed the experience after the first four weeks. The first four weeks I wasn't enjoying it. That might have been because we kept losing. At the same time, I'm really motivated by challenge and I think this is a super challenge, albeit an intimidating one. If you want to find out what you can bring to a group, what better way to do it than to take on one of the big jobs in world rugby?' As the briefing concluded, Schmidt loosened his shirt collar and joked, 'Jeez, it's a bit hotter in here than I'm used to.'

With Schmidt an engrossed tourist in North America, Kiss' Ireland edged a win over the United States, and were rewarded for an expansive game by defeating Canada 42–14. Rory Best had been named captain of the touring squad, but was replaced by Peter O'Mahony after receiving a late call-up to the Lions tour. Simon Zebo featured against the United States before packing a bag and flying out to Australia to join the Ulster hooker. The squad contained players such as Felix Jones, Chris Henry, Dan Tuohy, Andrew Trimble, Devin Toner and Fergus McFadden. There was no summer off for the overworked Mike Ross, while promising young stars Robbie Henshaw, Kieran Marmion and Stuart Olding were all included.

Schmidt's first match in charge saw Samoa front up at the Aviva Stadium, and a shirtless Brian Lima lead a passionate Siva Tau war dance. Nine of the Irish match-day squad had toured under Kiss that summer, with Schmidt able to call on six Lions to start and another three, including the fit-again Paul O'Connell, on the bench. The visitors ran Ireland hard for sixty minutes until a McFadden try and a double from debutant Dave Kearney made it 40–9. 'I didn't want to have to come in here afterwards,' admitted a relieved Schmidt, 'and face up to a first-up loss. That can never happen to me now, but I don't want to do it for a second-up loss or any loss.'

McKenzie's Australia were next up. In the lead-up to the match Schmidt spoke of developing thirty to thirty-five international-class players. On 16 November in Dublin, fifteen looked a stretch. The Wallabies assembled on wooden benches, passing around orange segments at half-time, and gave Schmidt his first taste of Test agony. Ireland never looked like scoring a try, while the Australians ran in four in the space of forty-eight minutes. Open-side Michael Hooper was the stand-out forward, while Nick Cummins and Israel Folau broke lines and made huge gains at will. The All Blacks – having already beaten Japan, France and England on tour – would touch down at Dublin Airport forty-eight hours later.

Schmidt had named O'Connell as his permanent captain ahead of the November internationals. The Munster second row had been in fantastic form during the Lions tour until he broke his arm, and played on, in the closing stages of the first Test. He had played New Zealand eight times (thrice as a Lion in 2005), and – having missed the gut-twister in Christchurch in 2012 – came closest to beating them at Waikato Stadium in 2006. The secret to beating the Kiwi men and myth, he said, was to 'do nearly everything right, all the time'. O'Connell expanded, 'We spoke about the opportunity of creating history. It's something we addressed very early on in the week. Joe has spoken about it. If there's ever an Irish team that is capable of doing it, that I've been on, I think it's this one. We're an excellent side with a lot of talent that just isn't playing well at the moment. That needs to stop somewhere.'

From the first seconds of that weekend's match, Ireland were inspired. The clock read 9:58 as Best stretched an arm out to score Ireland's second try of the game. Conor Murray had smashed over to reward early pressure, and Sean O'Brien featured twice in an unstoppable surge that Best finished off. The home crowd had seen their country poke the black bear before, and – deafeningly positive as they were – dared not believe a winning platform had been established. All that changed on sixteen minutes as Israel Dagg fumbled a pass and Rob Kearney gripped and ripped up the touchline. The fullback sprinted eighty metres and touched down before spiking the ball into the turf. Aaron Cruden found Julian Savea with a sublime grubber to bump Irish fans down to cloud eight, but a Sexton kick made it 22–7 at the break.

Cruden reduced arrears to twelve points with a fifty-second minute penalty, and Ben Franks shunted over from close range with fifteen minutes to go. O'Driscoll had been replaced by Luke Fitzgerald at this stage. He had suffered a concussive blow and could not talk team doctor Eanna Falvey into allowing him to continue. Ireland were creaking, but players such as Heaslip, O'Brien and Toner were pouring themselves into rucks and tackles around the fringes. Their defensive efforts were rewarded with eight minutes remaining after the All Blacks hauled down a rolling maul. Sexton, conscious of the kick's significance, stood over his penalty attempt for well over a minute before skewing it right and wide. The score stood at 22–17 as New Zealand captain Richie McCaw invoked one last drive from his teammates.

Ireland wrested possession back from their guests with three minutes of normal time remaining, and sought to run out the clock with picks and drives. The tactic was working up until 79:30 when Nigel Owens, the same referee from the Christchurch Test, penalised Jack McGrath for going off his feet at the ruck. Ireland were sixty-two metres from their tryline. New

Zealand had the ball back and Ben Smith made three vital carries in sixty seconds to bring play deep into the Irish half. The home defence were scrambling, but clearly out on their feet. Sensing weakness, the All Blacks players lined up for carries. Ma'a Nonu and Owen Franks made gains and drew in green shirts. Scrum half Aaron Smith got away with a low-flung pass to Nonu, but – having been left vulnerable out wide right – Ireland looked to have covered the left flank.

Modern professionals often preach about the one per cent that makes the difference between winning and losing. At 81:17, Cruden sourced that extra percentage to locate replacement hooker Dane Coles with a wonderful, flat pass that skipped Kieran Read and took two Irishmen out of the move. Ian Madigan, on the pitch for six minutes after replacing the spent Sexton, gravitated to Coles rather than sticking on the wing. O'Brien reached the forward, but not before the ball was offloaded to Ryan Crotty. With Madigan committed, the Crusaders winger scurried over to level the scores. The video replays gave broken Irish players four slow-motion chances to watch their world unravel. Three green jerseys mustered enough strength to race from the tryline as Cruden sized up a touchline conversion that missed the target. Owens gave him a second chance that soared over to make it 24–22 and delivered New Zealand their fourteenth straight win of an immense calendar year.

'Yeah, I'd say I am angry,' O'Brien agreed post match as glum-faced Irish reporters picked over the bones of another close call. 'We should have trusted each other in the last couple of minutes. I'd say a lot of the lads are angry at the way it finished. We weren't getting set early enough, not coming off the line at them again, and we just needed to want it that little bit more for the last two or three minutes of the game. That's where you should be trying even harder.'

The flanker concluded, 'I think it's time lads grew up and know what's expected when they put on an Irish jersey. That performance today, we can be proud, but it still wasn't good enough.'

# 26

## ANDREW TRIMBLE:
## OVERNIGHT SUCCESS, NINE YEARS ON

Andrew Trimble made his way up the steep tunnel steps onto the Lansdowne Road pitch and cast a glance to his left. 'There had been a fire on the north terrace, so some of it was closed off,' he recalls. 'To cover it up someone had placed a huge banner there with a picture of Brian O'Driscoll on it. I thought, "Jesus, that guy's kind of a big deal."'

Six months after O'Driscoll was spear-tackled into a shoulder dislocation on the 2005 British & Irish Lions' tour to New Zealand, Eddie O'Sullivan was assessing replacements. Gordon D'Arcy had featured at outside centre in a 45–7 flaking at the hands of the All Blacks on the previous Saturday [12 November 2005]. The Irish coach shook up his backline by moving Shane Horgan from inside centre to the right wing. Tommy Bowe switched wings, with Anthony Horgan surplus to requirements. D'Arcy took the vacated No. 12 jersey and was joined by a twenty-one-year-old, Trimble, who had made his Ulster debut two months before.

Trimble says, 'It was a few days after my birthday when I got the call and was asked to come down to Dublin to train with Ireland. Everything had ramped up, from my first full pre-season and friendlies to playing in the Celtic League and then the Heineken Cup. It seemed like I was being thrown in at the deep end against Australia, but it honestly didn't feel that way for me. Every two weeks I was experiencing something new, so the Ireland call-up felt no different. Almost natural. I was really excited about it and not that nervous at all.

'There had been a few questions asked about my filling Brian's shoes. I don't know if I didn't fully appreciate how big a role it was – putting that No. 13 jersey on your back. I hadn't fully thought about it and was a bit naive, but – in a way – it helped to keep the pressure off.'

Bowe was eight months older than Trimble, and had made a try-scoring debut against the United States in November 2004. He missed out on the following Six Nations, but O'Sullivan felt he was the strike-running winger Ireland were searching for. Australia at home was his fifth cap. David Humphreys, coming to the end of his international career, took his young Ulster teammates aside before the game to impart words of advice. Bowe nodded non-stop during his pep talk before Humphreys turned to Trimble. He says, 'David told me to take a few seconds to look around when I got out there. To really soak it in and appreciate where I was. I had gone from playing in front of 10,000 fans at Ravenhill to over 40,000 against Australia in O'Driscoll's spot. It was amazing.'

Australia's twenty-one-year-old winger, Drew Mitchell, was the scoring difference that afternoon as Ireland went down 14–30. Trimble held his own in the Irish midfield and kept his jersey for the visit of Romania the following week. Given that extra shaft of space by the second-tier nation, the Belfast native cut loose. He crossed for two tries, while provincial teammate Neil Best dotted down. Humphreys kicked thirteen points in a 43–12 win; it was his final Test match.

The out-half stayed on at Ulster, and – along with Trimble, Bowe and Neil Best – won the Celtic League by beating Ospreys on the final day of the season. Trimble comments, 'I won the league and the Triple Crown with Ireland in my first season. I had limited experience of professional rugby, but had it in my head that every time we were on the pitch we would win.'

Ulster failed to build on their league success, and would eventually go through four coaches (including caretaker Steve Williams) in four seasons. By the end of 2008, Bowe and Neil Best had departed as the province struggled to meet wage demands. O'Driscoll returned to the international stage in 2006, shifting Trimble out to the wing. He started the 2007 Six Nations on the right wing, but was relegated to the bench after the opening round win over Wales.

O'Sullivan spared O'Driscoll in the wretched, ill-deserved World Cup warm-up win over Italy. Paired with D'Arcy in midfield, Trimble scored a try, but Ireland still needed a late Ronan O'Gara drop goal to eek home. Another try followed in the World Cup game with Namibia, but he missed out on the close call against Georgia. He replaced Denis Hickie on the left wing for the pool match against France, but was part of an abject team performance. 'We never thought for a moment that we would underperform so badly,' he concedes. 'It is still hard to figure out how we fell so short. We didn't get enough rugby in beforehand. We spent too much time in the gym, doing weights, when we should have been on the pitch, working on our skills and speed.

'We were based in a hotel in an industrial estate outside of Bordeaux. There was no chance to get out of that zone and have any craic. When you compare it to 2011, it was so much better in New Zealand. We got out on daytrips and tours to take our minds off the rugby. There were coffee shops to go out to and chat, meet fans. In Bordeaux, there might have been a truck-stop.'

Trimble adds, 'Argentina played unbelievably well at that World Cup. We always knew they would be a handful. We never figured Georgia would be such a handful. The France and Georgia games were our measure. Our performances in those two games summed up our tournament. Just flat.'

D'Arcy broke his arm in five places at the beginning of the 2008 Six Nations, affording Trimble a run at inside centre for the remainder of the campaign. He enjoyed dovetailing with O'Driscoll and pitching himself into defensive efforts, but poor results drove O'Sullivan out. Following a summer in which the Irish were under caretakers, Declan Kidney arrived. Trimble featured off the bench against Fiji that November, but missed out on selection for Ireland's Grand Slam glory in 2009. It wasn't until the warm-ups for the 2011 World Cup that Trimble made four consecutive starts under Kidney. Once in New Zealand, he found it hard to shift Bowe or Keith Earls from their positions out wide.

'I couldn't get that run of games and was finding it frustrating,' Trimble admits. 'With Eddie, I felt he appreciated what I brought to the team. I struggled to stay involved for a while after that. At the same time, we had six or seven wingers playing out of their skins. They were doing well while I was struggling for form, putting myself under pressure.' The year 2012 represented the fairest crack of the whip from Kidney, but Trimble's confidence looked brittle. He rarely took the attack to his opponents or went looking for work, preferring often to linger on the outskirts of battle. Club form for Ulster – they had reached the Heineken Cup final only to lose out to Leinster – was not replicated in the Test arena. Kidney was far from convinced.

When the head coach moved on, Trimble's prospects improved. 'Things had been made simple in 2012/13 because I was out of favour with Ireland. I knew I wouldn't be involved there, so I threw all my energies into Ulster – "This is all I've got and I'm not going to let them down."'

Joe Schmidt was named as Ireland's head coach, but Les Kiss would oversee the summer tour to North America. 'I got the call and there was no way I would be missing that tour,' says Trimble. 'I had been sitting on forty-nine caps for a while. I was very anxious to reach fifty, and thought it would never happen. It was a good opportunity for game time and a chance to show the new guys what I was worth.

'The tour was great exposure for lads like Chris Henry and Devin Toner, too. I'm the same age as them and had played a lot of underage rugby with them. I was very much aware of how good both could be. Chris had been doing the job for Ulster for a number of years, already. They made the most of their starts and took a lot of confidence from that tour. We struggled in Houston against the United States, but finished – and performed – well against Canada.'

Trimble credits Schmidt with bringing out the best in him personally and in his game: 'He tells you exactly what he wants from you – accuracy, all-round game, looking for work, being sensible with your plays, making the most of yourself. Those were the things drilled into me during the autumn and pre-Six Nations camps. He expects perfection. Those training sessions are intense. It is really unpleasant being in that environment when you are trying things, pushing yourself and getting it wrong. It prepares you, though, for the level of intensity you need at Test level. Joe expects so much more of me than any coach I have ever worked with. You very rarely get to where he wants, but – because of that – your standards go through the roof.'

At the turn of the year, when it came to conversations on Ireland's starting fifteen for the Six Nations, Trimble, Toner and Henry barely raised a whisper. Injuries provided a pause and the trio responded with a roar.

# 27

## FAIRYTALES AND 'KILLER DRILLS': SIX NATIONS 2014

It's certainly going to be a massive task, but fairytales do come true sometimes.

*Joe Schmidt, March 2014*

Opening press conferences of Six Nations campaigns are jolly affairs as colleagues catch up, the foreign press add lilting accents to affairs, players flush with optimism and someone from the union splashes out on biscuits. Add an impending chat with Brian O'Driscoll into the afternoon and a home opener against a poor Scottish side. The atmosphere in Carton House is positively giddy. The outside centre has left no one in doubt that he is about to embark on his final Six Nations. This is it.

Team manager Mick Kearney provides the injury updates ahead of the opener against Scotland. He then sits back and listens as O'Driscoll considers aloud the end of a championship journey that began with a 50–18 reverse to England in February 2000: 'It's great driving through the [hotel] gates, last week and this week, knowing it's game-week. I still get as much of a buzz. Maybe more so now that I'm retiring. I have huge belief in the squad and the coaching ticket that we're going to go in the right direction, building with the lads for the World Cup.'

O'Driscoll adds, 'I was really unsure last year and there were strange emotions, but it is nice knowing that you can empty the tank in this Six Nations, knowing it will definitely be the last one … Just because it is the last one, it doesn't add any more incentive. As professionals, you're expected to deliver each time. There's always peaking and troughing throughout a career, and I'd like to think I've maintained a standard.'

Warren Gatland's Wales would be in town the weekend after, and the media dwell on O'Driscoll's getting axed during the British & Irish Lions tour. The Irishman returned home from Australia having won his first Lions Test series. Gatland, however, had selected Welshmen Jonathan Davies and Jamie Roberts in midfield for the deciding match, sparking sympathy in all rugby-playing nations, and irrational outrage in Ireland. Time proves a healer as O'Driscoll jokes, 'Why do you think I'm doing interviews this week?'

Scotland and Wales are bombarded with garryowens and flattened by rolling mauls, giving Joe Schmidt's men a great start to the championship. England win a Twickenham 'slog-fest', in round three, and Grand Slam headlines are packed up for another year. The collective focus of a nation swivels back to O'Driscoll. He will face Italy in his final international at home, so pops out to have another natter with the press. 'It will be difficult; leaving something you've done all your adult life will be hard,' he says. 'Being in that environment, one day you're part of it, the next day you're not. No matter who you are or what you've done, that's always going to be a difficult situation. But it is fortunate that I have been able to call it on my terms. I can see it's time to move on to pastures new, and not many people get to do that. I'm thankful for that.'

Approaching his one-hundred-and-fortieth Test cap, O'Driscoll downplays his role in transforming Irish rugby since his debut. He comments, 'I was very lucky to play at a time when there was great young talent coming through, and you can see the guys who began at the same time. Someone like Gordon D'Arcy, who's still here, the ROGs, the Strings, the Shane Horgans, Simon Easterby, [John] Hayes. All those guys came in within six months of my first cap, and I think we all had a big say in guiding expectation levels, first of all, and then performance levels after that, to where we felt they should be. Now the onus is on every young guy coming through, seeing that as the benchmark to carry on and make it better.'

Ireland went into '#Thirteen' overdrive ahead of O'Driscoll's Lansdowne Road farewell. Paul O'Connell remarks that he may hug his teammate tighter than usual before kick-off, Adidas commission a new pair of boots for their client, and a Fair City actor – reminiscing like nobody's business in 2054 – tells his fictitious grandson all about 'BOD'. One gulp, one hard exhale and O'Driscoll gets through the national anthem intact.

Each of the 51,022 supporters lucky or accredited enough to witness O'Driscoll's final home game comes away raving about a ravishing performance of guile and ingenuity. A reverse pass sets up Johnny Sexton for his first try, he dishes a basketball pass to send Andrew Trimble racing free up the left wing and saves his best for last. Italy are 27–7 behind and all but spent. Ireland are relentless and press for further scores. O'Driscoll swoops into a backline move just outside the Italian twenty-two and continues to pump the legs despite the grappling attentions of hooker Leonardo Ghiraldini. He somehow frees his left arm and dishes out a sublime offload to Rob Kearney in support. He links up with Dave Kearney on the left wing, who pops a pass to Sexton for a simple score.

O'Driscoll is withdrawn on sixty-one minutes, and Fergus McFadden, his replacement, later thanks fans for the standing ovation. A retired Ronan O'Gara, on commentary duty for RTÉ, seeks his former rival and teammate outside for a hug. McFadden, Sean Cronin and Jack McGrath contribute late scores to blow the score out to 46–7. Floating banners drop to acclaim O'Driscoll at the final whistle and Ireland tingles as he walks through a guard of honour with daughter Sadie in his arms.

Schmidt comments, 'In the modern day of the powerful, direct-running centre, he still showed that character and class can take you a long way. He had a hand in three tries, and it was a pretty important hand in all of them.' The Six Nations title awaits if Ireland can see off a tempestuous France in

Paris the following weekend. 'We've made a nice habit in Paris, winning once in forty-two years,' the coach quips.

Back at Carton House, Schmidt and his coaching staff ramp up the training intensity early in the week. Speaking four months after the championship, Ulster's Darren Cave recalled a particular drill the New Zealander focused on. The Killer Drill takes place within a twenty-two and has fifteen attackers against fifteen defenders with pads. It involves one-out runners off the scrum half and requires the attacking player to dominate and win the contact. The defenders have licence to pile through and disrupt. It means the attacking players need to clear them out in order to present clean, quick ball.

Cave commented, 'Joe said that the passage of play that the All Blacks scored from was two minutes forty seconds. That was the length of the drill. That passage of play against England, where Jonny May went over in the corner but the ball was dislodged, was three minutes ten seconds. So that became the new length of the drill. That is what Joe says – that is how long passages of play take in international rugby.'

England shred Italy in Rome on the championship's final afternoon, but a Leonardo Sarto try halts their momentum. The result means Ireland can claim the title if they beat their hosts by as little as a point. Peter O'Mahony is back at blindside after Iain Henderson deputised for the Italy game. It is a night of excruciating tension and of unsung heroes taking to the stage. Maxime Machenaud pops over two early penalties before Ireland's training pays off. They unload on the French inside their twenty-two and go through eleven phases in the space of one minute and thirty-nine seconds. As green jerseys heave into their hosts, Conor Murray is almost swallowed up. Ireland clear the French out and Chris Henry picks from the base before flicking a pass back for Sexton, who steps inside Mathieu Bastareaud and holds off Damien Chouly to score.

A 6–0 deficit is a 12–6 lead five minutes later as a mixture of Irish tactics, strike and support running breach France. Ireland wheel an attacking scrum to all but take the French pack out of the ensuing attack. A line break is still required to press home the numerical advantage. O'Driscoll provides it before Murray arrives to pick and snipe. France are scrambling but Maxime Médard and Brice Dulin are back to block Murray. Trimble is screaming in on his right shoulder and receives a perfectly judged pass before sliding over for his third crucial try of the tournament.

Roared on by a partisan crowd of 78,337, France force an attacking, five-metre line-out, and draw in bodies, before Rémi Talès unfurls a beautiful cross-field kick. Rob Kearney is left with a two-on-one and gambles on tackling Yoann Huget. The winger manages to bat the ball back for Dulin to dive over. Ireland trail 13–12 at the break, despite their attacking intentions. Sexton has missed a conversion and penalty attempt in the town he now calls home.

Huget looks for a score of his own after the break, but cannot control a high pass. Rob Kearney counters and – following a surge by Cian Healy – Murray recognises the space to his right and feeds Sexton, who in turn passes to D'Arcy. Trimble is next to receive the ball and he bursts through Pascal Papé and Médard. The Ulster winger spots O'Driscoll in support, but passes a mite too early rather than drawing in his man. O'Driscoll cuts inside but is hauled down a metre short and a turnover seems certain until O'Connell and Rory Best race onto the scene to clear men out. Murray gets to the ruck and turns to find a mismatch – Sexton on the charge versus a static Yoann Maestri. A try under the posts makes for a simple conversion. A fifty-second minute penalty makes it 22–13, but Ireland will not score again.

France look to their forwards to get back into the contest and are rewarded on sixty-two minutes when Dimitri Szarzewski touches down against the base of Ireland's right-hand post. A Machenaud conversion makes it 22–20, but he is withdrawn for Jean-Marc Doussain soon after. Schmidt springs four off his bench – Henderson, McFadden, Marty Moore and Eoin Reddan. Over in Rome, the English players are engrossed in proceedings. A narrow French win will see Stuart Lancaster's men claim the trophy. With twelve minutes to go, Ireland lose Sexton to concussion after an ill-fated meeting with a bulldozing Bastareaud. Ian Madigan replaces him, and curbs his attacking instinct to pitch in to a committed effort to preserve the Irish line.

Doussain has a chance to nudge his team ahead as Moore is penalised at the scrum. His kick is thirty metres out and slightly to the left of the posts. The hero at Murrayfield a week before, Doussain shanks it right and wide. Schmidt sends on Jack McGrath for Cian Healy. Only Jordi Murphy remains on the bench. Ireland play the kicking game as they attempt to see out the match in France's half. The tactic eats up three minutes before Les Bleus rumble beyond halfway in search of one last scoring opportunity. Henderson's presence at a seventy-fifth minute ruck forces blue shirts to come in from the side and a clearing penalty is won.

Ireland go through seventeen phases to take the match up to 77:28 before Henderson is whistled by Steve Walsh for going off his feet. Dulin gets greedy with a kick to the line and fails to find touch. Rob Kearney should seek contact and support, but he injudiciously pumps a speculator into the Parisian sky. On 77:58 the ball lands into Bastareaud's paws. The play is broken and green shirts are leaping into tackles, but within thirty seconds the French are within five metres of the Irish tryline. Huget shows great hands to link up with Pape, and Ireland are exposed on the right. The lock flings a pass to Chouly, who beats McGrath to the corner and dives over. Walsh calls for the Television Match Official (TMO) amid a cacophony of French celebration. The clock is stopped on 78:48. Replays show a forward pass, but the wait is interminable. In consultation with TMO Gareth Simmons, Walsh says 'It definitely left his hands forward but did it drift forward?' The longer it takes, the more Ireland fear another late heart-melter. Recalling last November's New Zealand match, Rob Kearney thinks, 'Christ, here we go again.' Up on the stadium's big screen, Simmons and Walsh are dwarfed by the shattered, pensive visage of O'Driscoll.

Forward pass is the call, but Ireland have a scrum to survive on their twenty-two. Ireland wind the clock down as Walsh calls for a reset. Reddan feeds with sixteen seconds of regular time to go, and the Irish pack are immediately in trouble. Vincent Debaty tears into Moore. The ball squirts out to Doussain, but he is shunted back by Henderson and Madigan. The clock ticks red as Sébastien Vahaamahina barrels towards the Irish twenty-two, only to be met by Henry and Toner. With O'Connell pitching in, the flanker is held up long enough for Walsh to call it a maul. Vahaamahina crumples to the floor and the ball is nowhere to be seen. Walsh has seen enough and ends the thriller. McFadden is the first to embrace O'Driscoll as O'Connell and Henry struggle to get to their feet.

Donal Lenihan, who was in Paris commentating for RTÉ that night, says, 'The most impressive part of the championship win was the players that were on the pitch for the final ten minutes of the game. You had the likes of McGrath, Moore, Henderson and Madigan all out there. The senior players got them into that position, and we could have lost it, still, on that last scrum. It was going to be a penalty [to France] until the ball came out. That experience, for those young players to be out on the field and to have the backing of their coach, will prove vital. It is further evidence of how far Ireland have progressed since 1995.'

O'Driscoll reflects on a fairytale finish with the French broadcaster. '*Je suis trés content*,' he declares.

He later reflects, 'I played on for one more year hoping to get a victory against the All Blacks – that didn't happen – and to win a Six Nations, and that did happen. You can't have it all, but you take the bits that you get. It's been a fantastic Six Nations for us; I've enjoyed every second. I don't really want to take this jersey off yet, because I know when I do it's the last time. I'm dragging the arse out of it a little bit.

'I got a frog in my throat on the final whistle all right,' O'Driscoll admits. 'You're not yourself sometimes when you're being interviewed. It feels as though you're trying to present a certain way. After scenarios like today it comes out a bit more, particularly when it's the end, you have to be as natural as you can. Over the course of the next while, when it sinks in, I'm sure [the emotion] will flood out. When I pull the jersey off it will be hard, but it will come with a great sense of happiness to finish off with a great high after a lot of "nearly" moments.

'I have lots of good memories in between, but to have had 2000 and our first victory there in twenty-eight years, having not won since then, to finish up here fourteen years later is incredibly special. Not many people get to finish their career on their own terms, certainly not with high emotions like today. I feel very fortunate and thankful to be part of a great, great team that has massive potential to go on and do more special things.'

O'Connell adds, 'We've achieved a lot of provincial success with Munster and Leinster, but this is where you really want to achieve it as an Irishman. To have made the progress we have in a year is great, but also [to] have that progress endorsed with a trophy is a great feeling. It gives the younger guys in the squad a winning habit, and that's an important thing to have.'

Jerry Flannery was in London that night, basking in a state of euphoria. 'I was delighted as an Irish fan, first of all, that they were successful,' he says. 'Also, the nature of how we won. It wasn't down to one guy. For me, Andrew Trimble and Devin Toner were two of the stand-out guys for us, and they wouldn't have been lauded as anything before the tournament. I really enjoyed that aspect of it.

'And particularly then with guys like Darce and Drico, I remember a few years ago when Darce had a lot of injuries and thought he wouldn't play again. And to see him now, he has outlasted everyone. The bastard. It was great; I was delighted for them.'

# 28

## ANIMAL INSTINCT: INTERPROVINCIAL BATTLE RAGES ON

**Leinster 19–15 Munster, 16 December 1995**

Thomond Park was the venue for the Munster–Leinster clash on 16 December 1995. Munster's Peter Clohessy had been playing interpros since he first travelled up to Ravenhill with the team in 1987. Ulster had taken the spoils that afternoon, but it had surprised few in attendance. The game may have been turning professional, but there were few signs on the ground of actual change.

A scant crowd was expected at Thomond Park. Shane Byrne, named as Leinster hooker, recalls Blue versus Red attendances as one-man-and-his-dog affairs, but 'Claw' feels 'Mullet' is selling the occasion short. 'You generally got fifty to a hundred people watching the interpro games,' he says. 'Maybe another lad who stopped by after picking up the Sunday paper.'

Former Ireland out-half Paul Dean's playing career had ended at the age of twenty-nine, courtesy of a torn anterior cruciate ligament, seven minutes into his first game on the 1989 British & Irish Lions tour to Australia. He quit his job with Smurfit upon returning to Ireland and went into business for himself. He combined his job with coaching at local club, St Mary's, and looking after Leinster's backs, for which he received a stipend of £40 per week. 'We used to try and avoid rugby for Leinster when I was playing,' he says. 'We preferred playing for our clubs as it was more fun; that's where our friends were. Club and national team were priorities,' he comments. 'The situation was slow to change in the early years of professionalism.'

A shoulder injury picked up at the World Cup meant Keith Wood missed out on the visit of Leinster to Limerick. Still, the Munster fifteen was studded with internationals in key positions. Clohessy started at tight-head with Mick Galwey and Gabriel Fulcher in the second row. David Corkery was Munster's open-side, with Richard Wallace on the right wing and Paul Burke joined in the half-back pairing by Stephen McIvor. The visitors mixed experience – from Chris Pim, Kurt McQuilkin and Neil Francis – with promise – from young players such as Victor Costello and Paul Wallace. Fullback Conor O'Shea would join up with London Irish in the New Year.

Niall Woods started on the left wing for Leinster. 'I didn't have a huge amount of fear about going there and winning,' he says. 'I had played with Blackrock against Shannon at Thomond Park. We had beaten them down there a couple of times. For me, it wasn't that intimidating … It was a physical enough game, and, of course, we were always deemed to have the weaker pack. The stigma of good backs, soft forwards didn't just spring up in the 2000s. A good few of the Leinster pack were from outside Dublin, but that didn't dispel the myth.'

Clohessy says, 'I was always raring to go whenever Leinster came to town. We needed little motivation there. They were the team you wanted to get one over on. We looked at a lot of them as stuck-up pricks. It was really a case of us versus them.'

Costello was named in the Leinster back row alongside Pim and Stephen Rooney. 'I had been with Connacht in the early nineties, but was interested in getting back home to Leinster when Jim Glennon came in,' he says. 'I was eager to get assurances that I'd get a fair crack at No. 8 as Phil Lawlor had been there for a while. We had a very tight squad and were in top form that season. You had O'Shea and Woods, Alain Rolland – who epitomised professionalism – even back then, Paul Wallace, the veterans like Pim, Rooney and Franno [Neil Francis]. You had Shane Byrne, who had been around as long as Fionn MacCumhaill. Still, we were up against the likes of Claw and Gaillimh. It was never going to be easy.'

Two Richard Wallace tries had the home side in the ascendancy, in front of a crowd Costello estimates at just shy of 2,000. He continues, 'We were pounding on their line near the end, and looking for a pushover try. As a No. 8, I often felt if you bent down to pick the ball up at the back of a scrum or maul, you were giving the opposition a chance. It would be easier to keep the ball at your foot and let your scrum half touch down. I remember saying to Rolland, "This is your try." We got the shove on and, with Rollers on the case, got the pushover try. Plenty of reason for a big night out in Limerick.'

## Operation Ticket Shift, October 2014

Fifty thousand seats to fill, and both Leinster and Munster were off to lacklustre starts. Sensing reticence from the paying public, Leinster summoned Shane Byrne and David Wallace to the Aviva Stadium to relive some of their warmest interprovincial memories. The Blues had beaten Welsh opposition with ease at the RDS, but had started the 2014/15 season with away slips to Glasgow Warriors and Connacht. Pat Lam had been so impressed with Connacht's humbling of Leinster at The Sportsground that he made his Irish tutor proud. 'Go raibh maith agat. Slán and, I will say, Rise up Eagles,' he beamed.

Matt O'Connor's second season as Leinster coach had begun with questions over Johnny Sexton's possible return, Johnny Sexton's confirmed return and how rival out-half Ian Madigan felt about Johnny Sexton's return. The Australian had snagged the northern hemisphere's best No. 10, but replacing the retired Brian O'Driscoll at outside centre was an immediate concern. He wedged Madigan into that hole and was rewarded with two virtuoso displays against Scarlets and Cardiff.

O'Connor was hampered by a spate of injuries across the deck. Cian Healy and Sean O'Brien had both been ruled out for six months with respective ankle and shoulder issues. Jordi Murphy was out until the end of the year, Shane Jennings was hamstrung and the backline was in greater trouble. Luke Fitzgerald was still a while away from return following summer surgeries and Zane Kirchner had picked up an injury against Cardiff. Dave Kearney and Noel Reid were training, but would not be ready in time for Munster.

Midway through a press briefing, in which he revealed the shoulder reconstruction needed to mend O'Brien, the coach shifted uncomfortably in his seat. O'Connor was asked if he was wary of the constant medical updates. 'Yeah,' he responded. 'Just write something else you guys. Write some sort of philosophical piece on the game ... but yeah, it's the game. Injuries are a part of it. Injuries impact on how teams play; injuries impact on who wins who loses. From that end it's a worthy news story.'

Having spent much of the previous season answering questions about an impressive beard or life after BOD, a freshly shaved Gordon D'Arcy showed up at Leinster's Newstead Building as the Blues' incumbent No. 13. Asked to reflect on his sixteen seasons of Leinster-versus-Munster service, he warmed to the task. 'Before I ever knew the intensity of it, Keith Wood turned me inside out in my first [derby] game – a hooker turning a fullback inside out,' he told the *Irish Mirror*. 'That was because I wasn't ready for the intensity of this level. We'd played a few games and then suddenly there's Munster and there's a huge spike. That was a huge learning curve for me. I told myself that I would never let that happen to me again – that I would never play against Munster and not be absolutely ready for it.'

Anthony Foley was up to his facial stubble with woes down in Munster. The regular midfield partnership of James Downey (released) and Casey Laulala (Racing Métro move) was no more and two candidates earmarked to replace them – Keith Earls and Kiwi import Tyler Bleyendaal – were long-term casualties. Donnacha Ryan's luckless run of injuries had seeped into a new season, so Foley was short of second-row nous, and bulk.

In early August, I met Foley and his coaching team at the Firgrove

Hotel in Mitchelstown. He told me, 'I do dream about Munster. It's a twenty-four/seven job now. It never leaves your head, even when you're at home, no matter what you're doing. Do you get any rest when you shut your eyes? Probably not. Your brain has to stay pretty active. There's a lot to be done – problem solving before problems have even occurred. That's part of the job I'm in. Trying to make sure stuff gets done and I'm on top of things.'

Three weeks later, Foley was attempting to diffuse the effect of a leaked player-review document that had been accidentally emailed to the entire squad. In his *Sunday Independent* column, Brendan Fanning revealed that the document included a colour-coding system on the playing squad's pecking order. A senior Munster source told Fanning, 'But it's not a crisis or anything like it. The senior players met to talk about it, and, yes, it might have been hurtful to one or two players, but we've moved on ... Anthony spoke to the group and said that it is what it is and it shouldn't have happened, rather than try to bullshit the players.'

Three of Munster's opening four Pro12 fixtures were at Thomond Park, but – with fans staying away in droves – only one home win was recorded. Simon Zebo laced in a hat-trick against Zebre, but Ospreys and Edinburgh left Limerick with the points. Before Munster boarded a bus for Dublin – a town they had not been victorious in for six seasons – Foley warned that simply 'beating your chest, roaring and shouting' would not cut it against Leinster. 'Hopefully,' he told the *Irish Examiner*, 'we can put in a performance that's worthy of the Munster jersey.'

The final build-up words were left to Rob Kearney and his expectations that 'a very different Munster' would take to the Aviva Stadium field that weekend: 'Munster have sort of reverted a little bit to the type of player they have. Over the last couple of years they have played that wide-wide very expansive game and it was hard for them to implement. They had some big centres who were much more suited to carrying direct than flinging twenty-yard passes. They have gone back to that this season.'

Forthright as ever, Kearney conceded that the rivalry between the two sides had been doused in recent years. 'Ten years ago in my first game there was a huge hatred, and it was probably more from them towards us and probably more envy on our part,' he says. 'I don't know … because we have had very good national success over the years, maybe it has brought guys together. The Munster guys would be friendly off the field now, whereas before they wouldn't. But that's not to say we won't be trying to bash lumps off each other on Saturday. It is the nature of the game, but I do think the relationship has improved over the years.

'When they were winning European Cups and competing with the best in Europe we were completely envious of them, and when we were doing the same I'm sure they were of us as well. That's just how sport works; you always envy the champions, the team on the up. Over the last few years, for the first few years in the last while, one of us is not the dominant force in Europe.'

## Game-night

You have to feel for the gang in the BT Sport marketing department as an advertising truck circles the Aviva Stadium with dates of Champions Cup fixtures and Sean O'Brien charging with ball in hand. O'Brien is in Manchester, recovering from his shoulder reconstruction as his image cruises past Raglan Road and takes a left up towards the Schoolhouse bar. I stop by Searsons pub on the way to the ground to watch a replay of Ben Smith touching down against South Africa. Trailing 21–13 at half-time in Ellis Park, the All Blacks are mounting another comeback. The scarf and flag sellers share hallowed trading ground with radio-station interns, handing out badges and flyers. Brian O'Driscoll Irish flags hang from railings, breaking up the Leinster blue and Munster red. Daylight is fading fast as families hurry to catch the warm-ups. The majority of the 43,817 crowd are still in the pub, and will filter in, roughly, around kick-off.

I chat with Simon Lewis of the *Irish Examiner* in the media room and learn I had not missed much at the A game in Donnybrook that afternoon. Donncha O'Callaghan was surplus to senior-team requirements, but helped his young teammates to an 18–8 win over Leinster, for whom Richardt Strauss was returning from injury. Shane Buckley and Luke O'Dea had scored the Munster tries, but – for Lewis' money – their captain, Jack O'Donoghue, was the outstanding performer. I catch the final three minutes of action at Ellis Park as Pat Lambie holds his nerve to kick a late, winning penalty against the All Blacks. Heyneke Meyer goes suitably nuts in the Springboks' control room. Game-time nears, so it is time to grab a lift and enter the fray. Taking my place in the press seats, I spot some former interpro stalwarts on media duty. Shane Horgan and Alan Quinlan are part of the Sky Sports squad, while Shane Byrne provides colour commentary for RTÉ Radio. Tony Ward sits among the rugby correspondents and jots notes for an *Irish Independent* feature.

Sky Sports are the main broadcaster for the Pro12 and have cameras set up inside the home and away dressing rooms. Felix Jones is Munster's captain for the evening as Peter O'Mahony is on the replacements' bench. Jones sits in reflection as Paul O'Connell stalks criss-crosses, inhaling and exhaling in slow, deliberate gallonfuls. Twenty metres away, Jamie Heaslip is doing all the talking for Leinster. The microphones are muted as captain Heaslip finger-jabs at teammates and the ground. 'Not in our house,' is the gist. Up in our cosy media seats there is a late tickle of excitement. O'Connor has taken a black pen to the Leinster team-sheet. A back twinge has dropped Kearney to the bench. Madigan shifts to fullback and Brendan Macken comes in at outside centre. D'Arcy will start the match in his familiar No. 12 jersey. Michael Bent also comes in at loose-head for Jack McGrath.

Rihanna's 'Yellow Diamonds' and a first fifteen of blue-clad cheerleaders welcome the teams onto the pitch. An early scrum collapse gives Madigan a chance to put Leinster 3–0 up, before Ian Keatley levels matters. A patently charged O'Connell is hunting ribcages and clatters Jimmy Gopperth and

Rhys Ruddock in the opening ten minutes. Injuries to O'Brien, Murphy and Jennings have afforded Dominic Ryan a run at open-side, and he rouses the home support with an aggressive hit that almost ejects Robin Copeland from his boots. A Madigan penalty edges Leinster ahead soon after, while Eoin Reddan is lucky to get away with a languid box-kick that O'Connell paws down. The lock's efforts are mirrored by his Munster teammates, and they are soon camped in the Leinster twenty-two and testing them around the fringes.

There is a break in play for a Munster penalty under the posts. Medics swarm onto the pitch to treat Fergus McFadden before grim replays confirm what they already know. The winger will play no more part in the game. His ankle jerks back and forth under the weight of a Munster ruck. Six weeks out is the Monday-morning prognosis, but – sitting high up in the hushed stands – I fear the worst for McFadden. Keatley chips over the penalty as play resumes and Munster come again after the restart. Jones and Dave Foley make profitable carries up the left before Denis Hurley glides through a yawning gap off Devin Toner's right shoulder. James Cronin finishes the attack by fending off Mike Ross and riding a Ruddock tackle to reach out and score.

Cronin's namesake, Sean, is the only Leinster player taking the game to Munster, but he is also part of a front row feeling the pressure. With twenty-three minutes on the clock, Munster's Cronin gets the scrummaging drop on Ross and a Keatley kick makes it 14–6. Substitute Leinster wing Mick McGrath is welcomed to the game by Conor Murray and picks himself unsteadily off the turf as play torrents around him. They may argue to the contrary, but the Munster midfield duo of Hurley and Andrew Smith are far from stealthy. Leinster have targeted them and one wrap-around move sees Smith drawn in before Gopperth streaks clear. A home score looks on as Leinster pile into the breakdown on the Red twenty-two, only for the penalty to go against them. C. J. Stander and Tommy O'Donnell are spoiling Leinster's plans for rapid recycles.

Munster respond in rousing fashion as Jones and Copeland made good carries. Blue jerseys are sucked in from their defensive positions to halt the picks and drives. Two minutes tick by and the progress is slow, but Murray urges the forwards on. Simon Zebo is doing star-jumps out on the left wing to get his scrum half's attention. Either that or he is trying to keep warm. The lads up front sense a score, and it eventually comes as Copeland burrows over under the posts despite a despairing Ruddock lunge. A simple conversion makes it 21–6 before a Madigan penalty claws three points back.

Reddan embarks on one of his cute snipes and makes twenty metres before he is hauled to the ground. O'Connell lingers on the wrong side of the ruck, reluctant to release the Leinster No. 9, before D'Arcy forcibly clears him out. There is a chance to even the score moments later with D'Arcy in transit, shifting left to right. O'Connell crumples him. Still Leinster press for a late score that will provide a second-half platform. Munster are playing their interpretation of onside. Gopperth feints to motor up the left again, but gets a call inside from Macken. His no-look pass is swallowed up by Keatley, who hares up field to score under the posts. His try is eerily reminiscent of Brian O'Driscoll's intercept on Ronan O'Gara's pass at Croke Park in 2009. Ian Davies blows for half-time, and Leinster are 28–9 behind. Perhaps the hatred is still there, but only one side are harnessing it.

Rob Kearney is sent on, early in the second half, as Leinster seek any sort of forward momentum. Sean Cronin makes one promising line break inside the Munster half, but a scoring chance is lost as D'Arcy knocks on. As both sets of forwards pack down, the veteran centre watches a replay of his fumble on the big screen and cringes. Munster's Damien Varley and B. J. Botha are both yellow-carded for separate infringements, on fifty-six and sixty minutes, and Gopperth takes advantage of the space to find winger Darragh Fanning on the charge for a try.

The next score is crucial, and Munster seize it, through a Keatley penalty. There is still time to flash a third yellow card, at Munster's Dave

Foley, for a Leinster penalty try and for substitute J. J. Hanrahan to land a late penalty. Murray is named man-of-the-match and directed to the sin-bin (yellow card number four) to bask. The seven-man Munster pack win the final scrum of the game and O'Connell claps the back of every red jersey he can find at the whistle. The scoreboard reads 34–23 in Munster's favour. The victors are applauded off the pitch, but wander to the Lansdowne Lane end to thank family, friends and supporters who made the trip. Leinster beat a hasty retreat. By the time Murray completes his Sky Sports interview on the field, the only people still in their seats are the Sunday sports journalists as they meet another deadline.

### 'He's just an animal'

The media briefing room is darkly lit and lacking in a single television camera as Foley takes his place. The first three rows are packed, with the print media hovering near a side door to catch five extra minutes with the Munster coach on the way out. Radio and online journalists get the first crack. 'I think it was the All-Ireland League against St Mary's was the last game I was involved in with four yellow cards,' remarks Foley. 'It is strange, but we handled it.' Asked about the incredible physicality his team brought to the contest, Foley replies, 'Let's do what we're good at … We made a couple of breaches. Why go away from that? That is the point of [Leinster's] weakness; let's go after that.'

Minutes later, surrounded by sixteen print journalists in the back room, that winning feeling is slowly sinking in. Foley cracks a few jokes while attempting to distil his coaching philosophy: 'There's no point trying to reinvent yourself to something you're not good at. At times we were very good at the wide-wide Canterbury-style game [under Rob Penney], and we got to two European Cup semi-finals with that, and the knock-outs of the Pro12 … I'm happy the boys are getting credit for the work they are doing. That's the players and the other coaches. At times we're easy targets, you know, because we're local. People know us; they know what we're about. They know our wrinkles and our good sides as well.' He adds, 'We're not by any means the finished article, but we're improving.'

Quizzed on a neck injury to Andrew Conway, Foley gets in a dig at his opposite number for some perceived brinkmanship. 'I'm not sure yet,' he says. 'It is obviously too early to tell, but we won't be changing our starting line-up five minutes before the game ... We knew last Tuesday what their team was. So it wasn't an issue for us; seeing Rob out there running around, but knowing that Madigan was No. 15. I think Jack McGrath was seen at the A game this morning ...'

'Ask Axel,' O'Connor shoots as he channels his unique brand of bemused frustration. The Leinster coach is still trying to get his head around his team's meek surrender, and accusations of team-sheet chicanery are swatted away. O'Connor does not for a moment suggest his side deserved to win the match, but he does take issue with Munster's manner of achieving victory. 'Every time we had any sort of ascendancy with the ball, they killed the ball,' he argues. 'You need strong officials and I don't think we had that tonight.'

It is put to O'Connor that one effective option to prevent Munster's spoiling tactics would be to self-police the breakdown. The Aussie replies, 'Yeah, it's very hard with the [video official] and everything that goes with the modern game. You know, a load of soccer moms sitting at home watching. It makes it very, very hard to deal with illegal play at the breakdown. That's the reality of it.'

'Out-passioned' is Jimmy Gopperth's take on the match as he bravely puts himself forward for questioning after a forgettable performance. The out-half concedes Munster bested his team at the breakdown. 'At the start of the game,' he says, 'they just came for us. Every breakdown they just hoed into us and really tried to kill our ball. They were very effective at it; all credit to them.' Asked what thoughts went through his head when Keatley intercepted his pass to score, he winces. 'I don't think I can say that word in the press.'

The final man through the room is Munster open-side Tommy O'Donnell, who had landed a staggering total of seventeen tackles. Fellow flanker C. J. Stander had contributed sixteen. Wins release honesty as much as pressure and O'Donnell admits toppling Leinster will ease pressure going into October's European fixtures. 'It's always great to get a win,' he says, 'especially to get one up in Leinster, away from home, playing against your Irish teammates and counterparts. You don't want to put two losses back to back, so it is great to stop the rot and show the people of Ireland what we're about and what we can do. They were kind of writing us off, saying we weren't on par, weren't that good, but in the first half they saw what we can do when we click. We knew all along we could do that.'

A bus ride home and a few celebratory beers await once O'Donnell answers his last question, which comes from me in the form of a statement: 'Paul O'Connell was a menace out there this evening. An old-school menace.'

O'Donnell laughs. 'Yeah,' he says. 'That man just shows up when he wants. He stole a line-out or deflected it there at a crucial part of the game. He's just an animal. He's still going, he's still training hard as ever, he's still that guy that everybody looks up to in the gym, in training. It's great to see him playing well and going as strong as ever.'

One of the final links to the amateur era, having played beside the likes of Clohessy, Galwey and Wood, Paul O'Connell still drives standards for a team that will never quit the fight.

# CONCLUSION

Malcolm O'Kelly was called into his first Ireland training squad in 1996. Six foot, eight inches in height, the twenty-one-year-old lock still found it a daunting experience to crouch his head, step onto a team bus, full of internationals and pick a seat. He nodded at a few of the fresh faces and was grateful to find a spare seat six rows from the front. Neutral; empty; his. Easing his lank frame into the seat, finally feeling the hour-long training session he had just completed, O'Kelly glanced to the back row – the source of all the laughter, slagging and bloody murder on the bus. Gabriel Fulcher of London Irish was in the thick of it, but the Munster lads dominated. Mick Galwey sat in the left-hand corner while, over the other side, Keith Wood draped his lineout-throwing arms over a seat in the next row. Holding court, slap, bang in the middle, was Peter Clohessy. Drowsy eyes offset by a crooked, mischievous grin, Claw's waving hands helped to tell a story he punctuated with expletives.

O'Kelly settled back for the journey ahead. His Test debut was still a year away and it took until the 1999 World Cup to establish himself as a regular. It would not be until 2001, however, with O'Kelly now a British & Irish Lion and Galwey's international career winding down, that he was able to claim that seat at the back of the bus. Wood was still there, so was Clohessy. They were joined by Brian O'Driscoll.

You can have all the Test caps you want, but you never feel truly settled until you are sitting in that back row.

\*\*\*

**16 March 2015**

The Monday morning after the Saturday before. Rob Kearney sat at the top table in one of the many high-ceilinged rooms at Carton House, a little under forty-eight hours since Ireland's Grand Slam hopes hit a brick-red wall in Cardiff. Kearney and his team-mates travelled to Wales on the back of a ten-match winning run. They were Six Nations champions, disposers of South Africa and Australia, ranked number three in the world and had, in Johnny Sexton, an out-half roundly declared as the best in the game. Wales, still coached by Warren Gatland, lay in wait. They got off to a lightning start, took every point offered and, when the Irish storm arrived, battened down the hatches. The Welsh team landed 289 tackles on green jerseys, in front of a thronged Millennium Stadium. Their 23–16 victory had blown the championship wide open.

Irish wins over Italy, France and England now meant little. The English now appeared to be favourites, with Wales and Ireland needing big wins to make the final day interesting. The Irish players were accused of lacking invention, Joe Schmidt's coaching was branded conservative and New Zealand-born centre Jared Payne was described, by one TV pundit, as a 'second-rate foreigner'.

For the first time in their history, Ireland had had the chance to win eleven Tests in a row. When they failed, the national mood plunged. The 1990s – two wins a year and sixty minutes of bluster – seemed centuries away. 'I think when you lose games and you under-perform,' Kearney reasoned, 'you're going to get criticism and some of it is probably warranted. So I'm not surprised at the criticism and the pessimism, we're fully aware of moods within our own camp. The main thing for us is that there's no pessimism within the team room.'

Schmidt named his team to face Scotland and included two men who had battled back from extended periods on the sideline. Cian Healy started at loose-head while Luke Fitzgerald would begin his first Ireland game since March 2011. After suffering three major injuries in the past three years, Fitzgerald was in a reflective mood. 'I was pretty close, with some major injuries, to quitting. I didn't really see a way back and I couldn't figure out what the problem was … It was too frustrating, coming in two or three times a day and working really, really hard and getting no results. I have worked really hard and I feel it is a nice result; I have been rewarded today.'

The final day of the Six Nations was exhausting to watch, let alone play a part in. Wales ripped Italy asunder at Stadio Olimpico, Rome. Their 60–21 demolition job set Ireland a tough benchmark. If they beat Scotland by 21 points, they would also finish on 8 points but with a superior points-scoring difference to the Welsh. Paul O'Connell, playing in his 101st Test match for Ireland, crashed over for a try after only four minutes. The tone was set and Scotland were powerless to halt the flow of points. Robbie Henshaw, who was eight years old when O'Connell made his debut, delivered another surging, incisive performance in midfield. Sean O'Brien thundered over for a try in each half, Payne burst through the Scottish midfield to score under the posts and Sexton overcame some goal-kicking nerves to pull Ireland clear. Jamie Heaslip lived up to his worker-bee role by making a crucial, last-ditch tackle on Stuart Hogg to prevent a certain try. At the final whistle, the Scots had been defeated 40–10. Nothing was won, however, until England and France went toe-to-toe in a game for the ages. England won 55–35 but fell short on points difference. For the first time since 1949, Ireland had retained their title outright.

Post-match, as Murrayfield Stadium bounced to the soft rock anthem 'Livin' on a Prayer', Schmidt took in the enormity of his team's achievement. 'We had the disappointment of missing out on a record [of Test wins]. On Paul's 100th cap, that would have had some synergy about it, but the big fella just decided to grab the group by the neck this week and drag them into this game with a fair bit of energy and resolve. Thankfully, it was enough to get us over the line.'

O'Connell said, 'It is the strangest, most bizarre way to win a trophy but when you do win one in those circumstances it is incredible. When you are sitting there at a table with a few of the lads around you and a beer in front of you, watching [England versus France] on TV, you are like a supporter. You are completely powerless to influence the result.

'Even with the crowd afterwards and the music, it was like Robbie Henshaw's twenty-first birthday with the 1980s hits coming out. It was an incredible day … a lot better craic than last year anyway.

'To go back-to-back is incredible,' O'Connell added. 'It is a very difficult thing to do. Ireland is a small island. We have four professional teams. It just goes to show how good the athletes and players we have are. It also goes to show, the way the provinces are run and the way, strength- and conditioning-wise, we are run [as players] too. We have smaller resources.'

O'Connell was asked if he would be happy, now, to finish up after the World Cup and leave the Six Nations as a winner. He let the question sink in; it had a nice ring to it. O'Connell, though, was not ready to set any retirement dates yet. 'If it does finish,' he said, 'it's a great way to finish. If it doesn't, it is still a great memory to have.' Media duties done with for the night, O'Connell sought the company of his team-mates. He patted the backs of Healy and Jordi Murphy as he passed. They shouted something at their captain but it was lost in music.

Three weeks before, I had interviewed Murphy ahead of his start, at No. 8, against England. We covered his upbringing in Barcelona, England's big threats and what he hoped to bring to the contest. As a relative newcomer to the squad, I asked him who now resides down the back of the Irish bus.

'It's usually Rob Kearney, Paulie O'Connell and Cian Healy,' he said. 'That's the back row and you are not going to be able to sneak in there with those boys. Brian O'Driscoll was there until last year.'

For most young players who break through, those back seats represent the pinnacle. The seniors and stars form a club with exclusive membership. The next generation know they will need to put their body on the line or prove a match-winner to gain passage. Money, sponsorships, media commitments, strict diet and training regimes have flooded the game over the past two decades. The journey to the back of the bus remains the constant. To get there, you need to be special.

# ACKNOWLEDGEMENTS

My thanks go to Dominic Perrem, Wendy Logue, Trish Myers Smith and everybody involved at Mercier Press.

Grenoble and Racing Métro were gracious hosts during my trip to France. Garryowen and each of the four Irish provinces opened their doors and kindly set up interviews. Louise Creedon, Neil Brittain, Marcus Ó Buachalla and Fiona Murphy, cheers for everything.

I am indebted to the research and interviews provided by Cillian O'Conchuir during the writing of this book. Peter O'Reilly and Hugh Farrelly were early, respective sounding boards and proof-readers. The assistance and encouragement of Ken Darley, Shane McCall, Rob Fields, Sean Farrell, Rory Keane, Stephen Doyle and Murray Kinsella must not go without mention.

To all the players and coaches, past, present, soon to be past and soon to be present, many thanks for your time, tales and insights.

Family, friends and all at Maximum Media have been extremely supportive throughout.

Caitriona, Caitlin and Patrick McCarry (Jr), I will see you at White Park Bay.

# INDEX OF KEY PLAYERS AND PERSONNEL

## A

Anderson, Willie 38, 75, 128
Ashton, Brian 29, 32, 33, 39,
    40, 44, 45, 78–80, 88, 92, 97

## B

Back, Neil 31, 84, 99
Barry, Ian 111, 114–116
Bell, Jonny 67, 72
Best, Rory 9, 12, 16, 103, 133,
    187, 266, 284, 286, 297
Betsen, Serge 62, 63
Bevan, John 40, 49
Blaney, Brian 133
Boss, Isaac 105, 278
Bowe, Tommy 9, 109, 187, 268,
    273, 288, 289, 291
Bradley, Michael 142–144
Brooke, Zinzan 37, 43, 46
Broun, Alex 23, 93, 94, 98
Browne, Philip 141, 190, 217
Buckley, Shane 112, 116, 280,
    307
Bunce, Paul 140, 175
Burke, Matt 5, 27
Burke, Paul 27, 47, 302
Byrne, Shane 80, 83, 130, 248,
    301–303, 307

## C

Campbell, Kieran 73, 84
Carolan, Nigel 140, 141, 144,
    166–168
Carr, Fionn 144, 147
Carr, Nigel 66
Cheika, Michael 121, 122, 131,
    132, 134, 136, 283
Clohessy, Peter 25, 28, 29,
    47–52, 62, 64, 78, 99, 186,
    247, 301–303, 312, 313
Contepomi, Felipe 86, 131, 132,
    134, 135, 158, 217
Cooper, Quade 10, 235, 260
Corkery, David 60, 61, 302
Corrigan, Reggie 40, 44, 87–90,
    129, 130, 133, 136, 248
Costello, Ian 169, 170
Costello, Victor 73, 74, 78, 84,
    87, 92, 130, 230, 248, 302,
    303

Coulson, Denis 153, 202, 207
Coulter, Sheldon 67
Cronin, James 169, 308
Cronin, Sean 144, 295, 308, 309
Crossan, Keith 67
Crotty, Dominic 59, 112
Crotty, Ryan 160, 287
Cullen, Leo 81, 134, 136, 230,
    232, 238, 277

## D

Danaher, Philip 24, 51, 111,
    112, 114
D'Arcy, Gordan 8, 10, 16, 28,
    31, 35, 61, 81, 82, 94, 103,
    129, 132, 135, 184, 248,
    260, 264, 276, 277, 282,
    288, 290, 294, 297, 300,
    304, 307, 309
Davidson, Jeremy 73, 74, 76,
    77, 98
Davidson, Jim 66
Davies, Jonathan 16, 294
Dawson, Kieron 39, 43, 71
Dawson, Mick 188
Dean, Paul 19, 80, 81, 301
Deans, Robbie 10, 283
Dempsey, Girvan 31, 32, 75,
    81–83, 102, 104–106, 129,
    132, 164, 165, 172, 237, 248
Diack, Robbie 218, 219
Duffy, Gavin 141–143, 273
Duffy, Johnny 144

## E

Earls, Keith 16, 117, 181–185,
    187, 199, 235, 291, 304
Easterby, Guy 96, 238
Easterby, Simon 96, 97, 101,
    103, 106, 294
Ella, Gary 90, 130, 131
Elwood, Eric 28, 29, 39, 141,
    142, 144, 146
Erskine, David 39, 78

## F

Falvey, Eanna 255–258, 260,
    263, 264, 286
Farley, Andrew 193, 204, 206
Farrell, Chris 153, 199, 200,

202–204, 207, 212, 215, 216
Farrell, Emmet 86, 237–244
Ferris, Stephen 7, 12–14, 16,
    109, 150, 178, 179, 229,
    231–235, 242, 272
Field, Maurice 67
Fitzgerald, Ciaran 19
Fitzgerald, Garret 114
Fitzgerald, Luke 135, 180, 229,
    232, 234–236, 286, 304, 314
Fitzgerald, Stephen 112
Fitzpatrick, Declan 266–271
Fitzpatrick, Sean 37–39, 46
Flannery, Jerry 11, 12, 63, 65,
    108, 258, 300
Flavin, Adrian 76, 77, 84,
    143–145, 173, 174
Foley, Anthony 25, 51, 53,
    55–57, 60, 65, 78, 112, 181,
    199, 273, 276, 304, 305,
    308, 310, 311
Fulcher, Gabriel 155, 302, 313

## G

Gaffney, Alan 31, 128, 130
Galwey, Mick 25, 48–52, 61,
    62, 64, 97, 99, 112, 114,
    302, 303, 312, 313
Gatland, Warren 15, 18, 31, 33,
    40, 75, 79, 85, 88, 92, 94,
    96–98, 100, 109, 141, 148,
    159, 197, 234, 294, 314
Genia, Will 10, 12, 261
Geoghegan, Simon 27
Glennon, Jim 25, 30, 81, 82, 302
Griffiths, Edward 20, 21

## H

Hagan, Jamie 144
Halpin, Gary 71, 78
Halstead, Trevor 60, 63, 134,
    217
Halvey, Eddie 27, 42, 51–53,
    56–58, 60, 61, 62, 78, 112
Hanrahan, J. J. 117, 203, 310
Hart, James 152–158, 193, 199,
    200, 207, 214, 215
Hart, John 37–39
Hayes, John 96, 97, 107, 110,
    112, 294

Healy, Cian 7, 10, 12, 13, 16, 180, 278, 297, 298, 303, 314, 316

Heaslip, Jamie 7, 108, 135, 136, 139, 171, 179, 180, 186–188, 209, 230–232, 234, 235, 241, 242, 244, 282, 286, 307, 315

Heenan, Jake 140, 219, 220–226

Henderson, Iain 164, 203, 268, 273, 296–299

Henderson, Rob 33, 43, 73

Hennessey, Ray 76

Hennessy, Liam 98, 247, 253

Henry, Chris 69, 284, 291, 292, 296, 299

Henshaw, Robbie 145, 147, 167, 168, 225, 261, 285, 315, 316

Hickie, Denis 28–35, 39–41, 79, 80, 86, 100, 121, 129, 132, 248, 290

Hill, Richard 51, 99

Hogan, Frank 30

Holland, Jason 60

Holland, Jerry 49

Horan, Marcus 64, 97, 101, 102, 104, 107, 108, 109, 112

Horgan, Anthony 58, 60, 63, 249, 288

Horgan, Shane 31, 82, 96–98, 105, 121, 122, 129, 132, 164, 229, 288, 294, 307

Humphreys, David 67–69, 71, 77, 79, 96, 97, 203, 231, 289

**I**

Irwin, David 66, 95

**J**

Jackman, Bernard 125, 132, 134, 156, 157, 193, 199–207, 212, 214, 215, 265, 266

Jackson, Paddy 175, 203, 268

Jennings, Shane 134, 136, 140, 242, 304, 308

Johnson, Martin 84, 99, 101, 104, 108

Johns, Paddy 27, 43

Jones, Felix 7, 117, 181, 261, 284, 307–309

Jones, Ian 36–38, 44, 46

Jones, Michael 37, 220

Jones, Stephen 109, 110

**K**

Keane, Killian 59, 85

Kearney, Dave 180, 226, 230, 237, 285, 295, 304

Kearney, Rob 10, 12, 16, 107, 108, 118–127, 135, 166, 187, 192, 230, 258, 260–262, 264, 286, 295, 297, 298, 305–307, 309, 311, 313, 314, 316

Keatley, Ian 144, 307–309, 311

Kelly, John 59

Kelly, John 'Rags' 50

Kidd, Murray 27, 32, 78, 114

Kidney, Declan 8–11, 13, 15–17, 49–51, 54, 58, 61, 62, 84, 91, 107–109, 130, 131, 133, 158, 183, 184, 194, 234, 235, 248, 278, 282–284, 290, 291

Kiernan, Tom 21, 24

Kingston, Terry 5, 27

Knox, David 27, 132

Kronfeld, Josh 21, 220

**L**

Lam, Pat 138–140, 146–148, 220, 222, 274, 303

Landreau, Fabrice 156–158, 201, 206

Langford, John 58, 64, 100, 217

Leamy, Denis 60, 133, 134

Lenihan, Donal 18, 19, 24, 25, 51, 53, 92–94, 96, 98, 99, 113, 299

Lomu, Jonah 5, 39, 46

Longwell, Gary 66–68, 69, 94, 95, 110, 163, 164

Lynagh, Michael 20, 51

**M**

Madigan, Ian 166, 226, 237, 261, 287, 298, 299, 303, 307, 308, 309, 311

Maggs, Kevin 39, 100, 103

Mallett, Nick 14, 43

Marmion, Kieran 145, 147, 168, 285

Marshall, Justin 36–38, 41–44, 46

Marshall, Luke 256, 259, 268

Mason, Simon 68, 69

Matthews, Phillip 66

McBride, Denis 24, 67

McCall, Mark 67–69, 71

McFadden, Fergus 180, 237, 245, 246, 284, 285, 295, 297, 299, 308

McGowan, Alan 25, 26

McGrath, Jack 226, 286, 295, 298, 299, 307, 311

McGuinness, Conor 39, 40

McLaughlin, Brian 164, 267

McLaughlin, Kevin 278

McMahon, Colm 60, 247

McQuilkin, Kurt 120, 302

McQuilkin, Noel 87

McWeeney, John 39, 40, 43, 84, 86

Mehrtens, Andrew 42, 43, 45, 46

Millar, Syd 18, 21, 22, 24

Miller, Eric 39, 42, 79, 84, 100, 130, 186

Moore, Marty 180, 271, 297–299

Morrow, Phillip 247

Morrow, Robin 67

Muldoon, John 141–147

Muliaina, Mils 138, 140, 145, 217

Mullin, Brendan 19, 24

Murphy, Geordan 10, 110, 124

Murphy, Jordi 140, 171, 237, 273, 298, 304, 308, 316

Murray, Conor 9, 16, 116, 117, 169, 170, 187, 260–263, 278, 286, 296, 297, 308–310

Murray, Pat 47, 51

**N**

Noone, Mick 226–228

Nowlan, Kevin 31, 39, 40, 43, 84

**O**

O'Brien, Sean 7, 10, 13, 16, 60, 140, 178–180, 187, 188, 190, 209, 230, 232, 242, 274, 278, 286, 287, 303, 304, 306, 308, 315

O'Callaghan, Donncha 12, 16, 50, 84, 101, 108, 162, 248, 251, 273, 280, 281, 307

O'Connell, Aidan 98, 133, 247–254

O'Connell, Paul 7, 8, 13, 17, 28, 61, 63, 95, 99, 101, 106, 107, 117, 133, 134, 135, 181, 199, 247, 248, 251, 252, 272, 274–276, 281,

285, 295, 297, 299, 300, 307–310, 312, 315, 316
O'Connor, Johnny 141, 144
O'Connor, Matt 125, 166, 179, 180, 191, 230, 278, 303, 304, 307, 311
O'Donnell, Tommy 170, 308, 312
O'Donovan, Niall 49
O'Driscoll, Brian 7, 8, 10, 13–15, 17, 28, 31, 34, 35, 60, 81, 84–86, 94–100, 103, 106, 108, 109, 119, 121, 122, 128, 129, 131–136, 150, 165, 171, 175, 177, 178, 183, 184, 189, 194, 202, 229, 232, 234, 235, 243–246, 248, 255, 256, 277, 278, 282, 284, 286, 288–290, 293–295, 297–300, 303, 304, 306, 309, 313, 316
O'Driscoll, Mick 64, 162, 166
O'Gara, Ronan 7, 8, 12, 13, 16, 17, 28, 35, 57–64, 96–101, 103–106, 108, 109, 133–135, 137, 149–152, 158, 188, 189, 193–195, 199, 200, 211–213, 231, 278, 282, 290, 294, 295, 309
O'Kelly, Malcolm 33, 39, 41, 43, 44, 52, 71–73, 75–78, 95, 98, 102, 128, 131, 223, 231, 313
Olding, Stuart 164, 175, 177, 203, 259, 285
O'Leary, Tomás 108, 278
O'Mahony, Peter 169, 170, 224, 226, 284, 296, 307
O'Meara, Brian 59
O'Reilly, Peter 46, 48, 71, 73, 85, 210
Osborne, Glen 39, 43, 45
O'Shea, Conor 26, 71, 72, 94, 104, 145, 302
O'Sullivan, David 31
O'Sullivan, Eddie 9, 33, 89, 100–103, 106, 107, 121, 140, 141, 206, 229–231, 234, 288–291

P

Payne, Jared 217, 219, 233, 314, 315
Penney, Rob 276, 279, 310
Phillips, Mike 16, 195, 196, 213, 214
Pienaar, Ruan 51, 217, 218

Popplewell, Nick 27, 39, 43, 44, 46
Prendergast, Mike 193, 199–202, 204, 212, 247
Prendergast, Neil 113, 114
Priestland, Rhys 15, 16, 211
Pugh, Vernon 22

Q

Quinlan, Alan 51, 53–55, 60, 78, 101, 112, 307

R

Reddan, Eoin 10, 12, 16, 260, 261, 278, 297, 299, 308, 309
Reid, Mike 68, 69
Reid, Noel 165, 304
Ringland, Trevor 66, 67
Ritchie, Stephen 67
Roberts, Jamie 15, 16, 190, 195–199, 212, 213, 215, 264, 294
Rossiter, Ed 112, 113
Ross, Mike 12, 178, 271, 284, 308
Ruddock, Mike 30, 40, 81–87, 128, 202, 226, 238
Ruddock, Rhys 226, 308, 309
Ryan, Dominic 226, 308
Ryan, Donnacha 199, 304
Ryan, Vinny 113, 114

S

Saverimutto, Chris 27
Schmidt, Joe 59, 123, 132, 136, 164, 166, 178, 182, 183, 187, 215, 218, 221, 261, 266, 268, 273, 277, 283–285, 291–298, 314, 315
Sexton, Johnny 7, 9, 12–14, 16, 120, 132, 134–137, 150, 153, 158–161, 175, 186–188, 190, 193, 199, 208–211, 245, 260–262, 265, 283, 286, 287, 295–298, 303, 314, 315
Sheahan, Frank 58
Sherry, Mike 112, 116, 185
Spicer, Kevin 71
Strauss, Richardt 218, 219, 238, 307
Stringer, Peter 50, 51, 58, 59, 63, 96, 97, 103, 110, 112, 278–280, 294

Swift, Michael 144, 274

T

Toner, Devin 241, 284, 286, 291, 292, 299, 300, 308
Topping, James 67, 121
Trimble, Andrew 103, 122, 272, 284, 288–292, 295, 297, 300
Tuohy, Greg 60

V

van der Westhuizen, Joost 5, 23
Varley, Damien 116, 309

W

Wallace, David 7, 33, 47, 49, 50, 52, 58, 60, 62, 64, 100, 108, 111, 112, 281, 303
Wallace, Paddy 69, 84, 108, 231
Wallace, Paul 27, 39, 44, 72, 79, 130, 186, 302
Wallace, Richard 72, 111, 112, 114, 302, 303
Walters, Aled 250, 251
Warwick, Paul 180, 181
Webb, Dr Michael 176, 177, 259, 260, 270
Whelan, Pa 74, 75, 92
Wigglesworth, Eddie 30, 217
Wilkinson, Jonny 84, 99, 159
Williams, Harry 67, 68
Williams, Jim 60, 217
Williams, Matt 31, 89, 90, 128–131, 248
Williams, Shane 16, 109
Wilson, Jeff 21, 37, 38, 41–43, 45
Wood, Keith 39, 41–43, 46, 48, 58–61, 64, 72, 79, 96–100, 111, 112, 186, 302, 304, 312, 313
Woods, Niall 25, 26, 71–75, 77, 171, 172, 186, 187, 189, 191, 192, 302
Woodward, Clive 71, 72, 74, 75, 77
Wyn Jones, Alun 15, 197

Y

Yachvili, Dimitri 62, 63, 146

Z

Zebo, Simon 181, 261, 284, 305, 309